C++ Memory Management

Len Dorfman
Marc J. Neuberger

Windcrest®/McGraw-Hill

New York San Francisco Washington, D.C. Auckland Bogotá
Caracas Lisbon London Madrid Mexico City Milan
Montreal New Delhi San Juan Singapore
Sydney Tokyo Toronto

To Barbara and Rachel,
for their love and spirited humor
To Stephen Moore, for his eagle's eye
Len

To Leah, Joe and Miriam
for their love, support, and friendship
Marc

FIRST EDITION
SECOND PRINTING

© 1994 by **Len Dorfman & Marc J. Neuberger**.
Published by Windcrest, an imprint of McGraw-Hill, Inc.
The name "Windcrest" is a registered trademark of McGraw-Hill, Inc.

Library of Congress Cataloging-in-Publication Data

Dorfman, Len.
    C++ memory management / by Len Dorfman and Marc J. Neuberger.
        p.   cm.
    Includes index.
    ISBN 0-8306-4288-9
    1. C++ (Computer program language) 2. Memory management (Computer science) I. Neuberger, Marc J. II. Title.
QA76.73.C153D67 1993
005.4'3—dc20   93-3277
                                              CIP

Acquisitions Editor: Stephen Moore
Editorial Team: Robert E. Ostrander, Executive Editor
               David M. McCandless, Book Editor
Production: Katherine G. Brown, Director
          Tina M. Sourbier, Typesetting
          Patsy D. Harne, Layout
          Lorie White, Proofreading
          N. Nadine McFarland, Quality Control
          Donna Gladhill, Assistant
Book Design: Jaclyn J. Boone
Associate Designer: Brian Allison   WP1
Cover Design and Illustration: Sandra Blair, Harrisburg, Pa.   4318

Contents

4 EMS 4.0   89

What you need to use this book

In order to benefit most from this book, you should have at least beginner's knowledge of the C++ programming language and its basic object-oriented features. The programs in this book were developed and tested using Borland C++ 3.1 and Microsoft C++ 7.0.

Although the assembly bindings were assembled using TASM and MASM, knowledge of assembly programming is not required to use the memory management functions presented in the book.

"MAKE" files have been provided for compiling and linking the programs found in this book. There is a make file for each library and associated example programs. A separate set of make files is provided for Borland C++ 3.1 and Microsoft C++ 7.0. The names of the make files are as follows:

MCB.MAK	Build Chapter 2 programs for BC++ 3.1
MCBMS.MAK	Build Chapter 2 programs for MSC++ 7.0
EMS.MAK	Build Chapters 3 & 4 programs for BC++ 3.1
EMSMS.MAK	Build Chapters 3 & 4 programs for MSC++ 7.0
XMS.MAK	Build Chapter 5 programs for BC++ 3.1
XMSMS.MAK	Build Chapter 5 programs for MSC++ 7.0
VM.MAK	Build Chapter 6 programs for BC++ 3.1
VMMS.MAK	Build Chapter 6 programs for MSC++ 7.0

The Borland make utility can be invoked to build the MCB library and example programs by typing

```
make -f MCB
```

The Microsoft make utility can be invoked to build the MCB library and example programs by typing

```
nmake -f MCB.MAK
```

Introduction

This practical, how-to book has been designed with the intent of providing C++ programmers with the practical tools required for seamless dynamic integration of high memory (expanded memory, extended memory, and the hard disk) into application programs. This book provides the tools required for expanded memory, extended memory, and virtual memory management in the 8086/8088 real mode.

EMS and XMS memory management functions provide the building blocks used to support the Virtual Memory Manager system presented in Chapter 6. The full source for the VMM system is presented along with the EMS and XMS interface. A comprehensive memory management library is also provided on disk.

When you finish this book, you will understand the workings of EMS, XMS and a Virtual Memory Management system. This understanding will allow you to take full advantage of EMS, XMS, and hard disk memory in your application programs. You'll have at your disposal a set of simple-to-use virtual dynamic memory allocation functions that will permit your program to access memory blocks in the multiple-megabyte range.

The book begins with a straightforward discussion of a PC's memory management scheme. Once the memory management overview is completed, Chapter 2 introduces the Memory Arena (as it's called by Microsoft) or the Memory Control Block (MCB—as is known by much of the industry). A full-blown Memory Control Block display program is presented.

Chapter 3 presents an explanation of the EMS 3.0 and 3.2 functions. The chapter's demonstration programs are designed to illustrate using the EMS 3.0 and 3.2 functions. The source code and function prototype for each EMS function are presented along with the demonstration programs' source listings.

Once you have a handle on using EMS 3.0 and 3.2 functions, Chapter 4 continues the EMS discussion by exploring the EMS 4.0 expanded memory standard. Similar to Chapter 3, most of the EMS 4.0 functions are prototyped and the source for the functions is presented. The sources for several EMS 4.0 demonstration programs are also presented in Chapter 4.

Chapter 5 introduces the Extended Memory Specification (XMS) 2.0. As with the EMS chapters, the full source for each function is presented along with XMS demonstration programs.

Chapter 6 presents the source code to a Virtual Memory Manager that enables you, for example, to open up a two-megabyte area of memory for use in your application program. This dynamically allocated memory may be opened, written to, read from, and freed as with standard dynamically allocated memory. The VMM interface functions are prototyped and two VMM demonstration programs are also presented. Great care has been taken in constructing the source code comments in this chapter, all in order to help facilitate your understanding of the VMM's complex inner workings.

1
Memory management overview

Although many programmers feel that the segment-offset architecture of the 80x86 series of CPUs is byzantine, the CPUs work just fine. In the vernacular, "They get the job done!"

Let's draw a thumbnail sketch of the 80x86 memory architecture: The 80x86 series of processors has three modes of operation. The least common denominator is "real mode," available to all 80x86 processors, in which the CPU acts like an 8086/8088, with addresses composed of a 16-bit segment and a 16-bit offset. These two words are combined to form a 20-bit physical address by shifting the segment left by 4 bits and adding the offset. This gives an address space of 1 megabyte.

In *16-bit protected mode*, available on 80286's and up, an address is comprised of a 16-bit selector and a 16-bit offset. Rather than being used directly to compute the physical address, the selector denotes a descriptor in a descriptor table. Among other things, the descriptor contains a 24-bit base address to be used in address computation. The offset is added to this base address. Thus 16 megabytes of memory can be addressed.

In *32-bit protected mode*, available on 80386's and up, an address is made up of a 16-bit selector and a 32-bit offset. Again, the selector denotes a descriptor, which now contains a 32-bit base address. The offset is added to this base address. This allows access to 4 gigabytes of physical memory. In addition, the 32-bit offsets allow memory to be configured into a 4 gigabyte linear address space, accessible through just an offset.

Most existing MS-DOS and PC-DOS programs run in real mode. This book deals with memory management in real mode.

When programming in the real mode, as opposed to the 80286- 80386- 80486 protected mode, the CPU cannot address memory above 1 megabyte.

1

Memory below 1 megabyte can be divided into two sections. Memory from 0 to 640K is generally referred to as *conventional memory* and the memory from 640K to 1024K (1Mb) is called *upper memory*. (Note that some sources, notably some Microsoft Press books, refer to the whole first megabyte of memory as conventional memory.) Memory above 1 megabyte can be called *extended memory*. The first 64K of extended memory (physical addresses 0x100000-0x10FFF0) is a special area known as the *high memory area*, or HMA. While not in the first megabyte of memory normally addressable, the HMA can be accessed by real-mode programs using techniques described in Chapter 5.

Memory range	Name
0 to 640K	Conventional memory
640K to 1Mb	Upper memory
Above 1Mb	Extended memory
1Mb to 1Mb+64K	High memory

Conventional memory is used for things like the PC BIOS's data area, DOS, interrupt vectors, device drivers, and TSRs. What remains for program use is called the Transient Program Area (TPA).

The upper memory area is reserved for BIOS code and hardware devices. Video display adapters require various amounts of upper memory for access to their screen refresh buffers. The system BIOS (Basic Input Output System), which provides low-level hardware access, resides in upper memory. Disk controllers also occupy some upper memory for their interface to the operating system.

The extended memory area is available to anyone with the know-how to exploit the EMS and/or XMS specifications.

Conventional memory is divided into blocks of memory. Each of these blocks is described by a Memory Control Block (MCB) structure. These control blocks contain information indicating the size of the memory block and whether the memory block is free or owned by a program.

With all of the various needs that must be filled by the lower memory area, space can run out. Pre-DOS 5.0 users could find themselves with 450K (or less!) for their application program's use (the TPA).

Although DOS 5.0 and commercial memory management utility programs improve the memory management situation considerably by allowing users to load TSRs, device drivers, and DOS into upper and extended memory, you're still limited by the paltry 640K boundary for the TPA.

Why the description of "paltry" for the 640K limit? Suppose you need to dynamically allocate 1Mb of memory for a program's use. Simply stated, 640K "won't get the job done." As the programs written by software designers become larger and increasingly complex, there is a crying need for ways to access more than 640K of memory.

Prior to the advent of EMS and XMS, one solution was to use disk storage as a substitute for RAM. Although this situation did work, using hard disk storage as a substitute for RAM proved very cumbersome. Disk access is a perceptible order of magnitude slower than RAM access. Programs that used the hard disk as a work-around the 640K limit were painfully slow. And, as they say, "time is money."

Hardware designers, however, proved up to the challenge of breaking the 640K boundary, and Expanded Memory (EMS) came into being. EMS is software specification for drivers that can provide access to memory in excess of the 1Mb addressable by real-mode programs. EMS provides a clever page flipping scheme where chunks of extended memory can be mapped to addresses in upper memory. Programs called Expanded Memory Managers (EMM) were designed to support this page-flipping memory management scheme, either through the use of hardware page mapping or the 80286/80386 paging capabilities.

This arrangement proved quite workable because Lotus, Intel, and Microsoft (LIM) together created the EMS standard. Having a standard for EMS proved essential for developing well-behaved programs that would not corrupt other programs' EMS-based data. Although page flipping was not as elegant as a linear addressing scheme, it certainly beat using the hard disk!

The 80286 chip's hitting the market heralded the arrival of Protected Mode programming by now allowing the CPU to access memory above the 1Mb boundary. Memory above 1Mb became known as extended memory. DOS, however, is not a protected mode operating system and does not have the means to access the area of memory above 1Mb. For a time using Extended Memory in your programs proved risky business because there wasn't a specification standard regulating Extended Memory usage.

In the late 1980's, however, the Extended Memory Specification (XMS) v2.0 appeared. The emergence of this XMS standard along with Microsoft's HIMEM.SYS XMS device driver allowed programmers to have access to extended memory in an orderly fashion.

DOS memory manager utility programs now allow inexpensive extended memory (XMS) to be reconfigured to function as expanded memory (EMS). This proves an economical solution. Many new-age 80x86 mother boards allow for installation of many megabytes of XMS memory. Memory manager utility programs allow this extended memory to be divided up into various combinations of XMS and EMS.

At the time of this writing, real mode programmers currently have three distinct ways of breaking the 640K boundary for dynamic memory allocation uses. They can use

- EMS together with hardware memory mapping
- extended memory (either with XMS or EMS software)
- the hard disk drive as substitute RAM

Using expanded memory for dynamic memory allocation

The software that implements the EMS standard is called an Expanded Memory Manager, or EMM. An EMM program allocates a 64K area of the address space between 640K and 1024K for use as what is called the *page frame area*. Four 16K blocks of RAM from above 1Mb may then be mapped to this page frame area by making calls to the EMM program.

This 64K page frame is composed of four 16K physical pages. The four physical pages are taken (really mapped) from a large collection of what are called *logical pages* (those of you familiar with operating systems will note that this terminology is somewhat backwards: here the program references physical pages that get mapped to logical pages instead of the other way around). Let's try to visualize the relationship between 16K logical pages, 16K physical pages, and 64K page frames. Figure 1-1 shows one way of viewing the EMS physical and logical page relationship.

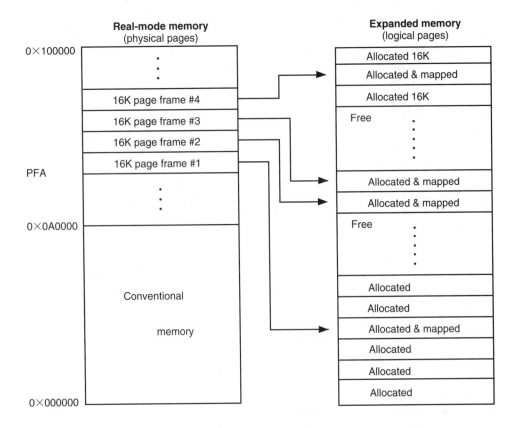

1-1 The EMS physical and logical page relationship

The EMS page mapping process may be thought of as follows:

1. Map up to four different 16K logical pages to the four different 16K physical pages using your EMM
2. Read from or write to physical pages
3. Map new 16K logical pages to physical pages
4. Go to Step 2

TABLE 1-1 presents a summary listing of the functions associated with EMS v3.0, v3.2, and v4.0.

Table 1-1   The EMS 3.0, 3.2, and 4.0 specification listing

Ver.	Funct.	Sub.	Description
3.0	40h		Get EMS status
3.0	41h		Get EMS page frame address
3.0	42h		Get number of EMS 16K pages
3.0	43h		Allocate EMS handle and 16K pages
3.0	44h		Map EMS logical pages to physical pages
3.0	45h		Free EMS handle and logical pages
3.0	46h		Get EMS version installed
3.0	47h		Save EMS page map
3.0	48h		Restore EMS page map
3.0	49h		(Reserved for future use)
3.0	4Ah		(Reserved for future use)
3.0	4Bh		Get EMS handle count
3.0	4Ch		Get EMS handle pages
3.0	4Dh		Get all EMS pages for all handles
3.2	4Eh	00h	Save EMS page map
3.2	4Eh	01h	Restore EMS page map
3.2	4Eh	02h	Save and restore EMS page map
3.2	4Eh	03h	Get size of EMS page map information
4.0	4Fh	00h	Save partial EMS page map
4.0	4Fh	01h	Restore partial EMS page map
4.0	4Fh	02h	Get size of partial EMS page map information
4.0	50h	00h	Map multiple EMS pages by number
4.0	50h	01h	Map multiple EMS pages by address
4.0	51h		Reallocate EMS pages for handle
4.0	52h	00h	Get EMS handle attribute
4.0	52h	01h	Set EMS handle attribute
4.0	52h	02h	Get EMS attribute capability
4.0	53h	00h	Get EMS handle name
4.0	53h	01h	Set EMS handle name
4.0	54h	00h	Get all EMS handle names
4.0	54h	01h	Search for EMS handle names
4.0	54h	02h	Get total EMS handles
4.0	55h	00h	Map EMS pages by number and JMP
4.0	55h	01h	Map EMS pages by address and JMP
4.0	56h	00h	Map EMS pages by number and CALL
4.0	56h	01h	Map EMS pages by address and CALL

Table 1-1   Continued

Ver.	Funct.	Sub.	Description
4.0	56h	02h	Get space for EMS map page and CALL
4.0	57h	00h	Move memory region
4.0	57h	01h	Exchange memory regions
4.0	58h	00h	Get addresses of mappable EMS pages
4.0	58h	01h	Get number of mappable EMS pages
4.0	59h	00h	Get hardware configuration
4.0	59h	01h	Get number of raw 16K pages
4.0	5Ah	00h	Allocate handle and standard EMS pages
4.0	5Ah	01h	Allocate handle and raw 16K pages
4.0	5Bh	00h	Get alternate EMS map registers
4.0	5Bh	01h	Set alternate EMS map registers
4.0	5Ch		Prep EMM for warm boot
4.0	5Dh	00h	Disable EMM Operating System functions
4.0	5Dh	01h	Enable EMM Operating System functions
4.0	5Dh	02h	Release EMS access key

We recommend that EMS be the first place a programmer look in order to break the 640K memory boundary limit for dynamic memory allocation.

Using extended memory for dynamic memory allocation

We rate using XMS for extended memory usage as a second choice to EMS for the following reasons:

1. EMS allows mapping pages into addressable memory while XMS requires data to be transferred to and from extended memory. Mapping is a much faster operation than transferring 16K of data.
2. EMS provides a richer set of functionality than XMS does.

Table 1-2 presents a listing of the XMS v2.0 specification.

Table 1-2   The XMS 2.0 specification list

Ver.	Funct.	Description
2.0	00h	Get XMS Version Number
2.0	01h	Request High Memory Area
2.0	02h	Release High Memory Area
2.0	03h	Global Enable A20
2.0	04h	Global Disable A20
2.0	05h	Local Enable A20
2.0	06h	Local Disable A20
2.0	07h	Query A20

Table 1-2 Continued

Ver.	Funct.	Description
2.0	08h	Query Free Extended Memory
2.0	09h	Allocate Extended Memory Block
2.0	0Ah	Free Extended Memory Block
2.0	0Bh	Move Extended Memory Block
2.0	0Ch	Lock Extended Memory Block
2.0	0Dh	Unlock Extended Memory Block
2.0	0Eh	Get Handle Information
2.0	0Fh	Reallocate Extended Memory Block
2.0	10h	Request Upper Memory Block
2.0	11h	Release Upper Memory Block

Using the hard disk
for dynamic memory allocation

Using file I/O in C++ is a relatively straightforward task. Building extended level memory management functions using DOS-based file I/O functions provides a useful back-up method for extended memory usage when the host computer doesn't have EMS or XMS memory available.

We deem the disk dynamic memory allocation management option as "back-up" because it is painfully slow compared to RAM-based methods.

Summary

DOS is a real mode operating system and allows no more than 640K for a program's use. The memory available for a program's use is called the TPA (Transient Program Area).

Many programs require far more memory than the 640K limit, and various memory management strategies come to the fore.

Using EMS for dynamic memory allocation proves both reliable and fast. The reliability of EMS was fostered by the emergence of the standard. Programming standards ensure well-behaved programs. EMS is our first choice for dynamic memory allocation because of the functionality associated with the EMS 3.0, 3.2, and 4.0 specifications, and the speed of mapping as opposed to the speed of data transfer.

Using XMS for dynamic memory allocation also proves fast and reliable. We rate using XMS for dynamic memory allocation second to using EMS because the XMS 2.0 specification has less functionality than the EMS specifications.

For these reasons, the following memory management rating list naturally follows:

1. EMS (expanded memory)
2. XMS (extended memory)
3. Hard disk drive

2
Understanding memory control blocks

A complete understanding of memory management must include a description of how DOS handles memory allocation in low memory. Simply stated, DOS divides the 640K of low memory into a series of contiguous memory blocks. These memory blocks are sized in multiples of 16-byte memory "paragraphs." This makes sense because the segment selector registers (DS,CS,ES,SS) work in paragraph boundaries and not single-byte boundaries (recall that in forming an address, the segment is shifted left by 4, or equivalently, multiplied by 16).

DOS creates a one-paragraph (16-byte) header at the beginning of each block of memory that describes certain attributes of the block. In this book, the one-paragraph memory block descriptor is called the MCB, or *Memory Control Block*. Other industry sources have referred to it as the *memory arena* and *arena header*.

Your PC's low memory has many memory blocks that describe memory held by programs, device drivers, and free memory. As there is an MCB for each block of memory, these multiple MCBs have come to be known collectively as the *MCB chain*.

In memory, the MCB is immediately followed by the block of memory that it describes. Let's have a look at the MCB structure as it seemed to behave in pre-DOS 4.0 days. Note that we use the term "seemed to behave" because in early Microsoft documentation the contents of the MCB were not described. In fact, the DOS call to locate the address of the first MCB is still an undocumented DOS service. Our C++ class `MCB_Mcb` provides a convenient method of traversing the MCB chain.

Pre-DOS 4.0 MCB

```
struct MCB_Mcb {
    char    chain_status;
    WORD    owner_psp;
    WORD    size_paragraphs;
    BYTE    dummy[3];
    char    reserved[8];

    };
```

The first element of the MCB structure is an 8-bit value that holds the status of the memory chain. If it holds an ASCII "M", this means that there are more memory blocks in the memory block chain. If it holds an ASCII "Z", then this MCB is the last MCB in the chain.

The second element in the MCB holds the segment value of the PSP (Program Segment Prefix) of the program that owns the block of memory described by the MCB. DOS creates this 256-byte PSP when a program is loaded. In this chapter, we will use the following information from a program's PSP:

PSP segment value is used as program owner ID
PSP:[0x2C] holds segment of program environment
PSP:[0x80] holds program command line length
PSP:[0x81] holds ASCII command line start

The third element in the MCB structure contains a 16-bit integer that contains the size of the memory block associated with the MCB in paragraphs. To calculate the size of the memory block in bytes, simply take the number of paragraphs and multiply that value by 16. (Of course, to assembly coders, shifting 4 bits left is a little slicker than multiplying by 16.)

Once you know the length of the memory block described by the MCB chain, it is very easy to find the next memory block in the chain. All you need to do is to take the MCB's segment, add the size (in paragraphs) of the MCB to that segment, and then add 1 (for the size of the MCB itself). Lo and behold, you'll then have the segment for the next MCB in the MCB chain.

Programs like MAPMEM, MEM, TDMEM and PROG2-3.CPP (a memory display utility program is presented in FIG. 2-3) work by getting the segment of the first MCB, displaying some information, getting the next MCB, displaying more information, and continuing with that process until the end of the MCB chain is reached. Once you have access to the MCB, PSP and program's environment, there are many things about the memory block owner that you can report.

In DOS 4.0 and later, the 8-byte fifth element holds the name (without extension) of the program that owns that MCB's memory block. This eases the task of finding the MCB's owner program name because you no longer need to search the owner program's environment for the owner name.

Here is the MCB structure for the DOS 4.0 and later MCB.

Post-DOS 4.0 MCB

```
struct MCB_Mcb {
    char    chain_status;
    WORD    owner_psp;
    WORD    size_paragraphs;
    BYTE    dummy[3];
    char    file_name[8];
    };
```

Now that we've introduced the MCB and its structure, let's write some code!

Preparatory memory management routines

Figure 2-1 presents the source code listing to MCB.H. This file contains a collection of definitions that will be useful in displaying information about the Memory Control Block chain.

2-1   The source code listing to MCB.H

```
////////////////////////////////////
//
// MCB.H
//
// Unit file for the MCB functions
//
////////////////////////////////////

//
//   Define the Memory Control Block Structure
//
struct MCB_Mcb {
    char                chain_status;
    WORD                owner_psp;
    WORD                size_paragraphs;
    BYTE                dummy[3];
    char                file_name[8];
    };

//
//   Define the MCB_McbPtr class. Which gives convenient access
//   to the MCB chain.
//
class  MCB_McbPtr {

    MCB_Mcb             *mcbPtr;

public:

        MCB_McbPtr() {
            mcbPtr= NULL;
            }
```

```
        MCB_McbPtr(WORD);
    void first();

    int  more() {
            return (mcbPtr != NULL);
            }

    void next();

    MCB_Mcb *operator->() {
            return mcbPtr;
            }

    WORD segment();

    };

DWORD        getVecPointer(BYTE);
```

Take a moment to review the source code to MCB.H. In addition to defining the layout of the MCB, we define a class, MCB_McbPtr, which makes MCB access easier. Objects of this class act like pointers to MCBs except that three methods are defined for making it easier to run through all of the MCBs. These methods are designed to be used together in "for" loops. MCB_McbPtr::first() initializes the pointer to the first MCB. MCB_McbPtr::more() returns a Boolean value indicating whether there are more MCBs left, and MCB_McbPtr::next() advances the pointer to the next MCB. Thus we can run through all of the MCBs with the following loop:

```
MCB_McbPtr    mcbPtr;
for (mcbPtr.first(); mcbPtr.more(); mcbPtr.next()) {
    //   Code executed once for each MCB
    printf("%d\n",
            mcbPtr->size_paragraphs); // for example
    }
```

Writing a memory chain display utility program

There are quite a few fine memory display utility programs on the market today. The purpose of the demonstration programs presented in this chapter is to clearly demonstrate how the information contained in the MCB and PSP may be obtained. We believe that a programming example is worth more than 1024 words.

Figure 2-2 presents the source code listing to PROG2-1.CPP. This program steps through the MCB memory chain and displays the MCB status, MCB segment value, PSP segment value and the size of the memory block in 16-byte paragraphs.

2-2 The source code listing to PROG2-1.CPP

```
////////////////////////////////////////
//
// prog2-1.cpp
//
// Demonstration of
//    getMcbPointer(...)
//
////////////////////////////////////////

extern "C" {
#include <stdio.h>
}

#include "gdefs.h"
#include "mcb.h"

void main()
{

    MCB_McbPtr          mcbPtr;


    //
    // print header
    //
    printf("\n");
    printf("\n");
    printf("Davy Jones' Memory Display Program  (Rev .1) \n");
    printf("\n");
    printf("CHAIN   MCB    PSP    PARAGRAPHS \n");
    printf("--------------------------------\n");


    //
    // Loop through the MCB's printing out the info they
    // contain.
    //
    for (mcbPtr.first(); mcbPtr.more(); mcbPtr.next()) {

        //
        // Print out the interesting stuff
        //
        printf("%c      %04X    %04X    %6u\n",
                mcbPtr->chain_status,
                mcbPtr.segment(),
                mcbPtr->owner_psp,
                mcbPtr->size_paragraphs);


    }
}
```

Now let's run PROG2-1.EXE. Figure 2-3 presents a sample output from PROG2-1.

Figure 2-4 presents the source code listing to PROG2-2.CPP. This program removes the MCB segment report from PROG2-1's display, calculates the memory block size in bytes, and prints the owner program's name.

2-3 The screen output for PROG2-1.EXE

```
Davy Jones' Memory Display Program  (Rev .1)

CHAIN   MCB    PSP    PARAGRAPHS
----------------------------------
M       04B6   0008      262
M       05BD   05BE      231
M       06A5   0000        3
M       06A9   05BE       64
M       06EA   05BE        5
M       06F0   0837       44
M       071D   071E      280
M       0836   0837      896
Z       0BB7   0000    37960
```

2-4 The source code listing to PROG2-2.CPP

```cpp
/////////////////////////////////////
//
// prog2-2.cpp
//
// Further demonstration of
//    getMcbPointer(...)
//
/////////////////////////////////////

extern "C" {
#include <stdio.h>
#include <dos.h>
}

#include "gdefs.h"
#include "mcb.h"

void main()
{

    MCB_McbPtr          mcbPtr;

    char                *env;
    WORD                envSeg;
    WORD                *temp;
    int                 i;

    //
    //   Print the header
    //
    printf("\n");
    printf("Davy Jones' Memory Display Program (Rev .2)\n");
    printf("\n");
    printf(" PSP   SIZE      PROGRAM  \n");
    printf("----- ------  ----------- \n");


    //
    //   Loop over the MCB"s printing out the info
    //
    for (mcbPtr.first(); mcbPtr.more(); mcbPtr.next()) {
```

```c
//
//  Print the easy stuff
//
printf("%04X  %6lu   ",
        mcbPtr->owner_psp,
        DWORD(mcbPtr->size_paragraphs) << 4);

//
//  If the PSP for this MCB is 0 then it represents
//  free memory
//
if (mcbPtr->owner_psp == 0) {
    printf("(free mem)");
    }

//
//  If the PSP is 8 then print config
//
else if (mcbPtr->owner_psp == 0x08) {
    printf("(config)");
    }

//
//  Otherwise it's a program, so print the program name
//
else {
    //
    //  Get pointer to environment segment
    //
    temp= WordPtr(MK_FP(mcbPtr->owner_psp, 0x2c));

    //
    //  Get program environment segment
    //
    envSeg= *temp;

    //
    //  Set pointer to environment
    //
    env= CharPtr(MK_FP(envSeg, 0));

    //
    //  Search environment for the program name
    //
    //  Scan to the double '\000' delimiter.
    //
    while (env[0] || env[1]) {
        env++;
        }

    //
    //  Skip the double delimiter:
    //
    env+= 2;

    //
    //  Search for executable filename.
    //
    while (env[0] != '.') {
        env++;
            }
```

2-4 Continued.

```
            //
            //  Backspace to backslash which precedes the
            //  executable filename
            //
            while (env[0] != '\\') {
                env--;
                }

            //
            //  Point to the first letter of the filename
            //
            env++;

            //
            //  Print the text up to the dot
            //
            i= 0;
            for (i= 0; i < 12 && env[0] != '.'; i++, env++) {
                printf("%c", env[0]);
                }

            //
            //  Print out the extension.
            //
            if (i < 12) {
                for (i= 0; i <= 3; i++, env++) {
                    printf("%c", env[0]);
                    }
                }
            }

    //
    //  Put out a Carriage return here
    //
    printf("\n");

    }

}
```

Figure 2-5 presents sample output for PROG2-2.

2-5 The screen output for PROG2-2.EXE

```
Davy Jones' Memory Display Program (Rev .2)

PSP    SIZE     PROGRAM
-----  ------   -----------
0008    4192    (config)
05BE    3696    pal.cfg
0000      48    (free mem)
05BE    1024    pal.cfg
05BE      80    pal.cfg
0837     704    PROG2-2.EXE
071E    4480    PROG2-2.EXE
0837   15360    PROG2-2.EXE
0000  606336    (free mem)
```

Figure 2-6 presents the source code listing to PROG2-3.CPP. This program presents a more polished, comprehensive, and flashier version of PROG2-1 and PROG2-2.

2-6 The source code listing to PROG2-3.CPP

```
/////////////////////////////////////
//
// prog2-3.cpp
//
// A slightly more comprehensive
// Memory Display Utility
//
/////////////////////////////////////

extern "C" {
#include <stdio.h>
#include <dos.h>
}

#include "gdefs.h"
#include "mcb.h"


extern WORD getProgPsp();
extern void getDosVersion(WORD *majRev, WORD *minRev);
extern int  isFNameChar(char c);


void main(int argc, char *argv[])
{
    MCB_McbPtr          mcbPtr;
    MCB_McbPtr          ownerMcbPtr;

    WORD                majRev;
    WORD                minRev;

    int                 help;

    char                *tmpStr;

    char                *f2e;
    WORD                seg2e;

    int                 i;

    WORD                *temp;
    WORD                 envSeg;
    char                *env;

    WORD                 charCount;

    char                *command;
    int                  expectCommand;

    WORD                 vectorsPrinted;
    WORD                 vecSeg;
    int                  remainder;
```

```
char                  padding[38];
//
//   Check help flag and set on '/h' command line
//   parameter
//
tmpStr= argv[1];
help= (argc != 0) &&
                (tmpStr[1] == '/') &&
                ((tmpStr[2] == 'H') ||
                    (tmpStr[2] == 'h') ||
                    (tmpStr[2] == '?'));

//
//   Get DOS version
//
getDosVersion(&majRev, &minRev);

//
//   Get pointer to int 2eh (points into command com code).
//   We'll use this to figure out whether a vector is hooked by
//   COMMAND.COM
//
f2e= CharPtr(getVecPointer(0x2e));
seg2e= FP_SEG(f2e) + (FP_OFF(f2e) >> 4);

//
//   Put out first header line:
//
//   Note that we assume ANSI.SYS to get colors.
//
printf("\033[30;46m");       // Set color to Black on Cyan
printf(
"          Davy Jones' Memory Display Program V3.0     DOS Rev %2d.%1d"
"                     ",
majRev, minRev);

//
//   Reset the attributes to normal:
//
printf("\033[m");

if (help) {

    //
    // place the cursor

    printf("\n");
    printf("\n");

    //
    //   Print help messages
    //
    printf("Program Syntax: prog2-3 [option]\n");
    printf("\n");
    printf("Options:\n");
    printf("    /H  => Help information\n");
    printf("    /?  => Help information\n");

    //
```

```
        // place the cursor
        //
        printf("\n");
        printf("\n");

        //
        // exit to DOS
        //
        return;
        }


    //
    //  Put out second header line:
    //
    printf("\033[30;47m");       // Set color to Black on Light Grey
    printf(
    "PSP   SIZE  PROGRAM    COMMAND LINE                 HOOKED  VECTORS");

    //
    //  Reset attributes.
    //
    printf("\033[m");

    //
    //  Loop and print MCB information
    //
    for (mcbPtr.first(); mcbPtr.more(); mcbPtr.next()) {

        //
        //   Get the owner's MCB address.
        //
        //   The segment number is automatically converted into
        //   an MCB_McbPtr
        //
        ownerMcbPtr= mcbPtr->owner_psp - 1;

        //
        //   Print out the basic information
        //
        printf("%04X|%6lu|",
                    mcbPtr->owner_psp,
                    DWORD(mcbPtr->size_paragraphs) << 4);


        expectCommand= TRUE;

        //
        //   If vector 2eh points within this block then
        //   it's COMMAND.COM
        //
        if ((seg2e >= mcbPtr.segment() &&
                seg2e <= mcbPtr.segment() + mcbPtr->size_paragraphs) ||
            (seg2e >= ownerMcbPtr.segment() &&
                seg2e <= ownerMcbPtr.segment())) {
            printf("COMMAND ");
            expectCommand= FALSE;
            }

        //
        //   If PSP is 0 then it's free
```

```
    //

    else if (mcbPtr->owner_psp == 0) {
        printf("(FREE)  ");
        expectCommand= FALSE;
        }

    //
    //  If PSP is 8 then it's config
    //
    else if (mcbPtr->owner_psp == 0x08) {

        printf("(SYSTEM)");
        expectCommand= FALSE;
        }

    //
    //  If we're running DOS 4.0 or better, then we can
    //  look in the owner's MCB structure for program name
    //
    else if (majRev >= 4) {
        i= 0;
        for (i= 0; i < 8 && isFNameChar(ownerMcbPtr->file_name[i]); i++) {
            putchar(ownerMcbPtr->file_name[i]);
            }
        if (i == 0) {
            printf("(N/A)   ");
            }
        else {
            while (i < 8) {
                putchar(' ');
                i++;
                }
            }
        }

    //
    //  Otherwise print the program name from the owner psp
    //
    else {

        //
        //  Get environment segment pointer
        //
        temp= WordPtr(MK_FP(mcbPtr->owner_psp, 0x2c));

        //
        //  Get program environment segment
        //
        envSeg= *temp;

        //
        //  Set pointer to environment
        //
        env= CharPtr(MK_FP(envSeg, 0));

        //
        //  Search environment for the program name
        //
```

```
        //  Scan to the double delimiter.
        //
        while (env[0] || env[1]) {
            env++;
            }

        //
        //  Skip the double delimiter:
        //
        env+= 2;

        //
        //  Search for executable filename.
        //
        while (env[0] != '.') {
            env++;
            }

        //
        //  Backspace to backslash which precedes the
        //  executable filename
        //
        while (env[0] != '\\') {
            env--;
            }

        //
        //  Point to the first letter of the filename
        //
        env++;

        //
        //  Print the text up to the dot
        //
        charCount= 0;
        for (charCount= 0; env[0] !=  '.'; charCount++, env++) {
            putchar(env[0]);
            }

        while (charCount < 8) {
            putchar(' ');
            charCount++;
            }
        }

    putchar('|');

    if (expectCommand) {
        //
        //  Get a pointer to the command line.
        //
        command= CharPtr(MK_FP(mcbPtr->owner_psp, 0x80));

        //
        //  Print it out
        //
        for (i= 1; i <= 20 && i <= command[0] && command[i]; i++) {
            putchar(command[i]);
            }

        //
```

```
                    //  Pad with spaces
                    //

                    while (i <= 20) {
                        putchar(' ');
                        i++;
                        }
                }
        else {
            printf("                        ");
            }


        printf("| ");


        //
        //   Now let's see if we have hooked vectors:
        //
        vectorsPrinted= 0;
        for (i= 0; i <= 255; i++) {
            vecSeg= FP_SEG(CharPtr(getVecPointer(i)));
            if (vecSeg >= mcbPtr.segment() &&
                    vecSeg <= mcbPtr.segment() + mcbPtr->size_paragraphs) {
                //
                //   See if we've filled the line:
                //
                if (vectorsPrinted > 0 &&
                        vectorsPrinted % 12 == 0) {
                    printf("      |      |      |                    | ");
                    }
                printf("%02X ", i);
                vectorsPrinted= vectorsPrinted + 1;
                }
            }

        //
        //   Clear the rest of the line and advance to next line
        //
        if (vectorsPrinted == 0) {
            remainder= 37;
            }
        else {
            remainder= 37 - 3 * (((vectorsPrinted + 11) % 12) + 1);
            }
        for (i= 0; i < remainder; i++) {
            padding[i]= ' ';
            }
        padding[i]= 0;
        printf(padding);
        }


    printf(
"____|_____|_____|_____|_____");

}
```

```
/*********************************************************************
***                                                               ***
***      getDosVersion() - Gets the DOS version                   ***
***                                                               ***
*********************************************************************/
void getDosVersion(WORD *majRev, WORD *minRev)
{

    REGISTERS;

    R_AL= 0x01;
    R_AH= 0x30;
    interrupt(0x21);

    *majRev= R_AL;
    *minRev= R_AH;

}


/*********************************************************************
***                                                               ***
***      isFNameChar()                                            ***
***                                                               ***
***      isFNameChar tells whether a character is a "reasonable"  ***
***      filename character. Filenames can have any character but ***
***      we exercise some judgement over what characters are      ***
***      acceptable.                                              ***
***                                                               ***
*********************************************************************/

int isFNameChar(char c)
{
    return ((c >= 'a') && (c <= 'z')) ||
                ((c >= 'A') && (c <= 'Z')) ||
                ((c >= '0') && (c <= '9')) ||
                (c == '_') ||
                (c == '-') ||
                (c == '$');
}
```

There are many instructive programming techniques used in this highly documented source file. The comments have been carefully written to aid in your understanding.

Summary

Low memory is organized into a sequence of memory blocks, each headed by a 16-byte Memory Control Block (MCB). The memory blocks follow one after another contiguously in memory. Thus, it is easy to go from one MCB to the next.

By looking at these MCBs, we can find out the owner program's PSP, whether the memory block is the last in the chain, the size of the memory block referred to by the MCB, the location of the next MCB in the chain, the owner program's command line, and the owner program's name.

Understanding how MCBs operate will lay a firm foundation for understanding low memory management.

Figure 2-7 presents the source code listing to PROG2-4.CPP. This program uses the standard library "spawnlp" function to invoke PROG2-3.EXE. Running the parent PROG2-4.EXE program will allow you to see the memory used both by PROG2-4 and by PROG2-3.

2-7 The source code listing to PROG2-4.CPP

```
/////////////////////////
//
// prog2-4.cpp
//
// test prog2-3 from
// system call showing
// how command.com
// is invoked
//
/////////////////////////

extern "C" {
#include <stdio.h>
#include <process.h>
#include <errno.h>
}

#include "gdefs.h"

void main(int argc, char *argv[])
{

    int                 i;

    //
    //  Print parameter 1 to the screen
    //
    for (i= 0; i < argc; i++) {
        printf("%s ", argv[i]);
        }
    printf("\n\nPress any key to continue...\n\n");

    //
    //  Wait for key press
    //
    getchar();

    //
    //  Invoke the memory display program from within this
    //  program.
    //
    if (spawnlp(P_WAIT, "PROG2-3.EXE", "PROG2-3.EXE", NULL) == -1) {
        printf("spawnlp() of PROG2-3 failed with DOS Error %d\n", errno);
        }
}
```

3
EMS 3.0 and 3.2

Chapter 3's content falls into three sections. The first portion of the chapter outlines the EMS classes that make up the EMS interface. We then present six EMS demonstration programs that show how several of the EMS 3.0 and 3.2 functions can be called from C++. The final section presents the EMS 3.0 and 3.2 programming interface in its entirety. The EMS interface code is primarily implemented in assembly language. The C++ classes are built on top of the assembly language EMS interface.

Peruse the sample programs before delving into the detailed description of the interface. You'll find that much of the interface is fairly intuitive.

About the EMS programmer's interface

The C++ EMS interface described in this book is based on two object classes. The first, EMS_Ems, contains all of the functions that are not targeted at a specific EMS handle. An object of type EMS_Ems can be considered to be an "EMS system." The object is initialized through a call to `EMS_Ems::init()`. Only one object of this type is required, because there is really only one EMS system.

The second object class is EMS_EmBlk. Objects of this type denote blocks of EMS memory. An EMS block is identified by a handle, so an object of this type contains an EMS handle. An EMS_EmBlk object is usually initialized via a call to `EMS_EmBlk::allocEM`, which allocates a specified amount of EMS memory, and associates the target object with that block of memory. Subsequent calls with that object as the target can map pages from the associated block, save the page map, get information about the block such as its size, etc.

In order to properly use the EMS_EmBlk class, you should understand the relationship between its objects and the actual EMS blocks obtained from the EMM. First of all, we do not use constructors to allocate EMS blocks because there is no natural way to return errors from constructors. When support of exception handling becomes common in C++ compilers, this difficulty will go away. For the time being, however, we must make do with what we have. The constructor for an EMS_EmBlk creates an object that does not denote an EMS block. There are several calls that will initialize the EMS_EmBlk.

In order to make the system as simple as possible to use, we have created a destructor for EMS_EmBlk. This will release the associated EMS block when the object goes out of scope. Sometimes, however, we do not want this to happen. For this reason, we added an additional flag to EMS_EmBlk's. An EMS_EmBlk can be either "attached" to an EMS block, or "detached." If it is attached, the associated EMS block will be released when the object is destroyed. If it is detached, no action will be taken when the object is destroyed. By default, functions that allocate EMS memory (EMS_EmBlk::allocEM(), for example) initialize the target object to be attached. Thus, if an object is initialized via allocEM(), the EMS memory will be freed when the object passes out of scope. If the object is initialized via a non-allocation call that returns a handle (EMS_EmBlk::searchHandleName(), for example), the object will be detached by default. This occurs so that a function that needs to look up an EMS block that it didn't allocate doesn't inadvertantly free it when it returns.

In addition to freeing attached blocks at destruction time, if an initialized attached block is reinitialized, the original EMS block is released. Thus if you issued block.allocEM(3) followed by block.allocEM(5), the first EMS block of 3 would be released before allocating the second block of 5. This helps prevent loss of EMS memory.

To override the defaults, functions EMS_EmBlk::attach() and EMS_EmBlk::detach() are provided, which attach and detach the object from the EMS block that it is associated with.

EMS 3.0 demonstration programs

There are six demonstration programs presented in this section of Chapter 3. The first program, PROG3-1.CPP, demonstrates the following EMS operations:

- Testing for the presence of EMS
- Getting the EMS status
- Getting the EMS page frame address
- Getting the EMS version number

PROG3-1 starts by attempting to initialize EMS using EMS_Ems::init(). If this fails, it prints a message indicating the EMS is not present. It then goes on to get the EMS status, using EMS_Ems::getStatus(), the version of EMS supported, using `EMS_Ems::getVersion()` and the page frame address, using `EMS_Ems::getPFA()`. We don't use any of this information yet; we just print it out.

Figure 3-1 presents the source code listing to PROG3-1.CPP.

3-1 The source code listing to PROG3-1.CPP

```
/////////////////////////////////////////
//
// prog3-1.cpp
//
//        Demonstrates
//           - Testing for presence of EMS
//           - Getting EMS status
//           - Getting Page Frame Address
//           - Getting EMS Version #
//
/////////////////////////////////////////

extern "C" {
#include <stdio.h>
#include <dos.h>
}

#include "gdefs.h"
#include "ems.h"



void main()
{

    EMS_Ems             ems;

    int                 ems_status;
    WORD                version;

    EMS_PageFrame       pfa;

    //
    //  First check to see whether EMS is there:
    //
    if (ems.init()) {
        printf("EMM is not present\n");
        return;
        }

    printf("EMM is present\n");

    //
    //  Now get the EMS status. This should be 0, indicating
    //  no problem.
    //
    ems_status= ems.getStatus();
    printf("EMS status is %02X\n", ems_status);

    //
    //  Now get the EMS version number and print it:
    //
```

3-1 Continued.

```
if (ems.getVersion(&version)) {
    ems_demoError("EMS_Ems::getVersion");
    }
printf("EMS version is %2d.%02d\n", (version>>4)&0xF,
                                    (version)&0xF);

//
//  Now get the Page Frame Address:
//
if (ems.getPFA(&pfa)) {
    ems_demoError("EMS_Ems::getPFA");
    }
printf("Page Frame address is %04X:%04X\n", FP_SEG(pfa), FP_OFF(pfa));

}
```

The next program, PROG3-2.CPP, demonstrates the following EMS operations:

- Allocating and freeing EMS pages
- Getting the number of available EMS pages
- Getting the number of pages allocated for each handle
- Getting the number of active page handles

PROG3-2 initializes EMS. It then allocates two blocks of EMS memory using EMS_EmBlk::allocEM(). Finally it frees the blocks with EMS_Em Blk::freeEM(). After each allocate and free, the program queries the EMM to get a list of all blocks that are allocated and their sizes using EMS_Ems::getPagesAllHandles(). It also uses EMS_Ems.getFreeEM() to determine the total amount of EMS memory available. Thus, you can see the display change as blocks are allocated and freed.

Figure 3-2 presents the source code listing to PROG3-2.CPP.

3-2 The source code listing to PROG3-2.CPP

```
/////////////////////////////////////////
//
// prog3-2.cpp
//
//      Demonstrates
//          - Alloc/Free of EMS pages
//          - Get # available EMS pages
//          - Get # pages for each handle
//          - Get # active handles
//
/////////////////////////////////////////

extern "C" {
#include <stdio.h>
#include <stdlib.h>
#include <dos.h>
}
```

```
#include "gdefs.h"
#include "ems.h"


extern void displayActiveHandles();
extern void pause();


EMS_Ems          ems;


void main()
{
    WORD               totalPages;
    WORD               freePages;
    EMS_EmBlk          handle1;
    EMS_EmBlk          handle2;

    //
    //  First check for presence of EMS
    //
    if (ems.init()) {
        printf("EMS is not present\n");
        return;
        }

    //
    //  Get the number of free pages
    //
    if (ems.getFreeEM(&totalPages, &freePages)) {
        ems_demoError("EMS_Ems::getFreeEM");
        }

    //
    //  Print header:
    //
    printf("      Operation          Avail Pages     Active Handles\n");
    printf("=========================================\n");
    printf("After initialization |    %3d     |   Handle    Pages  |\n",
            freePages);

    displayActiveHandles();
    pause();

    //
    //  Now allocate 5 pages.
    //
    if (handle1.allocEM(5)) {
        ems_demoError("EMS_EmBlk::allocEM");
        }

    //
    //  Get the number of free pages
    //
    if (ems.getFreeEM(&totalPages, &freePages)) {
        ems_demoError("EMS_Ems::getFreeEM");
        }

    //
```

```
//   Print header:
//
printf("       Operation        Avail Pages      Active Handles\n");
printf("=====================================================\n");
printf("After 5 page allocate   |    %3d    |   Handle   Pages   |\n",
          freePages);

displayActiveHandles();
pause();


//
//   Now allocate 7 pages.
//
if (handle2.allocEM(7)) {
    ems_demoError("EMS_EmBlk::allocEM");
    }


//
//   Get the number of free pages
//
if (ems.getFreeEM(&totalPages, &freePages)) {
    ems_demoError("EMS_Ems::getFreeEM");
    }


//
//   Print header:
//
printf("       Operation        Avail Pages      Active Handles\n");
printf("=====================================================\n");
printf("After 7 page allocate   |    %3d    |   Handle   Pages   |\n",
          freePages);

displayActiveHandles();
pause();


//
//   Now free the 5 page block.
//
if (handle1.freeEM()) {
    ems_demoError("EMS_EmBlk::freeEM");
    }


//
//   Get the number of free pages
//
if (ems.getFreeEM(&totalPages, &freePages)) {
    ems_demoError("EMS_Ems::getFreeEM");
    }


//
//   Print header:
//
printf("       Operation        Avail Pages      Active Handles\n");
printf("=====================================================\n");
printf("After 5 page free       |    %3d    |   Handle   Pages   |\n",
          freePages);

displayActiveHandles();
pause();
```

```
    //
    //  Now free the 7 page block.
    //
    if (handle2.freeEM()) {
        ems_demoError("EMS_EmBlk::freeEM");
        }

    //
    //  Get the number of free pages
    //
    if (ems.getFreeEM(&totalPages, &freePages)) {
        ems_demoError("EMS_Ems::getFreeEM");
        }

    //
    //  Print header:
    //
    printf("        Operation           Avail Pages     Active Handles\n");
    printf("=================================================\n");
    printf("After 7 page free    |    %3d    |   Handle   Pages  |\n",
                 freePages);

    displayActiveHandles();

}

void displayActiveHandles()
{

    EMS_HandleInfo      *handleInfoArray;
    WORD                numActiveHandles;
    WORD                numActiveHandles2;

    WORD                i;

    //
    //  First find out how many active handles there are:
    //
    if (ems.getNumActiveHandles(&numActiveHandles)) {
        ems_demoError("EMS_Ems::getNumActiveHandles");
        }

    //
    //  Now allocate a block of handleInfo packets big enough to
    //  hold them.
    //
    handleInfoArray= new EMS_HandleInfo[numActiveHandles];

    //
    //  Now get the info.
    //
    if (ems.getPagesAllHandles(handleInfoArray, &numActiveHandles2)) {
        ems_demoError("EMS_Ems::getNumActiveHandles");
        }

    //
    //  The following is a brief sanity clause (Everybody knows
    //  there ain't no sanity clause).
    //
    if (numActiveHandles2 != numActiveHandles) {
        printf("A most unusual situation has occurred...\n");
```

```
        exit(0);
        }

//
//  Finally, display it.
//
printf("                                         |          |         |\n");

for (i= 0; i < numActiveHandles; i++) {
    printf(
        "                                         |   %3d    |   %3d   |\n",
        handleInfoArray[i].handle,
        handleInfoArray[i].numPages);

    if (i+1 < numActiveHandles) {
        printf(
            "                                                 |          |         |\n");
    }
}

printf("==================================================\n");

//
//  Now free up the array.
//
delete handleInfoArray;

}

void pause()

{

    //
    //  Display a little message:
    //
    printf("Hit <CR> to continue...");
    fflush(stdout);

    //
    //  Wait for a <CR>
    //
    while (getchar() != '\n') {
        }

}
```

The third program, PROG3-3.CPP, demonstrates the following EMS operations:

- Mapping of EMS pages
- Transferring data to and from EMS

PROG3-3 shows how to get data in and out of EMS. It allocates two 64K blocks of EMS. It then maps the first into the page frame area using EMS_EmBlk::mapPage() and copies some text into it and prints it. It then maps the second block into the page frame area, copies some text into it and prints it. It then maps the first block again, this time mapping the 16K EMS pages in the reverse order. Thus, the first page of the EMS block is the last page in the page frame area. It prints out the text stored in the EMS block when the block was first mapped. Finally it maps the second block, again in reverse order, and prints the contents out. This program demonstrates the basic idea of using EMS: allocating, mapping, reading/writing, and re-mapping pages.

Figure 3-3 presents the source code listing to PROG3-3.CPP.

3-3 The source code listing to PROG3-3.CPP

```
/////////////////////////////////////////
//
// prog3-3.cpp
//
//        Demonstrates
//            - Mapping EMS pages
//            - Transfer of memory from/to EMS
//
/////////////////////////////////////////

extern "C" {
#include <stdio.h>
#include <stdlib.h>
#include <dos.h>
#include <string.h>
}


#include "gdefs.h"
#include "ems.h"


EMS_Ems          ems;


void main()
{
        EMS_PageFrame        page_frame;
        EMS_EmBlk            handle1;
        EMS_EmBlk            handle2;

        char                 *text;

        WORD                 i;


        //
        //  First check for presence of EMS
        //
        if (ems.init()) {
            printf("EMS is not present\n");
            return;
            }

        //
        //  Get the Page Frame Address.
```

```
//
if (ems.getPFA(&page_frame)) {
    ems_demoError("EMS_Ems::getPFA");
    }


//
//  Get a couple of 4 page blocks of memory (64K each).
//
if (handle1.allocEM(4)) {
    ems_demoError("EMS_EmBlk::allocEM");
    }
if (handle2.allocEM(4)) {
    ems_demoError("EMS_EmBlk::allocEM");
    }


//
//  Now let's map the first.
//
for (i= 0; i < 4; i++) {
    if (handle1.mapPage(i, i)) {
        ems_demoError("EMS_EmBlk::mapPage");
        }
    }


//
//  The memory is now mapped into the page frame. Let's
//  move some text into random spots in it.
//
text= "     I took a speed reading course and I";
strcpy(&page_frame[0][400], text);

text= "     read \"War and Peace\".";
strcpy(&page_frame[1][801], text);

text= "     It involves Russia.";
strcpy(&page_frame[2][4000], text);

text= "                 -- Woody Allen\n";
strcpy(&page_frame[3][2000], text);


//
//  Now print it back.
//
printf("%s\n", &page_frame[0][400]);
printf("%s\n", &page_frame[1][801]);
printf("%s\n", &page_frame[2][4000]);
printf("%s\n", &page_frame[3][2000]);


//
//  Now let's map the second block
//
for (i= 0; i < 4; i++) {
    if (handle2.mapPage(i, i)) {
        ems_demoError("EMS_EmBlk::mapPage");
        }
    }


//
//  The memory is now mapped into the page frame. Let's
```

```
    //  move some text into random spots in it.
    //
    text= "      Children make the most desirable opponents";
    strcpy(&page_frame[0][400], text);

    text= "      in Scrabble as they are both easy to beat";
    strcpy(&page_frame[1][801], text);

    text= "      and fun to cheat.";
    strcpy(&page_frame[2][4000], text);

    text= "                  -- Fran Lebowitz\n";
    strcpy(&page_frame[3][2000], text);

    //
    //  Now print it back.
    //
    printf("%s\n", &page_frame[0][400]);
    printf("%s\n", &page_frame[1][801]);
    printf("%s\n", &page_frame[2][4000]);
    printf("%s\n", &page_frame[3][2000]);

    //
    //  Now let's map the first, backwards this time.
    //
    for (i= 0; i < 4; i++) {
        if (handle1.mapPage(i, 3-i)) {
            ems_demoError("EMS_EmBlk::mapPage");
            }
        }


    //
    //  Now print it back.
    //
    printf("%s\n", &page_frame[3][400]);
    printf("%s\n", &page_frame[2][801]);
    printf("%s\n", &page_frame[1][4000]);
    printf("%s\n", &page_frame[0][2000]);

    //
    //  Now let's map the second block backwards.
    //
    for (i= 0; i < 4; i++) {
        if (handle2.mapPage(i, 3-i)) {
            ems_demoError("EMS_EmBlk::mapPage");
            }
        }

    //
    //  Now print it back.
    //
    printf("%s\n", &page_frame[3][400]);
    printf("%s\n", &page_frame[2][801]);
    printf("%s\n", &page_frame[1][4000]);
    printf("%s\n", &page_frame[0][2000]);

    //
    //  We're done. We could free the memory, but let's leave
    //  it for the destructors to do.
    //
    //  if (handle1.freeEM()) {
```

```
//        ems_demoError("EMS_EmBlk::freeEM");
//        }
//  if (handle2.freeEM()) {
//        ems_demoError("EMS_EmBlk::freeEM");
//        }
}
```

The fourth program, PROG3-4.CPP, demonstrates the following EMS operation:

- Saving and restoring of the EMS page map

PROG3-4 demonstrates saving and restoring the EMS page map. First an EMS block is mapped into the page frame area. Text is copied into it and printed. The page map is saved using EMS_EmBlk::savePageMap() and a second block is mapped. Text is copied to the second block and printed. Finally, the saved page map is restored with EMS_EmBlk::re storePageMap(). This brings the first EMS block into the page frame area. The text from this block is then printed.

Figure 3-4 presents the source code listing to PROG3-4.CPP.

3-4 The source code listing to PROG3-4.CPP

```
/////////////////////////////////////
//
// prog3-4.cpp
//
//       Demonstrates
//           - Save/Restore of the page map
//
/////////////////////////////////////

extern "C" {
#include <stdio.h>
#include <stdlib.h>
#include <dos.h>
#include <string.h>
}

#include "gdefs.h"
#include "ems.h"


EMS_Ems              ems;

void main()
{
    EMS_PageFrame        page_frame;
    EMS_EmBlk            handle1;
    EMS_EmBlk            handle2;

    char                *text;

    WORD                i;
```

```
//
//  First check for presence of EMS
//
if (ems.init()) {
    printf("EMS is not present\n");
    return;
    }

//
//  Get the Page Frame Address.
//
if (ems.getPFA(&page_frame)) {
    ems_demoError("EMS_Ems::getPFA");
    }

//
//  Get a couple of 4 page blocks of memory (64K each).
//
if (handle1.allocEM(4)) {
    ems_demoError("EMS_EmBlk::allocEM");
    }
if (handle2.allocEM(4)) {
    ems_demoError("EMS_EmBlk::allocEM");
    }

//
//  Now let's map the first.
//
for (i= 0; i < 4; i++) {
    if (handle1.mapPage(i, i)) {
        ems_demoError("EMS_EmBlk::mapPage");
        }
    }

//
//  The memory is now mapped into the page frame. Let's
//  move some text into random spots in it.
//
text= "     Be careful not to impart your wisdom to a guest";
strcpy(&page_frame[0][400], text);

text= "     whose background you do not know. You may be instructing";
strcpy(&page_frame[1][801], text);

text= "     a Nobel Laureate in his own field";
strcpy(&page_frame[2][4000], text);

text= "                    -- David Brown\n";
strcpy(&page_frame[3][2000], text);

//
//  Now print it back.
//
printf("%s\n", &page_frame[0][400]);
printf("%s\n", &page_frame[1][801]);
printf("%s\n", &page_frame[2][4000]);
printf("%s\n", &page_frame[3][2000]);

//
//  Save the map state. This will save the current map
//  of the PFA and associate the saved state with handle1.
//  We could as easily save it with handle2 as long as
```

3-4 Continued.

```
//   we restore it from the same place we saved it.
//
if (handle1.savePageMap()) {
    ems_demoError("EMS_EmBlk::savePageMap");
    }

//
//  Now let's map the second block
//
for (i= 0; i < 4; i++) {
    if (handle2.mapPage(i, i)) {
        ems_demoError("EMS_EmBlk::mapPage");
        }
    }
//
//  The memory is now mapped into the page frame. Let's
//  move some text into random spots in it.
//
text= "    I'm astounded by people who want to \"know\"";
strcpy(&page_frame[0][400], text);

text= "    the universe when it's hard enough to find your";
strcpy(&page_frame[1][801], text);

text= "    way around Chinatown.";
strcpy(&page_frame[2][4000], text);

text= "                    -- Woody Allen\n";
strcpy(&page_frame[3][2000], text);

//
//  Now print it back.
//
printf("%s\n", &page_frame[0][400]);
printf("%s\n", &page_frame[1][801]);
printf("%s\n", &page_frame[2][4000]);
printf("%s\n", &page_frame[3][2000]);

//
//  Now let's restore the old map.
//
if (handle1.restorePageMap()) {
    ems_demoError("EMS_EmBlk::restorePageMap");
    }

//
//  Now when we print out, we should get the first set
//  of lines.
//
printf("%s\n", &page_frame[0][400]);
printf("%s\n", &page_frame[1][801]);
printf("%s\n", &page_frame[2][4000]);
printf("%s\n", &page_frame[3][2000]);

//
//  We're done. Free the memory we've allocated.
//
if (handle1.freeEM()) {
    ems_demoError("EMS_EmBlk::freeEM");
```

```
        }
    if (handle2.freeEM()) {
        ems_demoError("EMS_EmBlk::freeEM");
        }
    }
```

The fifth program, PROG3-5.CPP, demonstrates the following EMS operation:

- Saving and restoring the EMS page map using EMS 3.2 calls

PROG3-5 shows how to use the EMS 3.2 calls to save and restore the page frame map. These calls allow the user to save the map to a specified area of memory. This allows the program to have an arbitrary number of saved maps, rather than one per EMS handle, as with the 3.0 calls. The program initializes two blocks of EMS by mapping and writing text to them. For each one, after writing the text, the page map is saved using EMS_Ems::savePageMap(). Then each saved map is restored with EMS_Ems::restorePageMap(), and the text is printed.

Figure 3-5 presents the source code listing to PROG3-5.CPP.

3-5 The source code listing to PROG3-5.CPP

```
///////////////////////////////////////
//
// prog3-5.cpp
//
//       Demonstrates
//           - Save/Restore of the page map using 3.2 calls
//
///////////////////////////////////////

extern "C" {
#include <stdio.h>
#include <stdlib.h>
#include <dos.h>
#include <string.h>
}


#include "gdefs.h"

#define     Uses_EMS32
#include "ems.h"


EMS_Ems             ems;


void main()
{
    EMS_PageFrame       page_frame;
    EMS_EmBlk           handle1;
    EMS_EmBlk           handle2;

    DWORD               *mapBuffer1;
```

```
DWORD                    *mapBuffer2;
WORD                      mapInfoSize;

char                     *text;

WORD                      i;

//
//  First check for presence of EMS
//
if (ems.init()) {
    printf("EMS is not present\n");
    return;
    }

//
//  Get the Page Frame Address.
//
if (ems.getPFA(&page_frame)) {
    ems_demoError("EMS_Ems::getPFA");
    }

//
//  Get a couple of 4 page blocks of memory (64K each).
//
if (handle1.allocEM(4)) {
    ems_demoError("EMS_EmBlk::allocEM");
    }
if (handle2.allocEM(4)) {
    ems_demoError("EMS_EmBlk::allocEM");
    }

//
//  Now let's map the first.
//
for (i= 0; i < 4; i++) {
    if (handle1.mapPage(i, i)) {
        ems_demoError("EMS_EmBlk::mapPage");
        }
    }

//
//  The memory is now mapped into the page frame. Let's
//  move some text into random spots in it.
//
text= "      Neurotic means he is not as sensible as I am,";
strcpy(&page_frame[0][400], text);

text= "      and psychotic means that he is even worse than";
strcpy(&page_frame[1][801], text);

text= "      my brother-in-law.";
strcpy(&page_frame[2][4000], text);

text= "                          -- Karl Menninger\n";
strcpy(&page_frame[3][2000], text);

//
//  Now print it back.
//
```

```
printf("%s\n", &page_frame[0][400]);
printf("%s\n", &page_frame[1][801]);
printf("%s\n", &page_frame[2][4000]);
printf("%s\n", &page_frame[3][2000]);

//
//   Save the map state. First we query as to how much
//   memory is required, allocate the memory, then do
//   the actual save.
//
if (ems.getMapInfoSize(&mapInfoSize)) {
    ems_demoError("EMS_Ems::getMapInfoSize");
    }
mapBuffer1= new DWORD[mapInfoSize/sizeof(DWORD)];
mapBuffer2= new DWORD[mapInfoSize/sizeof(DWORD)];

if (ems.savePageMap(mapBuffer1)) {
    ems_demoError("EMS_Ems::savePageMap");
    }

//
//   Now let's map the second block
//
for (i= 0; i < 4; i++) {
    if (handle2.mapPage(i, i)) {
        ems_demoError("EMS_EmBlk::mapPage");
        }
    }

//
//   The memory is now mapped into the page frame. Let's
//   move some text into random spots in it.
//
text= "    When I can no longer bear to think of the victims";
strcpy(&page_frame[0][400], text);

text= "    of broken homes, I begin to think of the victims";
strcpy(&page_frame[1][801], text);

text= "    of intact ones.";
strcpy(&page_frame[2][4000], text);

text= "                        -- Peter De Vries\n";
strcpy(&page_frame[3][2000], text);

//
//   Now print it back.
//
printf("%s\n", &page_frame[0][400]);
printf("%s\n", &page_frame[1][801]);
printf("%s\n", &page_frame[2][4000]);
printf("%s\n", &page_frame[3][2000]);

//
//   Now let's swap maps, saving the current map into mapBuffer2,
//   and loading the new map from mapBuffer1.
//
if (ems.swapPageMap(mapBuffer1, mapBuffer2)) {
    ems_demoError("EMS_Ems::swapPageMap");
    }

//
```

```
//   Now when we print out, we should get the first set
//   of lines.
//
printf("%s\n", &page_frame[0][400]);
printf("%s\n", &page_frame[1][801]);
printf("%s\n", &page_frame[2][4000]);
printf("%s\n", &page_frame[3][2000]);

//
//   Now let's finish by restoring the second page map.
//
if (ems.restPageMap(mapBuffer2)) {
    ems_demoError("EMS_Ems::restPageMap");
    }

//
//   And print the contents:
//
printf("%s\n", &page_frame[0][400]);
printf("%s\n", &page_frame[1][801]);
printf("%s\n", &page_frame[2][4000]);
printf("%s\n", &page_frame[3][2000]);

//
//   We're done. Free the memory we've allocated.
//
if (handle1.freeEM()) {
    ems_demoError("EMS_EmBlk::freeEM");
    }
if (handle2.freeEM()) {
    ems_demoError("EMS_EmBlk::freeEM");
    }
}
```

The last program, PROG3-6.CPP, demonstrates the following EMS operation:

- Relying on the EMS_EmBlk destructor to free EMS memory

PROG3-6 is similar to PROG3-2, except that it calls a procedure to allocate EMS blocks. When that procedure returns, destructors are called for the EMS_EmBlk's, which free the EMS blocks.

Figure 3-6 presents the source code listing to PROG3-6.CPP.

3-6 The source code listing to PROG3-6.CPP

```
////////////////////////////////////////
//
// prog3-6.cpp
//
//      Demonstrates
//          - Use of destructor to release EMS pages
//
////////////////////////////////////////

extern "C" {
```

```c
#include <stdio.h>
#include <stdlib.h>
#include <dos.h>
}

#include "gdefs.h"
#include "ems.h"


extern void displayActiveHandles();
extern void pause();
extern void destructorTest();

EMS_Ems          ems;

void main()
{

    WORD                totalPages;
    WORD                freePages;

    //
    //  First check for presence of EMS
    //
    if (ems.init()) {
        printf("EMS is not present\n");
        return;
        }

    //
    //  Get the number of free pages
    //
    if (ems.getFreeEM(&totalPages, &freePages)) {
        ems_demoError("EMS_Ems::getFreeEM");
        }

    //
    //  Print header:
    //
    printf("        Operation          Avail Pages     Active Handles\n");
    printf("===================================================\n");
    printf("After initialization |      %3d      |  Handle   Pages  |\n",
                freePages);

    displayActiveHandles();
    pause();

    //
    //  Call a routine which will allocate some pages.
    //
    destructorTest();

    //
    //  The memory allocated by destructorTest() should be released.
    //
    //  Get the number of free pages
    //
    if (ems.getFreeEM(&totalPages, &freePages)) {
        ems_demoError("EMS_Ems::getFreeEM");
        }
```

```
//
//   Print header:
//
printf("       Operation          Avail Pages        Active Handles\n");
printf("=================================================\n");
printf("After destructor called |     %3d    |   Handle   Pages  |\n",
              freePages);

displayActiveHandles();

}

void destructorTest()
{

    WORD                totalPages;
    WORD                freePages;

    EMS_EmBlk           handle;

    //
    //   Now allocate 5 pages.
    //
    if (handle.allocEM(5)) {
        ems_demoError("EMS_EmBlk::allocEM");
        }

    //
    //   Get the number of free pages
    //
    if (ems.getFreeEM(&totalPages, &freePages)) {
        ems_demoError("EMS_Ems::getFreeEM");
        }

    //
    //   Print header:
    //
    printf("       Operation          Avail Pages        Active Handles\n");
    printf("=================================================\n");
    printf("After 5 page allocate   |     %3d    |   Handle   Pages  |\n",
              freePages);

    displayActiveHandles();
    pause();

    //
    //   Note that we don't release the memory.
    //   The destructor will release it, since it is attached.
    //

}

void displayActiveHandles()
{

    EMS_HandleInfo      *handleInfoArray;
    WORD                numActiveHandles;
    WORD                numActiveHandles2;

    WORD                i;
```

```
    //
    //   First find out how many active handles there are:
    //
    if (ems.getNumActiveHandles(&numActiveHandles)) {
        ems_demoError("EMS_Ems::getNumActiveHandles");
        }

    //
    //   Now allocate a block of handleInfo packets big enough to
    //   hold them.
    //
    handleInfoArray= new EMS_HandleInfo[numActiveHandles];

    //
    //   Now get the info.
    //
    if (ems.getPagesAllHandles(handleInfoArray, &numActiveHandles2)) {
        ems_demoError("EMS_Ems::getNumActiveHandles");
        }

    //
    //   The following is a brief sanity clause (Everybody knows
    //   there ain't no sanity clause).
    //
    if (numActiveHandles2 != numActiveHandles) {
        printf("A most unusual situation has occurred...\n");
        exit(0);
        }

    //
    //   Finally, display it.
    //
    printf("                              ─────────┼─────────┤\n");

    for (i= 0; i < numActiveHandles; i++) {
        printf(
            "                                      |   %3d   |   %3d   |\n",
            handleInfoArray[i].handle,
            handleInfoArray[i].numPages);

        if (i+1 < numActiveHandles) {
            printf(
                "                              ├─────────┼─────────┤\n");
            }
        }

    printf("══════════════════════════════╧═════════╧═════════╝\n");

    //
    //   Now free up the array.
    //
    delete handleInfoArray;

}

void pause()

{

    //
    //   Display a little message:
```

```
//
printf("Hit <CR> to continue...");
fflush(stdout);

//
//  Wait for a <CR>
//
while (getchar() != '\n') {
    }

}
```

The EMS 3.0 and 3.2 interface

All of the EMS related assembly files presented in Chapters 3 and 4 have been assembled and have had their resultant object modules included in EMSL.LIB.

Note that the assembly source file naming convention follows a consistent format. All EMS source names begin with the "EMS" prefix. This prefix is followed by two or three hexadecimal numbers. The first two numbers refer to the EMS Interrupt 67h function number. If there is a third number, it refers to the subfunction number. For example, the source file EMS5D2.ASM contains the source code to invoke interrupt 67h function 5Dh subfunction 2h. Simple as that.

Note that the naming convention for the EMS 4.0 interface is similar. For example, source file EMS5D2.ASM contains the code to function EMS_Ems.releaseAccessKey40(). The numerical suffix refers to the EMS version number. In this case, function 5Dh subfunction 2h is supported only by EMS 4.0.

Finally, we have decided always to return the EMS function's error status via the global errno variable. If a function takes an error it returns a non-zero error code.

EMS function return status

== 0   Status OK, no error
!= 0   Status NOT OK, error occurred, error code in the variable errno

EMS functions that are required to return values to the calling function do so via pointer parameters in the function's definition.

Before presenting the EMS 3.0 and 3.2 programmer's interface code, we present three preparatory files. The first is a header file for the EMS interface. This file defines the functions, classes, types, and error codes for the EMS interface.

The second file is the C++ source to those class methods that are not defined inline.

The third file is a defines file for use by the assembly language modules.

Figure 3-7 presents the source code listing to EMS.H. This is a header file that defines the EMS interface for the EMS 3.0, 3.2, and 4.0 functionality.

3-7 The source code listing to EMS.H

```
///////////////////////////////////////
//
// ems.h
//
//   Ems and Emm related definitions,
//   structures and function prototypes
//
///////////////////////////////////////


/**********************************************************************
***                                                                ***
***        Constant #defines                                       ***
***                                                                ***
**********************************************************************/

#define EMS_STD_PAGE_SIZE      16384
#define EMS_PAGE_FRAME_SIZE    4
#define EMS_NULL_HANDLE        0xFFFF


//
//   Define a couple of constants for the move and exchange operations.
//
#define EMS_MOVE_CONV          0
#define EMS_MOVE_EMS           1

//
//   Define the EMS error codes.
//
#define EMSErrOK            0x00     // No error
#define EMSErrInternal      0x80     // Internal EMM error
#define EMSErrHardware      0x81     // EM Hardware error
#define EMSErrEMMBusy       0x82     // EMM Busy
#define EMSErrHandInv       0x83     // Handle Invalid
#define EMSErrUnimp         0x84     // Undefined EMS function
#define EMSErrNoHandles     0x85     // Handles Exhausted
#define EMSErrSaveRest      0x86     // Error in save/restore of context
#define EMSErrReqGTPhys     0x87     // Not enough physical EM for request
#define EMSErrReqGTAvail    0x88     // Not enough available EM for request
#define EMSErrReqIsZero     0x89     // Cannot allocate zero pages
#define EMSErrLogPgInv      0x8A     // Invalid logical page number
#define EMSErrPhysPgInv     0x8B     // Invalid physical page number
#define EMSErrSSAreaFull    0x8C     // Mapping save area is full
#define EMSErrSaveFail      0x8D     // Mapping save failed
#define EMSErrRestFail      0x8E     // Mapping restore failed
#define EMSErrParameter     0x8F     // Subfunction parameter not defined
#define EMSErrAttribute     0x90     // Attribute type not defined
#define EMSErrUnsupported   0x91     // Feature not supported
#define EMSErrOverlap       0x92     // Source/dest of move overlap, move done
```

3-7 Continued.

```
#define EMSErrLenInv          0x93    // Length of move request invalid
#define EMSErrOverlapCE       0x94    // Overlap of conventional and extended
#define EMSErrOffsetInv       0x95    // Offset outside logical page
#define EMSErrRegionGT1MB     0x96    // Region size > 1 megabyte
#define EMSErrOverlapFatal    0x97    // Source/dest overlap prevented move
#define EMSErrMemTypeInv      0x98    // Memory source/dest types invalid
#define EMSErrDMARegUnsupp    0x9A    // Specified register set unsupported
#define EMSErrNoDMARegs       0x9B    // No available alternate register sets
#define EMSErrAltRegsUnsupp   0x9C    // Alternate registers unsupported
#define EMSErrDMARegUndef     0x9D    // Specified register set undefined
#define EMSErrDMAChanUnsupp   0x9E    // Dedicated DMA channels unsupported
#define EMSErrChanUnsupp      0x9F    // Specified DMA channel unsupported
#define EMSErrNameNotFound    0xA0    // No handle found for name
#define EMSErrNameExists      0xA1    // Handle with same name already exists
#define EMSErrPointerInv      0xA3    // Invalid pointer or source array bogus
#define EMSErrAccess          0xA4    // Access denied by operating system


/***********************************************************************
***                                                                  ***
***        Structure and type definitions                           ***
***                                                                  ***
***********************************************************************/

//
//   Mapping packet element for ems_mapPagesByNumber
//
typedef struct {
    WORD    logicalPage;     // Logical page
    WORD    physicalPage;    // Physical page number
    }   EMS_MapByNumber;

//
//   Mapping packet element for ems_mapPagesByAddress
//
typedef struct {
    WORD    logicalPage;     // Logical page
    WORD    physicalSeg;     // Physical segment number
    }   EMS_MapByAddress;

//
//   Packet element for ems_getPagesAllHandles
//
typedef struct {
    WORD    handle;          // ems handle
    WORD    numPages;        // ems pages associated with handle
    }   EMS_HandleInfo;

//
//   Packet element for ems_getAddrsMappable40
//
typedef struct {
    WORD    pageSegment;     // Segment base address
    WORD    physNumber;      // Physical page number
    }   EMS_MappablePagesInfo;

//
```

```
//   Packet element for ems_getAllHandleNames40
//
typedef struct {
    WORD    handle;             // ems handle
    char    name[8];            // ems name (version 4.0)
    }    EMS_HandleNameInfo;


//
//   Packet for ems_moveMemRegion40 and ems_swapMemRegions40
//
typedef struct {
    DWORD   length;             // memory length
    BYTE    srcType;            // 0=conventional,1=expanded
    WORD    srcHandle;          // source handle
    WORD    srcOffset;          // source offset
    WORD    srcPage;            // source segment or logical page
    BYTE    destType;           // 0=conventional,1=expanded
    WORD    destHandle;         // destination handle
    WORD    destOffset;         // destination offset
    WORD    destPage;           // destination segment or logical page
    }    EMS_MoveMemoryInfo;


//
//   Packet for ems_getHWConfig40
//
typedef struct {
    WORD    rawPgSize;          // size of raw pages in paragraphs
    WORD    altRegSets;         // number of alternate reg sets
    WORD    saveAreaSz;         // size of mapping save area in bytes
    WORD    regsDma;            // num of regs can be assigned to dma
    WORD    dmaType;            // 0=alt dma regs OK,1=one dma reg only
    }    EMS_HardwareConfigInfo;



//
//   An EMS_PageFrame is a pointer to an array of four pages.
//
typedef char (*EMS_PageFrame)[EMS_STD_PAGE_SIZE];


/************************************************************************
***                                                                  ***
***     Function definitions for 'C' interface                       ***
***                                                                  ***
************************************************************************/

extern "C" {


//
//   EMS 3.0 'C' API
//


extern int ems_getStatus(void);
extern int ems_getPFA(EMS_PageFrame *page_frame);
extern int ems_getFreeEM(WORD *total, WORD *free);
extern int ems_allocEM(WORD pages, WORD *handle);
extern int ems_mapPage(WORD physical_page,
                       WORD logical_page,
                       WORD handle);
```

3-7 Continued.

```
extern int ems_freeEM(WORD handle);
extern int ems_getVersion(WORD *version);
extern int ems_savePageMap(WORD handle);
extern int ems_restorePageMap(WORD handle);
extern int ems_getNumActiveHandles(WORD *num_handles);
extern int ems_getPagesForHandle(WORD handle, WORD *num_pages);
extern int ems_getPagesAllHandles(EMS_HandleInfo info[],
                                  WORD *num_handles);

#if defined(Uses_EMS32) || defined(Uses_EMS40)

//
//   EMS 3.2 'C' API
//

extern int ems_savePageMap32(DWORD *save_buffer);
extern int ems_restPageMap32(DWORD *restore_buffer);
extern int ems_swapPageMap32(DWORD *rest_buffer, DWORD *save_buffer);
extern int ems_getMapInfoSize32(WORD *size);

#endif

#if defined(Uses_EMS40)

//
//   EMS 4.0 'C' API
//

extern int ems_savePartialMap40(WORD *map, void *buffer);
extern int ems_restPartialMap40(void *buffer);
extern int ems_getPMapInfoSize40(WORD pages, WORD *buffSize);

extern int ems_mapPagesByNum40(WORD handle, WORD pages,
                               EMS_MapByNumber *buffer);
extern int ems_mapPagesByAddr40(WORD handle, WORD pages,
                                EMS_MapByAddress *buffer);
extern int ems_reallocHandPages40(WORD handle, WORD pages);

extern int ems_getHandleAttr40(WORD handle, WORD *attribute);
extern int ems_setHandleAttr40(WORD handle, WORD attribute);
extern int ems_getAttrCapability40(WORD *capability);

extern int ems_getHandleName40(WORD handle, char *handle_name);
extern int ems_setHandleName40(WORD handle, char *handle_name);
extern int ems_getAllHandleNames40(EMS_HandleNameInfo *info_list);
extern int ems_searchHandleName40(WORD *handle, char *name);
extern int ems_getTotalHandles40(WORD *handles);

extern int ems_mapPagesJumpNum40(WORD handle, DWORD *buffer);
extern int ems_mapPagesJumpSeg40(WORD handle, DWORD *buffer);
extern int ems_mapPagesCallNum40(WORD handle, DWORD *buffer);
extern int ems_mapPagesCallSeg40(WORD handle, DWORD *buffer);
extern int ems_getStackNeeded40(WORD *stack_space);

extern int ems_moveMemRegion40(EMS_MoveMemoryInfo *buffer);
extern int ems_swapMemRegions40(EMS_MoveMemoryInfo *buffer);

extern int ems_getAddrsMappable40(EMS_MappablePagesInfo *buffer,
                                  WORD *num_entries);
```

```
        extern int ems_getNumMappable40(WORD *mappablePages);

        extern int ems_getHWConfig40(EMS_HardwareConfigInfo *buffer);

        extern int ems_getNumRawPages40(WORD *total_pages, WORD *free_pages);

        extern int ems_allocHandleStd40(WORD *handle, WORD pages);
        extern int ems_allocHandleRaw40(WORD *handle, WORD pages);

        extern int ems_getAltMapRegs40(BYTE *active_map, BYTE *regs_area);
        extern int ems_setAltMapRegs40(BYTE alt_set, BYTE *regs_area);
        extern int ems_getAltMapRegSize40(WORD *buf_size);
        extern int ems_allocAltMapRegs40(BYTE *alt_map);
        extern int ems_releaseAltMapRegs40(BYTE alt_map);

        extern int ems_allocDMARegs40(BYTE *set);
        extern int ems_enableDMA40(BYTE set, BYTE channel);
        extern int ems_disableDMA40(BYTE set);
        extern int ems_releaseDMARegs40(BYTE set);

        extern int ems_prepEmmWarmBoot40(void);
        extern int ems_enableEmmOSFuncs40(WORD a1, WORD a2, WORD *a3, WORD *a4);
        extern int ems_disableEmmOSFuncs40(WORD a1, WORD a2, WORD *a3, WORD *a4);
        extern int ems_releaseAccessKey40(WORD a1, WORD a2);

        #endif

        }    // End of 'C' definitions


        /************************************************************************
        ***                                                                  ***
        ***      Class definitions                                           ***
        ***                                                                  ***
        ************************************************************************/

        class    EMS_Ems;
        class    EMS_EmBlk;

        //
        //   First define the XMS_XmBlk class, which defines Expanded memory
        //   blocks as objects.
        //
        class    EMS_EmBlk {

            WORD                handle;
            BYTE                attached;

        public:
            friend class    EMS_Ems;

                EMS_EmBlk() {
                    handle= EMS_NULL_HANDLE;
                    attached= FALSE;
                    }

                EMS_EmBlk(WORD handleNumber) {
                    handle= handleNumber;
                    attached= FALSE;
                    }
```

3-7 Continued.

```
#if defined(Uses_EMS40)
        EMS_EmBlk(char *handleName) {
            if (ems_searchHandleName40(&handle, handleName)) {
                handle= EMS_NULL_HANDLE;
                }
            attached= FALSE;
            }
#endif


        EMS_EmBlk(const EMS_EmBlk &old) {
            handle= old.handle;
            attached= FALSE;
            }

    ~EMS_EmBlk() {
            if (attached) {
                ems_freeEM(handle);
                }
            }

    EMS_EmBlk &operator=(const EMS_EmBlk &rhs) {
            if (attached) {
                ems_freeEM(handle);
                }
            handle= rhs.handle;
            attached= FALSE;
            return *this;
            }

    EMS_EmBlk &operator=(const WORD handleNum) {
            if (attached) {
                ems_freeEM(handle);
                }
            handle= handleNum;
            attached= FALSE;
            return *this;
            }

    void attach() {
            attached= TRUE;
            }

    void detach() {
            attached= FALSE;
            }

    WORD num() {
            return handle;
            }


    int allocEM(WORD pages);

    int mapPage(WORD physical_page,
                        WORD logical_page) {
            return ems_mapPage(physical_page, logical_page, handle);
            }
```

```
        int freeEM();

        int savePageMap() {
                return ems_savePageMap(handle);
                }

        int restorePageMap() {
                return ems_restorePageMap(handle);
                }

        int getPagesForHandle(WORD *num_pages) {
                return ems_getPagesForHandle(handle, num_pages);
                }


#if defined(Uses_EMS40)

        int mapPagesByNum(WORD pages, EMS_MapByNumber *buffer) {
                return ems_mapPagesByNum40(handle, pages, buffer);
                }

        int mapPagesByAddr(WORD pages, EMS_MapByAddress *buffer) {
                return ems_mapPagesByAddr40(handle, pages, buffer);
                }

        int reallocHandPages(WORD pages) {
                return ems_reallocHandPages40(handle, pages);
                }

        int getHandleAttr(WORD *attribute) {
                return ems_getHandleAttr40(handle, attribute);
                }

        int setHandleAttr(WORD attribute) {
                return ems_setHandleAttr40(handle, attribute);
                }

        int getHandleName(char *handle_name) {
                return ems_getHandleName40(handle, handle_name);
                }

        int setHandleName(char *handle_name) {
                return ems_setHandleName40(handle, handle_name);
                }

        int searchHandleName(char *name);

        int allocHandleStd(WORD pages);

        int allocHandleRaw(WORD pages);
#endif
        };


//
//  Define the EMS_Ems class, which contains general EMS functions.
//
class    EMS_Ems {
```

3-7 Continued.

```
    //
    //   Prevent assignment and copy-initialization:
    //
    EMS_Ems      &operator=(const EMS_Ems &);
                 EMS_Ems(const EMS_Ems &);

public:

        EMS_Ems() {};

    int init();

    int getStatus() {
            return ems_getStatus();
            }

    int getPFA(EMS_PageFrame *page_frame) {
            return ems_getPFA(page_frame);
            }

    int getFreeEM(WORD *total, WORD *free) {
            return ems_getFreeEM(total, free);
            }

    int getVersion(WORD *version) {
            return ems_getVersion(version);
            }

    int getNumActiveHandles(WORD *num_handles) {
            return ems_getNumActiveHandles(num_handles);
            }

    int getPagesAllHandles(EMS_HandleInfo info[],
                                    WORD *num_handles) {
            return ems_getPagesAllHandles(info, num_handles);
            }


#if defined(Uses_EMS32) || defined(Uses_EMS40)

    //
    //   EMS 3.2 functions:
    //
    int savePageMap(DWORD *save_buffer) {
            return ems_savePageMap32(save_buffer);
            }

    int restPageMap(DWORD *restore_buffer) {
            return ems_restPageMap32(restore_buffer);
            }

    int swapPageMap(DWORD *rest_buffer, DWORD *save_buffer) {
            return ems_swapPageMap32(rest_buffer, save_buffer);
            }

    int getMapInfoSize(WORD *size) {
            return ems_getMapInfoSize32(size);
            }
```

```
#endif

#if defined(Uses_EMS40)

    //
    //    EMS 4.0 functions:
    //
    int savePartialMap(WORD *map, void *buffer) {
            return ems_savePartialMap40(map, buffer);
            }

    int restPartialMap(void *buffer) {
            return ems_restPartialMap40(buffer);
            }

    int getPMapInfoSize(WORD pages, WORD *buffSize) {
            return ems_getPMapInfoSize40(pages, buffSize);
            }


    int getAttrCapability(WORD *capability) {
            return ems_getAttrCapability40(capability);
            }


    int getAllHandleNames(EMS_HandleNameInfo *info_list) {
            return ems_getAllHandleNames40(info_list);
            }

    int getTotalHandles(WORD *handles) {
            return ems_getTotalHandles40(handles);
            }


    int getStackNeeded(WORD *stack_space) {
            return ems_getStackNeeded40(stack_space);
            }


    int moveMemRegion(EMS_MoveMemoryInfo *buffer) {
            return ems_moveMemRegion40(buffer);
            }

    int swapMemRegions(EMS_MoveMemoryInfo *buffer) {
            return ems_swapMemRegions40(buffer);
            }


    int getAddrsMappable(EMS_MappablePagesInfo *buffer,
                                     WORD *num_entries) {
            return ems_getAddrsMappable40(buffer, num_entries);
            }

    int getNumMappable(WORD *mappablePages) {
            return ems_getNumMappable40(mappablePages);
            }


    int getHWConfig(EMS_HardwareConfigInfo *buffer) {
            return ems_getHWConfig40(buffer);
```

```
            }

    int getNumRawPages(WORD *total_pages, WORD *free_pages) {
            return ems_getNumRawPages40(total_pages, free_pages);
            }

    int prepEmmWarmBoot() {
            return ems_prepEmmWarmBoot40();
            }

#endif

    };


/**********************************************************************
***                                                                ***
***      Declare functions which are not class members             ***
***                                                                ***
**********************************************************************/

//
//  ems_demoError() is used by the demo programs to report any errors
//  which might occur.
//
extern void       ems_demoError(char *);

//
//  ems_errorText() returns the text associated with an EMS error.
//
extern char       *ems_errorText(WORD);
```

Figure 3-8 presents the source code listing to EMSLIB.CPP. This file defines all of the EMS_Ems and EMS_EmBlk methods that are not defined inline in EMS.H.

3-8 The source code listing to EMSLIB.CPP

```
/////////////////////////////////////////
//
// emslib.cpp
//
//  Provides error handling for demo programs.
//
/////////////////////////////////////////

extern "C" {
#include <stdio.h>
#include <stdlib.h>
#include <fcntl.h>
#include <io.h>
#include <dos.h>
#include <sys/types.h>
#include <sys/stat.h>
}
```

```
#include "gdefs.h"

#define Uses_EMS40
#include "ems.h"


int EMS_Ems::init()
{

    int         emmxxxx0_handle;

    REGISTERS;

    //
    //   All we need to do is make sure that EMS is present:
    //


    //
    //   First try opening the device "EMMXXXX0"
    //
    emmxxxx0_handle= open("EMMXXXX0", O_RDONLY);
    if (emmxxxx0_handle == -1) {
        //
        //   There was some kind of error. EMS must be unavailable.
        //
        return EMSErrUnimp;
        }


    //
    //   Now we've got something. We need to make sure it's not
    //   a file, but a device. ioctl() can give us this info.
    //
    R_AH= 0x44;
    R_DS= 0;
    R_DX= 0;
    R_CX= 0;
    R_BX= emmxxxx0_handle;
    R_AL= 0;
    interrupt(0x21);
    if (R_CY || !(R_DX & 0x80)) {
        //
        //   Error occurred, or status was for a file. Close
        //   handle, and return EMSErrUnimp.
        //
        close(emmxxxx0_handle);

        return EMSErrUnimp;
        }

    //
    //   Finally, check the output status. If it's 0 that's bad.
    //
    R_AH= 0x44;
    R_DS= 0;
    R_DX= 0;
    R_CX= 0;
    R_BX= emmxxxx0_handle;
    R_AL= 7;
    interrupt(0x21);
```

3-8 Continued.

```
    if (R_CY !! R_AL == 0) {
        //
        //   Error occurred, or status was bad. Close
        //   handle, and return EMSErrUnimp.
        //
        close(emmxxxx0_handle);

        return EMSErrUnimp;
        }

    //
    //   If we got here, we must be golden. Close the handle
    //   and return True.
    //
    close(emmxxxx0_handle);

    return EMSErrOK;
}



/***********************************************************************
***                                                                 ***
***      EMS_EmBlk::allocEM() - Allocates a block of EMS memory     ***
***      The block is attached to the EMS_EmBlk object, so that when ***
***      that object is destroyed, the ems block will be freed.     ***
***                                                                 ***
***********************************************************************/

int EMS_EmBlk::allocEM(WORD pages)
{
    int              rval;


    if (attached) {
        ems_freeEM(handle);
        handle= EMS_NULL_HANDLE;
        attached= FALSE;
        }

    rval= ems_allocEM(pages, &handle);
    if (rval == EMSErrOK) {
        attached= TRUE;
        }
    return rval;
}

/***********************************************************************
***                                                                 ***
***      EMS_EmBlk::freeEM() -  Frees the memory associated with    ***
***      the EMS_EmBlk object. If the free is successful, the object ***
***      becomes uninitialized and unattached, so destruction will  ***
***      do nothing.                                                ***
***                                                                 ***
***********************************************************************/

EMS_EmBlk::freeEM()
{
    int              rval;
```

```
        if (handle != EMS_NULL_HANDLE) {
            rval= ems_freeEM(handle);
            if (rval == EMSErrOK) {
                handle= EMS_NULL_HANDLE;
                attached= FALSE;
                }
            return EMSErrOK;
            }

    return EMSErrOK;
    }

/***********************************************************************
 ***                                                                 ***
 ***     EMS_EmBlk::allocHandleStd() -  Same as allocEM except that  ***
 ***     the EMS 4.0 interface call is used.                         ***
 ***                                                                 ***
 ***********************************************************************/

int EMS_EmBlk::allocHandleStd(WORD pages)
{
    int                 rval;


    if (attached) {
        ems_freeEM(handle);
        handle= EMS_NULL_HANDLE;
        attached= FALSE;
        }

    rval= ems_allocHandleStd40(&handle, pages);
    if (rval == EMSErrOK) {
        attached= TRUE;
        }
    return rval;
    }

/***********************************************************************
 ***                                                                 ***
 ***     EMS_EmBlk::allocHandleRaw() - Like allocEM except that the  ***
 ***     EMS 4.0 RAW page interface is used.                         ***
 ***                                                                 ***
 ***********************************************************************/

int EMS_EmBlk::allocHandleRaw(WORD pages)
{
    int                 rval;


    if (attached) {
        ems_freeEM(handle);
        handle= EMS_NULL_HANDLE;
        attached= FALSE;
        }

    rval= ems_allocHandleRaw40(&handle, pages);
    if (rval == EMSErrOK) {
        attached= TRUE;
        }
    return rval;
    }
```

```
/**********************************************************************
***                                                                ***
***      EMS_EmBlk::searchHandleName() -  Looks up an ems block     ***
***      by its name. Initializes the EMS_EmBlk to denote that      ***
***      block if found. The EMS_EmBlk is not attached to the ems   ***
***      block, so if the EMS_EmBlk object is destroyed, the EMS    ***
***      block won't be freed.                                      ***
***                                                                ***
**********************************************************************/

int EMS_EmBlk::searchHandleName(char *name)

{
    int              rval;


    if (attached) {
        ems_freeEM(handle);
        handle= EMS_NULL_HANDLE;
        attached= FALSE;
        }

    rval= ems_searchHandleName40(&handle, name);
    return rval;
}

/**********************************************************************
***                                                                ***
***      ems_errorText() - Returns the text associated with an EMS  ***
***      error.                                                     ***
***                                                                ***
**********************************************************************/

char  *ems_errorText(WORD err)
{
    static char buff[64];

    switch (err) {
    case EMSErrOK:
        return "No error";
    case EMSErrInternal:
        return "Internal EMM software error";
    case EMSErrHardware:
        return "EM Hardware error";
    case EMSErrEMMBusy:
        return "EMM Busy";
    case EMSErrHandInv:
        return "Handle Invalid";
    case EMSErrUnimp:
        return "Undefined EMS function";
    case EMSErrNoHandles:
        return "Handles Exhausted";
    case EMSErrSaveRest:
        return "Error in save/restore of context";
    case EMSErrReqGTPhys:
        return "Not enough physical EM for request";
    case EMSErrReqGTAvail:
        return "Not enough available EM for request";
    case EMSErrReqIsZero:
```

```
            return "Cannot allocate zero pages";
        case EMSErrLogPgInv:
            return "Invalid logical page number";
        case EMSErrPhysPgInv:
            return "Invalid physical page number";
        case EMSErrSSAreaFull:
            return "Mapping save area is full";
        case EMSErrSaveFail:
            return "Handle already has a saved state associated with it";
        case EMSErrRestFail:
            return "Handle has no saved state associated with it";
        case EMSErrParameter:
            return "Subfunction parameter not defined";
        case EMSErrAttribute:
            return "Attribute type not defined";
        case EMSErrUnsupported:
            return "Feature not supported";
        case EMSErrOverlap:
            return "Source/dest of move overlap, move performed";
        case EMSErrLenInv:
            return "Length of move request invalid";
        case EMSErrOverlapCE:
            return "Overlap of conventional and extended memory";
        case EMSErrOffsetInv:
            return "Offset outside logical page";
        case EMSErrRegionGT1MB:
            return "Region size > 1 megabyte";
        case EMSErrOverlapFatal:
            return "Source/dest overlap prevented move";
        case EMSErrMemTypeInv:
            return "Memory source/dest types invalid";
        case EMSErrDMARegUnsupp:
            return "Specified alternate register set unsupported";
        case EMSErrNoDMARegs:
            return "No available alternate register sets";
        case EMSErrAltRegsUnsupp:
            return "Alternate registers unsupported";
        case EMSErrDMARegUndef:
            return "Specified alternate register set undefined";
        case EMSErrDMAChanUnsupp:
            return "Dedicated DMA channels unsupported";
        case EMSErrChanUnsupp:
            return "Specified DMA channel unsupported";
        case EMSErrNameNotFound:
            return "No handle found for name";
        case EMSErrNameExists:
            return "Handle with same name already exists";
        case EMSErrPointerInv:
            return "Invalid pointer or source array bogus";
        case EMSErrAccess:
            return "Access denied by operating system";
        default:
            sprintf(buff, "Unknown error 0x%X", err);
            return buff;
            }
}


/***********************************************************************
***                                                                 ***
***     ems_demoError() - Used by the demo programs to report an    ***
```

The EMS 3.0 and 3.2 interface 61

```
***      error and terminate.                                      ***
***                                                                ***
*********************************************************************/

void ems_demoError(char *function)
{

    //
    //  Report the error:
    //
    printf("Error on %s(): \"%s\"\n", function, ems_errorText(errno));
    exit(0);

}
```

Figure 3-9 presents the source code listing to EMSDEFS.ASM. This definition file will be included in all the EMS-based assembly bindings. It defines error codes and EMS function and subfunction values for assembly language programming.

3-9 The source code listing to EMSDEFS.ASM

```
;**************************************************
;***                                          ***
;***      EmsDefs.ASM                         ***
;***                                          ***
;***      Contains definitions for EMS routines ***
;***                                          ***
;**************************************************


;
;    Define the EMS interrupt:
;
Ems           equ      67h


;
;    Now define the 3.0 EMS function codes.
;    These are 8 bit values which are loaded into
;    AH before calling the EMS interrupt.
;
GetStatus            equ      40h
GetPFA               equ      41h
GetPSEG              equ      41h
GetFreeEM            equ      42h
AllocateEM           equ      43h
MapEMPage            equ      44h
FreeEM               equ      45h
GetVersion           equ      46h
SavePageMap          equ      47h
RestorePageMap       equ      48h
Reserved1            equ      49h
Reserved2            equ      4ah
GetNumActHandles     equ      4bh
GetPagesForHandle    equ      4ch
GetPagesAllHandles   equ      4dh
```

```
;
;    Define the 3.2 and 4.0 EMS function codes:
;
;    Note that these are 16 bit values which
;    are loaded into AX prior to calling
;    the EMS interrupt. (These can be regarded
;    as an 8 bit function plus an 8 bit sub-
;    function.
;
;    The 3.2 codes:
;

SavePageMap32       equ     4e00h
RestPageMap32       equ     4e01h
SwapPageMap32       equ     4e02h
GetMapInfoSize32    equ     4e03h


;
;    The 4.0 codes:
;
SavePartialMap40    equ     4f00h
RestPartialMap40    equ     4f01h
GetPMapInfoSize40   equ     4f02h

MapPagesByNum40     equ     5000h
MapPagesByAddr40    equ     5001h

ReallocHandPages40  equ     5100h

GetHandleAttr40     equ     5200h
SetHandleAttr40     equ     5201h
GetAttrCapability40 equ     5202h

GetHandleName40     equ     5300h
SetHandleName40     equ     5301h

GetAllHandleNames40 equ     5400h
SearchHandleName40  equ     5401h
GetTotalHandles40   equ     5402h

MapPagesJumpNum40   equ     5500h
MapPagesJumpSeg40   equ     5501h

MapPagesCallNum40   equ     5600h
MapPagesCallSeg40   equ     5601h
GetStackNeeded40    equ     5602h

MoveMemRegion40     equ     5700h
SwapMemRegions40    equ     5701h

GetAddrsMappable40  equ     5800h
GetNumMappable40    equ     5801h

GetHWConfig40       equ     5900h
GetNumRawPages40    equ     5901h

AllocHandleStd40    equ     5a00h
AllocHandleRaw40    equ     5a01h
GetAltMapRegs40     equ     5b00h
SetAltMapRegs40     equ     5b01h
GetAltMapRegSize40  equ     5b02h
```

```
AllocAltMapRegs40      equ      5b03h
ReleaseAltMapRegs40    equ      5b04h
AllocDMARegs40         equ      5b05h
EnableDMA40            equ      5b06h
DisableDMA40           equ      5b07h
ReleaseDMARegs40       equ      5b08h

PrepEmmWarmBoot40      equ      5c00h

EnableEmmOSFuncs40     equ      5d00h
DisableEmmOSFuncs40    equ      5d01h
ReleaseAccessKey40     equ      5d02h
```

We now present the EMS 3.0 and 3.2 interface functions.

C++ interface functions

Initialize EMS

Function EMS_Ems::init() checks for the presence of EMS. If there is no Expanded Memory Manager present in the system, it will return an error.

Function EMS_Ems::init()

```
EMS_Ems    ems;

error= ems.init();
```

This function is defined in EMSLIB.CPP (FIG. 3-8).

Get the EMM status

Function EMS_Ems::getStatus() is used to get the status of the Expanded Memory Manager. It should be called only after function EMS_Ems::init() has been called successfully. If the status indicates an error, EMS_Ems::getStatus() returns the error, and errno is set the error code. This function calls ems_getStatus(), defined in EMS40.ASM.

Figure 3-10 presents the source code list to EMS40.ASM.

Function EMS_Ems::getStatus()

```
EMS_Ems    ems;

error= ems.getStatus();
```

3-10 The source code listing to EMS40.ASM

```
;*****************************************************************
;***      EMS40.ASM                                        ***
;***                                                       ***
;***      int ems_getStatus()                              ***
```

```
;***                                                           ***
;***      Returns 0 for OK status or an error                  ***
;***      code.                                                ***
;***                                                           ***
;***      (Ems Version 3.0)                                    ***
;****************************************************************

;----------------------------------------
;
; Declare memory model and language
;

        .model  large,C

;----------------------------------------
;
; Include ems definition file
;

        include emsdefs.asm

;----------------------------------------
;
; Declare errno as extrn to this
; module
;

        extrn   errno:WORD

;----------------------------------------
;
; Declare function as PUBLIC
;

        public  ems_getStatus

;----------------------------------------
;
; Begin code segment
;

        .code

ems_getStatus   proc

        mov     ah,GetStatus            ; Move function code
        int     Ems                     ; Do the ems call

;
;   Return AH to caller
;
        mov     al,ah
        xor     ah,ah                   ; Zero high byte
        mov     errno,ax                ; Save in errno too
        ret                             ; Return to caller

ems_getStatus   endp                    ; End of procedure

        end                             ; End of source file
```

Get the page frame address

Function EMS_Ems::getPFA() is used to obtain a pointer to the EMS page frame. This pointer will be used by the caller to write data to and read data from the EMS pages that have been mapped into the page frame area. This function calls ems_getPFA(), defined in EMS41.ASM.

Figure 3-11 presents the source code listing to EMS41.ASM.

Function EMS_Ems::getPFA()

```
EMS_Ems          ems;
EMS_PageFrame    page_frame;

error= ems.getPFA(&page_frame);
```

where

page_frame   Receives pointer to the EMS page frame

3-11   The source code listing to EMS41.ASM

```
;******************************************************************
;***      EMS41.ASM                                        ***
;***                                                       ***
;***      int ems_getPFA(void **pfa_ptr)                   ***
;***                                                       ***
;***      Returns PFA through pfa_ptr parameter.           ***
;***      Gives 0 if no error, or an error code.           ***
;***                                                       ***
;***                                                       ***
;***      (Ems Version 3.0)                                ***
;******************************************************************
;
          .model   large,C

          include emsdefs.asm

          extrn    errno:WORD


;
;    Define entry point
;
          public   ems_getPFA

          .code

ems_getPFA        proc     pfa:far ptr dword

          mov      ah,GetPFA              ; Move function code
          int      Ems                    ; Do the ems call


;
;    Check AH to see if an error occurred:
;
          or       ah,ah                  ; Set flags
          jnz      error


;
;    BX has a segment address, put it in the high word
```

```
;       of the caller's location, and put zero in the low
;       word giving BX:0000 for an address.
;
            mov     ax,bx                   ; Save bx
            les     bx,pfa                  ; Get address for return
            mov     es:[bx+2],ax            ; Put segment down
            xor     ax,ax                   ; AX gets a zero
            mov     es:[bx],ax              ; Put offset down

            ret                             ; Return to caller (AX == 0)

error:
            mov     al,ah
            xor     ah,ah                   ; Zero high byte
            mov     errno,ax                ; Save in errno too
            ret                             ; Return to caller

ems_getPFA      endp                        ; End of procedure

            end                             ; End of source file
```

Get the number of free EMS pages

Function EMS_Ems::getFreeEM() gets the total number of EMS pages installed and the number of EMS pages available. It calls ems_getFreeEM(),
defined in EMS42.ASM.

Figure 3-12 presents the source code listing to EMS42.ASM.

Function EMS_Ems::getFreeEM()

```
EMS_Ems     ems;
WORD        total;
WORD        free;

error= ems.getFreeEM(&total, &free);
```

where

total	Receives number of EMS pages installed
free	Receives number of free EMS pages available

3-12 The source code listing to EMS42.ASM

```
;******************************************************************
;***      EMS42.ASM                                          ***
;***                                                         ***
;***      int ems_getFreeEM(int *total,                      ***
;***                        int *free)                       ***
;***                                                         ***
;***      Returns the total number of EMS pages and the      ***
;***      number of pages available. Returns 0 if no error   ***
;***      or an error code.                                  ***
;***                                                         ***
;***                                                         ***
;***      (Ems Version 3.0)                                  ***
;******************************************************************
```

```
        .model  large,C

        include emsdefs.asm

        extrn   errno:WORD

;
;   Define entry point
;
        public  ems_getFreeEM
        .code

ems_getFreeEM   proc    total:far ptr word, free:far ptr word

        mov     ah,GetFreeEM            ; Move function code
        int     Ems                     ; Do the ems call

        or      ah,ah                   ; Set flags
        jnz     error

;
;   BX now has the number of free EMS pages, DX has the total
;   number of EMS pages. Return the values:
;
        mov     ax,bx                   ; Save free pages
        les     bx,free                 ; Get address of free
        mov     es:[bx],ax              ; Put free pages down
        les     bx,total                ; Get address of total
        mov     es:[bx],dx              ; Put total pages down

        xor     ax,ax
        ret                             ; AX has zero

error:
        mov     al,ah
        xor     ah,ah                   ; Zero high byte
        mov     errno,ax                ; Save in errno too
        ret

ems_getFreeEM   endp                    ; End of procedure

        end                             ; End of source file
```

Allocate EMS handle and pages

Funtion EMS_EmBlk::allocEM() is used to allocate a specified number of EMS pages required for use by your program. This function initializes an object of type EMS_EmBlk by allocating EMS memory for it. Subsequent operations work on the EMS_EmBlk object. Note that the EMS_EmBlk object will be attached to the EMS block, and so the EMS block will be released when the object is destroyed. To override this behavior, use EMS_Em-Blk::detach(). EMS_EmBlk::allocEM() calls ems_allocEM. defined in EMS43.ASM.

Figure 3-13 presents the source code listing to EMS43.ASM.

Function EMS_EmBlk::allocEM()

```
EMS_EmBlk    block;
WORD         pages
error= block.allocEM(pages);
```

where

pages **The number of 16K pages you want to allocate**

3-13 The source code listing to EMS43.ASM

```
;******************************************************************
;***     EMS43.ASM                                           ***
;***                                                         ***
;***     int ems_allocEM(WORD pages, WORD *handle)           ***
;***                                                         ***
;***     Takes the number of pages to allocate and returns   ***
;***     a handle with that number of pages. On error,       ***
;***     returns a non-zero error code.                      ***
;***                                                         ***
;***                                                         ***
;***     (Ems Version 3.0)                                   ***
;******************************************************************

        .model  large,C

        include emsdefs.asm

        extrn   errno:WORD

;
;   Define entry point
;
        public  ems_allocEM

        .code

ems_allocEM     proc    pages:word, handle:far ptr word

;
;   BX takes the number of pages to allocate:
;
        mov     bx,pages

        mov     ah,AllocateEM       ; Move function code
        int     Ems                 ; Do the ems call

        or      ah,ah               ; Set flags
        jnz     error

;
;   DX now has the EMM handle. Return it:
;
        les     bx,handle           ; Get address of handle
        mov     es:[bx],dx          ; Put handle down

        xor     ax,ax               ; AX gets 0
        ret                         ; Return to caller
```

```
error:
        mov     al,ah               ; Transfer return code to al
        xor     ah,ah               ; Zero high byte
        mov     errno,ax            ; Save in errno too
        ret                         ; Return to caller

ems_allocEM     endp                ; End of procedure

        end                         ; End of source code
```

Map an expanded memory page

Function `EMS_EmBlk::mapPage()` is used to map EMS logical pages from the target EMS block to one of the four physical pages located in the 64K page frame segment. This function calls `ems_mapPage()`, defined in EMS44.ASM.

Figure 3-14 presents the source code listing to EMS44.ASM.

Function EMS_EmBlk::mapPage()

```
EMS_EmBlk    block;
WORD         physical_page;
WORD         logical_page;

error= block.mapPage(physical_page, logical_page);
```

where

```
physical_page   The physical page number (0–3)
logical_page    The EMS logical page to be mapped
```

3-14 The source code listing to EMS44.ASM

```
;****************************************************************
;***      EMS44.ASM                                         ***
;***                                                        ***
;***      int ems_mapPage(WORD physical_page,               ***
;***                      WORD logical_page,                ***
;***                      WORD handle);                     ***
;***                                                        ***
;***      Maps a physical page into a specified logical page. ***
;***                                                        ***
;***                                                        ***
;***      (Ems Version 3.0)                                 ***
;****************************************************************

        .model  large,C

        include emsdefs.asm

        extrn   errno:WORD
```

```
;
;    Define entry point
;
        public  ems_mapPage

        .code
ems_mapPage proc    physical_page:Word, logical_page:Word, handle:Word

;
;    AL takes the physical page number, BX, the logical page number,
;    and DX, the handle.
;
        mov     ax,physical_page
        mov     bx,logical_page
        mov     dx,handle

        mov     ah,MapEMPage            ; Move function code
        int     Ems                     ; Do the ems call

        or      ah,ah                   ; Set flags
        jnz     error

        xor     ax,ax                   ; AX gets 0
        ret                             ; Return to caller

error:
        mov     al,ah                   ; Transfer return code to al
        xor     ah,ah                   ; Zero high byte
        mov     errno,ax                ; Save in errno too
        ret                             ; Return to caller

ems_mapPage endp                        ; End of procedure

        end                             ; End of source listing
;
;----------------------------------------
```

Free a handle and the associated EMS pages

Function EMS_EmBlk::freeEM() frees all the EMS memory that had been previously allocated and associated with a specified handle. Note that the memory will be released whether or not the object is attached. The object is returned to an uninitialized, unattached state. This function calls ems_freeEM(), defined in EMS45.ASM.

Figure 3-15 presents the source code listing to EMS45.ASM.

Function EMS_EmBlk::freeEM()

```
EMS_EmBlk   block;
WORD        pages;

error= block.allocEM(pages);
...
error= block.freeEM();
```

3-15 The source code listing to EMS45.ASM

```
;******************************************************************
;***      EMS45.ASM                                         ***
;***                                                        ***
;***      int ems_freeEM(WORD handle)                       ***
;***                                                        ***
;***      Releases an EMM handle along with the associated  ***
;***      pages.                                            ***
;***                                                        ***
;***                                                        ***
;***      (Ems Version 3.0)                                 ***
;******************************************************************

        .model  large,C

        include emsdefs.asm

        extrn   errno:WORD

;
;   Define entry point
;
        public  ems_freeEM

        .code

ems_freeEM      proc    handle:Word

;
;   DX takes the number of pages to allocate:
;
        mov     dx,handle

        mov     ah,FreeEM           ; Move function code
        int     Ems                ; Do the ems call

        or      ah,ah              ; Set flags
        jnz     error

        xor     ax,ax              ; AX gets 0
        ret                        ; Return to caller
error:
        mov     al,ah              ; Transfer return code to al
        xor     ah,ah              ; Zero high byte
        mov     errno,ax           ; Save in errno too
        ret                        ; Return to caller

ems_freeEM      endp               ; End of procedure

        end                        ; End of source listing
```

Get the EMS version number

Function EMS_Ems::getVersion() returns the current version number in Binary Coded Decimal (BCD) format. So, for example, 4.13 would be represented by 0x0413. This function calls ems_getVersion(), defined in EMS46.ASM.

Figure 3-16 presents the source code listing to EMS46.ASM.

Function EMS_Ems::getVersion()

```
EMS_Ems   ems;
WORD      version;

error= ems.getVersion(&version);
```

where

version   Receives the EMS version number in BCD format

3-16   The source code listing to EMS46.ASMx

```
;****************************************************************
;***     EMS46.ASM                                      ***
;***                                                    ***
;***     int ems_getVersion(int *version)               ***
;***                                                    ***
;***     Gives the EMS version.                         ***
;***                                                    ***
;***                                                    ***
;***     (Ems Version 3.0)                              ***
;****************************************************************

        .model  large,C

        include emsdefs.asm

        extrn   errno:WORD

;
;   Define entry point
;
        public  ems_getVersion

        .code

ems_getVersion proc     version:Far Ptr Word

        mov     ah,GetVersion          ; Move function code
        int     Ems                    ; Do the ems call

        or      ah,ah                  ; Set flags
        jnz     error

;
;   AL now has the EMS version.
;
        xor     ah,ah                  ; Zero extend
        les     bx,version             ; Get address of version
        mov     es:[bx],ax             ; Return it

        xor     ax,ax                  ; AX gets 0
        ret                            ; Return to caller
error:
        mov     al,ah                  ; Transfer return code to al
```

3-16 Continued.

```
        xor     ah,ah                   ; Zero high byte
        mov     errno,ax                ; Save in errno too
        ret                             ; Return to caller

ems_getVersion endp                     ; End of procedure

        end                             ; End of source file
```

Save the contents of page map registers

Function EMS_EmBlk::savePageMap() saves the page map (the mapping of physical pages to logical pages) to a save area associated with the specified EMS_EmBlk. This function calls ems_savePageMap(), defined in EMS47.ASM.

Figure 3-17 presents the source code listing to EMS47.ASM.

Function EMS_EmBlk::savePageMap()

```
EMS_EmBlk   block;

error= block.savePageMap();
```

3-17 The source code listing to EMS47.ASM

```
;******************************************************************
;***      EMS47.ASM                                          ***
;***                                                         ***
;***      int ems_savePageMap(WORD handle)                   ***
;***                                                         ***
;***      Saves the page map state for the                   ***
;***      specified handle.                                  ***
;***                                                         ***
;***                                                         ***
;***      (Ems Version 3.0)                                  ***
;******************************************************************

        .model  large,C

        include emsdefs.asm

        extrn   errno:WORD

;
;   Define entry point
;
        public  ems_savePageMap

        .code

ems_savePageMap proc     handle:Word

;
;   DX takes the handle
;
        mov     dx,handle
```

```
        mov     ah,SavePageMap          ; Move function code
        int     Ems                     ; Do the ems call

        or      ah,ah                   ; Set flags
        jnz     error

        xor     ax,ax                   ; AX gets 0
        ret                             ; Return to caller

error:
        mov     al,ah                   ; Transfer return code to al
        xor     ah,ah                   ; Zero high byte
        mov     errno,ax                ; Save in errno too
        ret                             ; Return to caller

ems_savePageMap endp                    ; End of procedure

        end                             ; End of source file
```

Restore the contents of page map registers

Function `EMS_EmBlk::restorePageMap()` restores the map registers
that had previously been saved using the `EMS_EmBlk::savePage-`
`Map()` function. This function calls `ems_restorePageMap()`, defined in
EMS48.ASM.

Figure 3-18 presents the source code listing to EMS48.ASM.

Function EMS_EmBlk::restorePageMap()

```
EMS_EmBlk   block;

error= block.savePageMap();
...
error= block.restorePageMap();
```

3-18 The source code listing to EMS48.ASM

```
;****************************************************************
;***    EMS48.ASM                                           ***
;***                                                        ***
;***    int ems_restorePageMap(WORD handle)                 ***
;***                                                        ***
;***    Saves the page map state for the                    ***
;***    specified handle.                                   ***
;***                                                        ***
;***                                                        ***
;***    (Ems Version 3.0)                                   ***
;****************************************************************

        .model  large,C

        include emsdefs.asm

        extrn   errno:WORD


;
;   Define entry point
```

```
;
        public  ems_restorePageMap

        .code

ems_restorePageMap proc    handle:Word

;
;   DX takes the handle
;
        mov     dx,handle

        mov     ah,RestorePageMap       ; Move function code
        int     Ems                     ; Do the ems call

        or      ah,ah                   ; Set flags
        jnz     error

        xor     ax,ax                   ; AX gets 0
        ret                             ; Return to caller
error:
        mov     al,ah                   ; Transfer return code to al
        xor     ah,ah                   ; Zero high byte
        mov     errno,ax                ; Save in errno too
        ret                             ; Return to caller

ems_restorePageMap endp                 ; End of procedure

        end                             ; End of source file
```

Get the number of active EMM handles

Function EMS_Ems::getNumActiveHandles() **gives the number of active EMM handles. This function calls** ems_getNumActiveHandles(), **defined in EMS4B.ASM.**

Figure 3-19 presents the source code listing to EMS4B.ASM.

Function EMS_Ems::getNumActiveHandles()

```
EMS_Ems   ems;
WORD      num_handles;

error= ems.getNumActiveHandles(&num_handles);
```

where

num_handles **Receives number of active handles**

3-19 The source code listing to EMS4B.ASM

```
;****************************************************************

;***    EMS4B.ASM                                          ***
```

```
;***                                                              ***
;***       int ems_getNumActiveHandles(WORD *num_handles)         ***
;***                                                              ***
;***       Gives the number of active EMM handles                 ***
;***                                                              ***
;***                                                              ***
;***       (Ems Version 3.0)                                      ***
;*******************************************************************

            .model  large,C

            include emsdefs.asm

            extrn   errno:WORD

;
;   Define entry point
;
            public  ems_getNumActiveHandles

            .code

ems_getNumActiveHandles proc      num_handles:Far Ptr Word


            mov     ah,GetNumActHandles     ; Move function code
            int     Ems                     ; Do the ems call

            or      ah,ah                   ; Set flags
            jnz     error

;
;   Return the result:
;
            mov     ax,bx                   ; Number of handles
            les     bx,num_handles
            mov     es:[bx],ax              ; Give it back

            xor     ax,ax                   ; AX gets 0
            ret                             ; Return to caller

error:
            mov     al,ah
            xor     ah,ah                   ; Zero high byte
            mov     errno,ax                ; Save in errno too
            ret                             ; Return to caller

ems_getNumActiveHandles endp                ; End of procedure

            end                             ; End of source file
```

Get number of pages for handle

Function EMS_EmBlk::getPagesForHandle() gets the number of extended memory pages associated with a given handle. This function calls ems_getPagesForHandle(), defined in EMS4C.ASM.

Figure 3-20 presents the source code listing to EMS4C.ASM.

Function EMS_EmBlk::getPagesForHandle()

```
EMS_EmBlk    block;
WORD         num_pages;

error= block.getPagesForHandle(&num_pages);
```

where

num_Pages **Receives number of pages associated with handle.**

3-20 The source code listing to EMS4C.ASM

```
;**********************************************************************
;***      EMS4C.ASM                                        ***
;***                                                       ***
;***      int ems_getPagesForHandle(WORD handle,           ***
;***                           WORD *num_pages)            ***
;***                                                       ***
;***      Gives the number of pages associated with a      ***
;***      given EMM handle.                                ***
;***                                                       ***
;***                                                       ***
;***      (Ems Version 3.0)                                ***
;**********************************************************************
;

        .model  large,C

        include emsdefs.asm

        extrn   errno:WORD

;
;   Define entry point
;
        public  ems_getPagesForHandle

        .code

ems_getPagesForHandle proc    handle:Word, num_pages:Far Ptr Word

;
;   DX takes the handle
;
        mov     dx,handle

        mov     ah,GetPagesForHandle    ; Move function code
        int     Ems                     ; Do the ems call

        or      ah,ah                   ; Set flags
        jnz     error

;
;   Return the result:
;
        mov     ax,bx                   ; Number of pages
        les     bx,num_pages
        mov     es:[bx],ax              ; Give it back

        xor     ax,ax                   ; AX gets 0
```

```
        ret                         ; Return to caller
error:
        mov     al,ah               ; Transfer return code to al
        xor     ah,ah               ; Zero high byte
        mov     errno,ax            ; Save in errno too
        ret                         ; Return to caller

ems_getPagesForHandle endp          ; End of procedure

        end                         ; End of source file
```

Get number of pages for all handles

Function `EMS_Ems::getPagesAllHandles()` gives the number of active handles and the number of pages associated with each of those handles. This function calls `ems_getPagesAllHandles()`, defined in EMS4D.ASM.

Figure 3-21 presents the source code listing to EMS4D.ASM.

Function EMS_Ems::getPagesAllHandles()

```
EMS_Ems         ems;
EMS_HandleInfo  *info;
WORD            num_handles;

error= ems.getNumActiveHandles(&num_handles);
info= new EMS_HandleInfo[num_handles];
error= ems.getPagesAllHandles(info, &num_handles);
```

where

info   Is an array big enough to accommodate each handle/
                page count pair
num_handles   Receives the number of active handles

3-21 The source code listing to EMS4D.ASM

```
;****************************************************************
;***    EMS4D.ASM                                           ***
;***                                                        ***
;***    typedef struct {                                    ***
;***        WORD    handle;                                 ***
;***        WORD    num_pages;                              ***
;***        }   HandleInfo_type;                            ***
;***                                                        ***
;***    int ems_getPagesAllHandles(HandleInfo_type         ***
;***                                      info[],           ***
;***                            WORD *num_handles)          ***
;***                                                        ***
;***    Gives the number of pages associated with each     ***
;***    active EMM handle, and the number of active        ***
;***    EMM handles.                                        ***
;***                                                        ***
```

3-21 Continued.

```
;***                                                        ***
;***      (Ems Version 3.0)                                 ***
;************************************************************************

        .model  large,C

        include emsdefs.asm

        extrn   errno:WORD

;
;   Define entry point
;
        public  ems_getPagesAllHandles

        .code

ems_getPagesAllHandles proc     info:Far Ptr DWord, num_handles:Far Ptr Word

        push    di                          ; Save DI, we need it

;
;   ES:[DI] gets the buffer address
;
        les     di,info

        mov     ah,GetPagesAllHandles       ; Move function code
        int     Ems                         ; Do the ems call

        or      ah,ah                       ; Set flags
        jnz     error

;
;   Return the number of handles:
;
        mov     ax,bx                       ; Number of handles
        les     bx,num_handles
        mov     es:[bx],ax                  ; Give it back

        xor     ax,ax                       ; AX gets 0
        pop     di                          ; Restore di
        ret                                 ; Return to caller

error:
        pop     di                          ; Restore di

        mov     al,ah                       ; Transfer return code to al
        xor     ah,ah                       ; Zero high byte
        mov     errno,ax                    ; Save in errno too
        ret                                 ; Return to caller

ems_getPagesAllHandles endp                 ; end of procedure

        end                                 ; end of source file
```

EMS 3.2 functions

There are four functions added with EMS 3.2. These functions provide greater flexibility in saving and restoring the map state. In order to use the

3.2 functionality, the program must #define either Uses_EMS32 or Uses_EMS40 before the #include of EMS.H.

Save page map to a buffer

Function EMS_Ems::savePageMap() allows the programmer to save the map registers into a specified buffer. The 3.0 function only allowed them to be saved in a special area associated with a handle. This function calls ems_savePageMap32(), defined in EMS4E0.ASM.

Figure 3-22 presents the source code listing to EMS4E0.ASM.

Function EMS_Ems::savePageMap()

```
EMS_Ems    ems;
WORD       map_size;
char       *save_buffer;

error= ems.getMapInfoSize(&map_size);
save_buffer= new char[map_size];
error= ems.savePageMap(save_buffer);
```

where

> save_buffer Is a pointer to an area of sufficient size (the size can be determined via a call to EMS_Ems::getMapInfoSize)

3-22 The source code listing to EMS4E0.ASM

```
;*****************************************************************
;***    EMS4E0.ASM                                        ***
;***                                                      ***
;***    int ems_savePageMap32(DWORD *save_buffer)         ***
;***                                                      ***
;***    Returns 0 for OK status or an error               ***
;***    code.                                             ***
;***                                                      ***
;***    (Ems Version 3.2)                                 ***
;*****************************************************************

        .model  large,C

        include emsdefs.asm

        extrn   errno:WORD

;
;   Define entry point
;
        public  ems_savePageMap32

        .code
ems_savePageMap32   proc save_buff:Far Ptr DWord

        push    di                      ; Save di
```

```
            les     di,save_buff                ; Get address of buffer into ES:DI

            mov     ax,SavePageMap32            ; Make the EMS call to save the map
            int     Ems

            or      ah,ah                       ; Check for error
            jnz     error

            xor     ax,ax                       ; AX gets 0
            pop     di                          ; Restore di
            ret                                 ; Return to caller

error:
            pop     di                          ; Restore di

            mov     al,ah
            xor     ah,ah                       ; Zero high byte
            mov     errno,ax                    ; Save in errno too
            ret                                 ; Return to caller

ems_savePageMap32   endp                        ; End of procedure

            end                                 ; End of source file
```

Restore page map from a buffer

Function EMS_Ems::restPageMap() allows the programmer to restore the map registers from a buffer previously filled by a call to EMS_Ems::savePageMap(). This function calls ems_restPageMap32(), defined in EMS4E1.ASM.

Figure 3-23 presents the source code listing to EMS4E1.ASM.;

Function EMS_Ems::restPageMap()

```
EMS_Ems     ems;
WORD        map_size;
char        *save_buffer;

error= ems.getMapInfoSize(&map_size);
save_buffer= new char[map_size];
error= ems.savePageMap(save_buffer);
...
error= ems.restPageMap(save_buffer);
```

where

> restore_buffer Is a pointer to an area initialized by a call to EMS_Ems::savePageMap32

3-23 The source code listing to EMS4E1.ASM

```
****************************************************************
;***    EMS4E1.ASM                                        ***
```

```
;***                                                           ***
;***      int ems_restPageMap32(DWORD *restore_buffer)         ***
;***                                                           ***
;***      Returns 0 for OK status or an error                 ***
;***      code.                                                ***
;***                                                           ***
;***      (Ems Version 3.2)                                    ***
;****************************************************************

          .model  large,C

          include emsdefs.asm

          extrn   errno:WORD

;
;    Define entry point
;
          public  ems_restPageMap32

          .code

ems_restPageMap32   proc restore_buff:Far Ptr DWord

          push    ds                    ; Save ds
          push    si                    ; Save si

          lds         si,restore_buff       ; Get buffer address into DS:SI

          mov         ax,RestPageMap32
          int     Ems

          or      ah,ah                 ; Check for error
          jnz     error

          xor     ax,ax                 ; Return a zero meaning no error

          pop         si                      ; Restore si
          pop         ds                      ; Restore ds
          ret                           ; Return to caller
error:
          pop     si                    ; Restore si
          pop     ds                    ; Restore ds

          mov     al,ah
          xor     ah,ah                 ; Zero high byte
          mov     errno,ax              ; Save in errno too
          ret                           ; Return to caller

ems_restPageMap32   endp                ; End of procedure

          end                           ; End of source file
```

Swap page maps

Function EMS_Ems::swapPageMap() allows the programmer to save the current page map in a buffer and restore the page map from another buffer in one call. This function calls ems_swapPageMap32(), defined in EMS4E2.ASM.

Figure 3-24 presents the source code listing to EMS4E2.ASM.

Function EMS_Ems::swapPageMap()

```
EMS_Ems    ems;
char       *rest_buffer;
char       *save_buffer;

...
error= ems.swapPageMap(rest_buffer, save_buffer);
```

where

rest_buffer Is the map register buffer to be restored
save_buffer Is the buffer in which to save the current map state.

3-24 The source code listing to EMS4E2.ASM

```
;****************************************************************
;***     EMS4E2.ASM                                        ***
;***                                                        ***
;***     int ems_swapPageMap32(DWORD *restore_buffer,       ***
;***                     DWORD *save_buffer)                ***
;***                                                        ***
;***     Returns 0 for OK status or an error               ***
;***     code.                                              ***
;***                                                        ***
;***     (Ems Version 3.2)                                  ***
;****************************************************************

        .model  large,C

        include emsdefs.asm

        extrn   errno:WORD

;
;   Define entry point
;
        public  ems_swapPageMap32

        .code

ems_swapPageMap32  proc restore_buff:Far Ptr DWord, save_buff:Far Ptr DWord

        push    ds                      ; Save ds
        push    si                      ; Save si
        push    di                      ; Save di

        lds     si,restore_buff         ; Get map to restore into DS:SI
        les     di,save_buff            ; Get save area address into ES:DI

        mov     ax,SwapPageMap32        ; Call EMS to swap
        int     Ems
```

```
        or      ah,ah                   ; Check for error
        jnz     error

        xor     ax,ax                   ; Return a zero meaning no error

        pop     di                      ; Restore di
        pop     si                      ; Restore si
        pop     ds                      ; Restore ds
        ret                             ; Return to caller
error:
        pop     di                      ; Restore di
        pop     si                      ; Restore si
        pop     ds                      ; Restore ds

        mov     al,ah
        xor     ah,ah                   ; Zero high byte
        mov     errno,ax                ; Save in errno too
        ret                             ; Return to caller

ems_swapPageMap32    endp               ; End of procedure

        end                             ; End of source file
```

Get the size of a map register save area

Function `EMS_Ems::getMapInfoSize()` returns the number of bytes required to save a page map. This function should be called before calling `EMS_Ems::savePageMap()` in order to ensure that sufficient buffer space is being provided. This function calls `ems_getMapInfoSize32()`, defined in EMS4E3.ASM.

Figure 3-25 presents the source code listing to EMS4E3.ASM.

Function EMS_Ems::getMapInfoSize()

```
EMS_Ems   ems;
WORD      size;

error= ems.getMapInfoSize(&size);
```

where

   `size`   Gets the size in bytes of the space required to save the page
            map.

3-25 The source code listing to EMS4E3.ASM

```
;****************************************************************
;***     EMS4E3.ASM                                        ***
;***                                                       ***
;***     int ems_getMapInfoSize32(WORD *map_size)          ***
;***                                                       ***
```

3-25 Continued.

```
;***    Returns 0 for OK status or an error              ***
;***    code.                                            ***
;***                                                     ***
;***    (Ems Version 3.2)                                ***
;*************************************************************

        .model  large,C

        include emsdefs.asm

        extrn   errno:WORD

;
;   Define entry point
;
        public  ems_getMapInfoSize32

        .code

ems_getMapInfoSize32  proc map_size:Far Ptr Word

        mov     ax,GetMapInfoSize32     ; Make the call to get the size
        int     Ems

        or      ah,ah                   ; Check for an error
        jnz     error

;
;   Return the info. Size is in AL. We zero extend it to
;   16 bits and return it.
;
        les     bx,map_size             ; Get address of return spot
        xor     ah,ah                   ; Zero extend to 16 bits
        mov     es:[bx],ax              ; Return the size

        xor     ax,ax                   ; Return a zero meaning no error
        ret                             ; Return to caller
error:
        pop     di                      ; Restore di
        pop     es                      ; Restore es

        mov     al,ah
        xor     ah,ah                   ; Zero high byte
        mov     errno,ax                ; Save in errno too
        ret                             ; Return to caller

ems_getMapInfoSize32    endp            ; End of procedure

        end                             ; End of source file
```

Summary

This chapter presented a C++ interface to the EMS 3.0 and 3.2 functions. Some of the routines presented allow you to determine if an EMM is installed, if the EMM's status is OK, to allocate a specified number of EMS pages, to map logical pages to the EMS page frame, to get a far pointer to the page frame, and release the previously allocated memory.

These routines will form the foundation for the EMS portion of the Virtual Memory Management system presented in Chapter 6.

4

EMS 4.0

In a fashion similar to that of Chapter 3, which presented the EMS 3.0 and 3.2 functions, this chapter will present the functional capabilities of EMS 4.0. Although EMS 4.0 adds wide-ranging capabilities to your memory management bag of tricks, you must be thoughtful about using EMS 4.0 functions in commercial application programs.

The reason, of course, is that there might still be some computers in the market with EMMs supporting only EMS 3.0 or 3.2. If your program will be reaching the commercial marketplace, then you will have to think hard about whether you must support pre-revision 4.0 EMM.

On the other hand, if you're writing a program to work in a known environment that does indeed support EMS 4.0, then it makes great sense to use as many features of EMS 4.0 as you want to.

If you intend to use the EMS 4.0 functions, you must `#define Uses_EMS40` before you `#include ems.h`. If you do not have this symbol defined, you will get a compile error if you attempt to use a 4.0 function. This has been done so that programmers wanting to adhere to the 3.0 or 3.2 specifications can do so, and receive errors if they attempt to use functionality not supported by those revisions.

EMS 4.0 enhancements

There are two important enhancements in EMS 4.0 that merit some discussion. In EMS 3.0 and 3.2, the only place in addressable memory where an EMS page can be mapped is the Page Frame Area. This means that only four EMS pages can be mapped at any given time. In EMS 4.0, many or most of the pages in conventional memory (below 640K) can be remapped.

Thus, a programmer can, for example, replace the normal memory at segment 0x4000 with a page from an EMS block. Several calls are required to support this functionality. First, calls are required to determine which physical pages are mappable. Second, calls are required for saving the map status of a specified set of physical pages. In EMS 3.0 and 3.2, the save page map routines only save the page map for the Page Frame Area.

The second major enhancement for applications programmers is the existence of handle names. The programmer can associate a name with an EMS handle. This proves useful in two ways: memory display utilities can provide more meaningful information if names are associated with EMS blocks, and, more importantly, a program can avoid having to pass handle numbers to every part of the program that requires access to an EMS block. Instead, a meaningful name for the EMS block can be agreed upon by all parts of a program.

We now turn to the demonstration programs which illustrate the use of the enhancements.

EMS 4.0 demonstration programs

The programs presented in this section of Chapter 4 demonstrate the use of many EMS 4.0 functions. The source code has been heavily documented to facilitate your understanding of these functions.

PROG4-1.CPP demonstrates the following operations:

- Getting the number of mappable pages
- Getting the addresses of mappable pages

PROG4-1 first gets the number of mappable pages in conventional memory via a call to EMS_Ems::getNumMappable(). It then allocates a block of memory large enough to hold an array of information for these pages. EMS_Ems::getMappablePagesInfo() is then called to get the addresses and physical page #'s of each of the mappable pages. In PROG4-6, we will use this information to do page mapping in conventional memory. Previously, we have only mapped pages into the Page Frame Area that resides in upper memory.

Figure 4-1 presents the source code listing to PROG4-1.CPP.

4-1 The source code listing to PROG4-1.CPP

```
/////////////////////////////////////////
//
// prog4-1.cpp
//
//      Demonstrates
//          - Get number of mappable pages
//          - Get addresses of mappable pages
//
/////////////////////////////////////////
```

```cpp
extern "C" {
#include <stdio.h>
#include <stdlib.h>
#include <dos.h>
#include <string.h>
}

#include "gdefs.h"

#define Uses_EMS40
#include "ems.h"


EMS_Ems                 ems;

void main()
{

    WORD                numMappablePages;
    WORD                numMappablePages2;

    WORD                i;

    EMS_MappablePagesInfo
                        *pageAddress;


    //
    //  First check for presence of EMS
    //
    if (ems.init()) {
        printf("EMS is not present\n");
        return;
        }

    //
    //  Find out how many mappable pages we have all together. In
    //  4.0, we do not have a fixed size page frame, we may have
    //  many more than 4 mappable pages.
    //
    if (ems.getNumMappable(&numMappablePages)) {
        ems_demoError("EMS_Ems::getNumMappable");
        }

    //
    //  Now allocate a buffer big enough to hold the addresses
    //  of these pages.
    //
    pageAddress= new EMS_MappablePagesInfo[numMappablePages];

    //
    //  Get the info
    //
    if (ems.getAddrsMappable(pageAddress, &numMappablePages2)) {
        ems_demoError("EMS_Ems::getAddrsMappable");
        }

    //
    //  Sanity check that the page counts match.
    //
```

```
if (numMappablePages != numMappablePages2) {
    printf("There is something really wrong here!\n");
    return;
    }

//
//  Now print the info out:
//
printf("┌═══Segment═Address════════Physical═Page═#══┐\n");

for (i= 0; i < numMappablePages; i++) {
    printf("║         0x%04X        |        %4d        ║\n",
            pageAddress[i].pageSegment,
            pageAddress[i].physNumber);

    if (i < numMappablePages-1) {
        printf("║────────────────────────+──────────────────║\n");
        }
    }
    printf("└────────────────────────┴──────────────────┘\n");
}
```

PROG4-2.CPP demonstrates the following operations:

- Getting the hardware configuration
- Getting the number of raw pages

PROG4-2 demonstrates the use of EMS_Ems::getHWConfig() to get **EMS** hardware information, EMS_Ems::getNumRawPages() to get the number of raw pages (raw page size might differ from 16K), and EMS_Ems::getTotal Handles() to get the total number of handles available.

Figure 4-2 presents the source code listing to PROG4-2.CPP.

4-2 The source code listing to PROG4-2.CPP

```
////////////////////////////////////////////
//
// prog4-2.cpp
//
//      Demonstrates
//          - Get hardware configuration
//          - Get number of raw pages
//
////////////////////////////////////////////

extern "C" {
#include <stdio.h>
#include <stdlib.h>
#include <dos.h>
#include <string.h>
}
```

```c
#include "gdefs.h"

#define Uses_EMS40
#include "ems.h"

EMS_Ems             ems;

void main()
{

    EMS_HardwareConfigInfo
                    hwConfig;

    WORD            freeRawPages;
    WORD            totalRawPages;

    WORD            totalHandles;

    //
    //  First check for presence of EMS
    //
    if (ems.init()) {
        printf("EMS is not present\n");
        return;
        }

    //
    //  Start by getting the hardware configuration
    //
    if (ems.getHWConfig(&hwConfig)) {
        ems_demoError("EMS_Ems::getHWConfig");
        }

    //
    //  Now get the raw page counts
    //
    if (ems.getNumRawPages(&totalRawPages, &freeRawPages)) {
        ems_demoError("EMS_Ems::getNumRawPages");
        }

    //
    //  Get the total handles that can be used.
    //
    if (ems.getTotalHandles(&totalHandles)) {
        ems_demoError("EMS_Ems::getTotalHandles");
        }

    //
    //  Print the info out:
    //
    printf("Total # of raw pages:       %d\n", totalRawPages);
    printf("# of free raw pages:        %d\n\n", freeRawPages);
    printf("Total # of handles:         %d\n\n", totalHandles);
    printf("Raw page size (bytes):      %d\n", 16*hwConfig.rawPgSize);
    printf("Alternate reg sets:         %d\n", hwConfig.altRegSets);
    printf("Context Save area size:     %d\n", hwConfig.saveAreaSz);
    printf("# Regs assignable to DMA:   %d\n\n", hwConfig.regsDma);
    printf("DMA %s be used with alternate registers",
                (hwConfig.dmaType) ? "cannot" : "can");

}
```

PROG4-3.CPP demonstrates the following operations:

- Getting and setting the handle name
- Searching for the handle name

PROG4-3 demonstrates the use of names for EMS blocks. It allocates three blocks of EMS giving each a unique name via EMS_EmBlk::set HandleName(). It then frees each one by looking it up by name, using EMS_EmBlk::searchHandleName() and freeing the resulting handle. At each step, it gets and displays the names of all of the EMS blocks using EMS_EmBlk::getHandleName().

Figure 4-3 presents the source code listing to PROG4-3.CPP.

4-3 The source code listing to PROG4-3.CPP

```
/////////////////////////////////////////
//
// prog4-3.cpp
//
//      Demonstrates
//          - Get/Set handle name
//          - Search for handle name
//
/////////////////////////////////////////

extern "C" {
#include <stdio.h>
#include <stdlib.h>
#include <dos.h>
}

#include "gdefs.h"

#define Uses_EMS40
#include "ems.h"


EMS_Ems             ems;


extern void displayActiveHandles(void);
extern void pause(void);

void main()
{
    WORD                totalPages;
    WORD                freePages;
    EMS_EmBlk           handle1;
    EMS_EmBlk           handle2;
    EMS_EmBlk           handle3;
    EMS_EmBlk           tmpHandle;

    //
    // First check for presence of EMS
    //
    if (ems.init()) {
```

```
        printf("EMS is not present\n");
        return;
        }

//
//  Get the number of free pages
//
if (ems.getFreeEM(&totalPages, &freePages)) {
    ems_demoError("EMS_Ems::getFreeEM");
    }


//
//  Print header:
//
printf("        Operation           Avail Pages          Active Handles\n");
printf("============================================================\n");
printf("After initialization  |      %3d      | Handle   Pages     Name   |\n",
        freePages);

displayActiveHandles();
pause();

//
//  Now allocate 5 pages.
//
if (handle1.allocEM(5)) {
    ems_demoError("EMS_EmBlk::allocEM");
    }

//
//  Set the name for the handle
//
if (handle1.setHandleName("Aramis  ")) {
    ems_demoError("EMS_EmBlk::setHandleName");
    }


//
//  Get the number of free pages
//
if (ems.getFreeEM(&totalPages, &freePages)) {
    ems_demoError("EMS_Ems::getFreeEM");
    }


//
//  Print header:
//
printf("        Operation           Avail Pages          Active Handles\n");
printf("============================================================\n");
printf("After 5 page allocate |      %3d      | Handle   Pages     Name   |\n",
        freePages);

displayActiveHandles();
pause();

//
//  Now allocate 7 pages.
//
if (handle2.allocEM(7)) {
    ems_demoError("EMS_EmBlk::allocEM");
    }
//
```

```
    //   Set the name for the handle
    //
    if (handle2.setHandleName("Athos    ")) {
        ems_demoError("EMS_EmBlk::setHandleName");
        }


    //
    //  Get the number of free pages
    //
    if (ems.getFreeEM(&totalPages, &freePages)) {
        ems_demoError("EMS_Ems::getFreeEM");
        }


    //
    //  Print header:
    //
    printf("       Operation          Avail Pages          Active Handles\n");
    printf("═══════════════════════════════════════════════════════════\n");
    printf("After 7 page allocate   |    %3d    | Handle   Pages     Name   |\n",
               freePages);

    displayActiveHandles();
    pause();


    //
    //   Now allocate 6 pages.
    //
    if (handle3.allocEM(6)) {
        ems_demoError("EMS_EmBlk::allocEM");
        }


    //
    //   Set the name for the handle
    //
    if (handle3.setHandleName("Porthos ")) {
        ems_demoError("EMS_EmBlk::setHandleName");
        }


    //
    //   Get the number of free pages
    //
    if (ems.getFreeEM(&totalPages, &freePages)) {
        ems_demoError("EMS_Ems::getFreeEM");
        }


    //
    //   Print header:
    //
    printf("       Operation          Avail Pages          Active Handles\n");
    printf("═══════════════════════════════════════════════════════════\n");
    printf("After 6 page allocate   |    %3d    | Handle   Pages     Name   |\n",
               freePages);

    displayActiveHandles();
    pause();
    //
    //   IMPORTANT!! We are now going to start freeing the blocks
    //   by looking them up by name. This will not refer back to the
    //   EMS_EmBlk objects which are attached to them. Thus, if we
```

```
//   don't detach them, we will attempt to free them again at
//   destruction time. Therefore we detach here.
//
handle1.detach();
handle2.detach();
handle3.detach();


//
//   Now find and free the "Aramis  " block.
//
if (tmpHandle.searchHandleName("Aramis  ")) {
    ems_demoError("EMS_EmBlk::searchHandleName");
    }
if (tmpHandle.freeEM()) {
    ems_demoError("EMS_EmBlk::freeEM");
    }


//
//   Get the number of free pages
//
if (ems.getFreeEM(&totalPages, &freePages)) {
    ems_demoError("EMS_Ems::getFreeEM");
    }


//
//   Print header:
//
printf("        Operation          Avail Pages          Active Handles\n");
printf("============================================================\n");
printf("After \"Aramis\" free    |    %3d    | Handle    Pages    Name    |\n",
            freePages);

displayActiveHandles();
pause();


//
//   Now free the "Athos   " block.
//
if (tmpHandle.searchHandleName("Athos   ")) {
    ems_demoError("EMS_EmBlk::searchHandleName");
    }
if (tmpHandle.freeEM()) {
    ems_demoError("EMS_EmBlk::freeEM");
    }


//
//   Get the number of free pages
//
if (ems.getFreeEM(&totalPages, &freePages)) {
    ems_demoError("EMS_Ems::getFreeEM");
    }


//
//   Print header:
//
printf("        Operation          Avail Pages          Active Handles\n");
printf("============================================================\n");
printf("After \"Athos\" free    |    %3d    | Handle    Pages    Name    |\n",
            freePages);

displayActiveHandles();
```

```
    pause();

    //
    //  Now free the "Porthos " block
    //
    if (tmpHandle.searchHandleName("Porthos ")) {
        ems_demoError("EMS_EmBlk::searchHandleName");
        }
    if (tmpHandle.freeEM()) {
        ems_demoError("EMS_EmBlk::freeEM");
        }

    //
    //  Get the number of free pages
    //
    if (ems.getFreeEM(&totalPages, &freePages)) {
        ems_demoError("EMS_Ems::getFreeEM");
        }

    //
    //  Print header:
    //
    printf("        Operation          Avail Pages        Active Handles\n");
    printf("================================================================\n");
    printf("After \"Porthos\" free  |   %3d   | Handle   Pages    Name   |\n",
            freePages);

    displayActiveHandles();

}

void displayActiveHandles()
{

    EMS_HandleInfo      *handleInfoArray;

    WORD                numActiveHandles;
    WORD                numActiveHandles2;

    WORD                i;

    char                nameBuff[8];

    //
    //  First find out how many active handles there are:
    //
    if (ems.getNumActiveHandles(&numActiveHandles)) {
        ems_demoError("EMS_Ems::getNumActiveHandles");
        }

    //
    //  Now allocate a block of handleInfo packets big enough to
    //  hold them.
    //
    handleInfoArray= new EMS_HandleInfo[numActiveHandles];

    //
    //  Now get the info.
    //
```

```cpp
    if (ems.getPagesAllHandles(handleInfoArray, &numActiveHandles2)) {
        ems_demoError("EMS_Ems::getNumActiveHandles");
        }

    //
    //   The following is a brief sanity clause (Everybody knows
    //   there ain't no sanity clause).
    //
    if (numActiveHandles2 != numActiveHandles) {
        printf("A most unusual situation has occurred...\n");
        exit(0);
        }

    //
    //   Finally, display it.
    //
    printf("                                        |               |               |               |\n");

    for (i= 0; i < numActiveHandles; i++) {

        //
        //   We need a EMS_EmBlk for the handle so we create one
        //   from the handle number and then look up the name.
        //
        EMS_EmBlk tmpHandle= handleInfoArray[i].handle;
        if (tmpHandle.getHandleName(nameBuff)) {
            ems_demoError("EMS_EmBlk::getHandleName");
            }

        printf(
            "                                      |  %3d  |  %3d  | %-8.8s |\n",
            handleInfoArray[i].handle,
            handleInfoArray[i].numPages,
            nameBuff);

        if (i+1 < numActiveHandles) {
            printf(
                                                    "|-------+-------+-------|/n");
            }
        }

    printf("========================================|===========|===========|\n");

    //
    //   Now free up the arrays.
    //
    delete handleInfoArray;
}

void pause()

{

    //
    //   Display a little message:
    //
    printf("Hit <CR> to continue...");
    fflush(stdout);

    //
```

```
    //  Wait for a <CR>
    //
    while (getchar() != '\n') {
        }

}
```

PROG4-4.CPP demonstrates the following operation:

- Getting all the handle names

PROG4-4 demonstrates the use of `EMS_Ems::getAllHandleNames()` to get the names of all existing EMS handles in one call.
Figure 4-4 presents the source code listing to PROG4-4.CPP.

4-4 The source code listing to PROG4-4.CPP

```
/////////////////////////////////////
//
// prog4-4.cpp
//
//      Demonstrates
//          - Get all handle names
//
/////////////////////////////////////

extern "C" {
#include <stdio.h>
#include <stdlib.h>
#include <dos.h>
}

#include "gdefs.h"

#define Uses_EMS40
#include "ems.h"


EMS_Ems             ems;


void main()
{
    WORD                i;

    EMS_EmBlk           handle1;
    EMS_EmBlk           handle2;
    EMS_EmBlk           handle3;

    WORD                numHandles;

    EMS_HandleNameInfo
                        *handleNameArray;

    //
```

```
//  First check for presence of EMS
//
if (ems.init()) {
    printf("EMS is not present\n");
    return;
    }


//
//  Allocate some handles and name them:
//
if (handle1.allocEM(1)) {
    ems_demoError("EMS_EmBlk::allocEM");
    }
if (handle2.allocEM(1)) {
    ems_demoError("EMS_EmBlk::allocEM");
    }
if (handle3.allocEM(1)) {
    ems_demoError("EMS_EmBlk::allocEM");
    }
if (handle1.setHandleName("Larry")) {
    ems_demoError("EMS_EmBlk::setHandleName");
    }
if (handle2.setHandleName("Moe")) {
    ems_demoError("EMS_EmBlk::setHandleName");
    }
if (handle3.setHandleName("Curly")) {
    ems_demoError("EMS_EmBlk::setHandleName");
    }


//
//  Allocate space for the names.
//
if (ems.getNumActiveHandles(&numHandles)) {
    ems_demoError("EMS_Ems::getNumActiveHandles");
    }

handleNameArray= new EMS_HandleNameInfo[numHandles];

//
//  Get the names for the handles.
//
if (ems.getAllHandleNames(handleNameArray)) {
    ems_demoError("EMS_Ems::getAllHandleNames");
    }

//
//  Now print the info out:
//
printf("┌─Handle──┬──Name──┐\n");

for (i= 0; i < numHandles; i++) {
    printf("║  %4d  |  %-8.8s  ║\n",
            handleNameArray[i].handle,
            handleNameArray[i].name);

    if (i < numHandles-1) {
        printf("║────────┼────────║\n");
        }
    }
printf("└────────┴────────┘\n");

//
```

4-5 Continued.

```
    //   Let the destructors deal with releasing the blocks.
    //
}
```

Figure 4-5 presents the source code listing to PROG4-5.CPP.

This program demonstrates the following operation:

- Resizing an expanded memory block

PROG4-5 uses `EMS_EmBlk::reallocHandPages()` to change the number of pages associated with a handle. It displays all of the handles and their sizes after each operation.

4-5 The source code listing to PROG4-5.CPP

```
/////////////////////////////////////
//
// prog4-5.cpp
//
//      Demonstrates
//          - Resize handle
//
/////////////////////////////////////

extern "C" {
#include <stdio.h>
#include <stdlib.h>
#include <dos.h>
}

#include "gdefs.h"

#define Uses_EMS40
#include "ems.h"


EMS_Ems              ems;

extern void displayActiveHandles(void);
extern void pause(void);

void main()
{
    WORD             totalPages;
    WORD             freePages;
    EMS_EmBlk        handle1;


    //
```

```
    //  First check for presence of EMS
    //
    if (ems.init()) {
        printf("EMS is not present\n");
        return;
        }


    //
    //  Now allocate 5 pages.
    //
    if (handle1.allocEM(5)) {
        ems_demoError("EMS_EmBlk::allocEM");
        }


    //
    //  Set the name for the handle
    //
    if (handle1.setHandleName("OurBlock")) {
        ems_demoError("EMS_EmBlk::setHandleName");
        }


    //
    //  Get the number of free pages
    //
    if (ems.getFreeEM(&totalPages, &freePages)) {
        ems_demoError("EMS_Ems::getFreeEM");
        }


    //
    //  Print header:
    //
    printf("      Operation          Avail Pages        Active Handles\n");
    printf("=========================================================\n");
    printf("After 5 page allocate    |    %3d    | Handle   Pages      Name    |\n",
            freePages);

    displayActiveHandles();
    pause();

    //
    //  Now resize the block:
    //
    if (handle1.reallocHandPages(8)) {
        ems_demoError("EMS_EmBlk::reallocHandPages");
        }


    //
    //  Get the number of free pages
    //
    if (ems.getFreeEM(&totalPages, &freePages)) {
        ems_demoError("EMS_Ems::getFreeEM");
        }


    //
    //  Print header:
    //
    printf("      Operation          Avail Pages        Active Handles\n");
    printf("=========================================================\n");
    printf("After Resize of handle   |    %3d    | Handle   Pages      Name    |\n",
            freePages);
```

```
    displayActiveHandles();

    if (handle1.freeEM()) {
        ems_demoError("EMS_EmBlk::freeEM");
        }
}

void displayActiveHandles()
{
    EMS_HandleInfo      *handleInfoArray;

    WORD                numActiveHandles;
    WORD                numActiveHandles2;

    WORD                i;

    char                nameBuff[8];

    //
    //   First find out how many active handles there are:
    //
    if (ems.getNumActiveHandles(&numActiveHandles)) {
        ems_demoError("EMS_Ems::getNumActiveHandles");
        }

    //
    //   Now allocate a block of handleInfo packets big enough to
    //   hold them.
    //
    handleInfoArray= new EMS_HandleInfo[numActiveHandles];

    //
    //   Now get the info.
    //
    if (ems.getPagesAllHandles(handleInfoArray, &numActiveHandles2)) {
        ems_demoError("EMS_Ems::getNumActiveHandles");
        }

    //
    //   The following is a brief sanity clause (Everybody knows
    //   there ain't no sanity clause).
    //
    if (numActiveHandles2 != numActiveHandles) {
        printf("A most unusual situation has occured...\n");
        exit(0);
        }

    //
    //   Finally, display it.
    //
    printf("                                    |_____|_____|_____|_____|\n");

    for (i= 0; i < numActiveHandles; i++) {

        EMS_EmBlk tmpHandle= handleInfoArray[i].handle;
        if (tmpHandle.getHandleName(nameBuff)) {
            ems_demoError("EMS_EmBlk::getHandleName");
            }

        printf(
```

```
            "                                    │ %3d    │ %3d   │ %-8.8s │\n",
            handleInfoArray[i].handle,
            handleInfoArray[i].numPages,
            nameBuff);

        if (i+1 < numActiveHandles) {
            printf(
              "
├─────┼─────┼─────────┤\n");
            }
        }

    printf("═════════════════════════════╧═════╧═════╧══════════╝\n");

    //
    //  Now free up the arrays.
    //
    delete handleInfoArray;

}

void pause()

{

    //
    //  Display a little message:
    //
    printf("Hit <CR> to continue...");
    fflush(stdout);

    //
    //  Wait for a <CR>
    //
    while (getchar() != '\n') {
        }

}
```

PROG4-6.CPP demonstrates the following operations:

- Mapping multiple pages by segment number
- Saving and restoring the partial map
- Mapping pages in low memory (below 640K)

PROG4-6 demonstrates mapping pages into conventional memory. There are three sets of pages that we work with—conventional pages and two EMS blocks. We start by finding six mappable conventional memory pages. We put text into those pages. We then save the current map that allows us to remap the conventional memory. We then remap those pages to point to EMS block pages. We put text into those pages and then map in other EMS pages and put text in those. We then restore the various maps that map the various sets of pages and print the contents.

Figure 4-6 presents the source code listing to PROG4-6.CPP.

4-6 The source code listing to PROG4-6.CPP

```
//////////////////////////////////////
//
// prog4-6.cpp
//
//       Demonstrates
//            - Map multiple pages by #/segment
//            - Save/restore partial map
//            - Mapping pages in lower 640K
//
//////////////////////////////////////

extern "C" {
#include <stdio.h>
#include <stdlib.h>
#include <dos.h>
#include <string.h>
}

#include "gdefs.h"

#define Uses_EMS40
#include "ems.h"


EMS_Ems              ems;

void main()
{

    WORD                 i;

    WORD                 numMappablePages;
    WORD                 numAvailableFrames;

    char                *frame[6];

    EMS_PageFrame       pfa;
    EMS_MappablePagesInfo
                        *pageAddress;
    EMS_MappablePagesInfo
                        *availableFrame;

    EMS_MapByNumber     mapByNumber[6];
    EMS_MapByAddress    mapByAddress[6];

    void                *restOfMem;
    long                 memLeft;

    WORD                 mapPageList[7];
    WORD                 mapSize;
    void                *mapSave1;
    void                *mapSave2;

    EMS_EmBlk            handle;


    //
    // First check for presence of EMS
```

```
//
if (ems.init()) {
    printf("EMS is not present\n");
    return;
    }

//
//  Now get the Page Frame Address:
//
if (ems.getPFA(&pfa)) {
    ems_demoError("EMS_Ems::getPFA");
    }

//
//  We'll want a dozen pages of EMS, so allocate them now.
//
if (handle.allocEM(12)) {
    ems_demoError("EMS_EmBlk::allocEM");
    }

//
//  Find out how many mappable pages we have all together. In
//  4.0, we do not have a fixed size page frame, we may have
//  many more than 4 mappable pages.
//
if (ems.getNumMappable(&numMappablePages)) {
    ems_demoError("EMS_Ems::getNumMappable");
    }

//
//  Now allocate a buffer big enough to hold the addresses
//  of these pages.
//
pageAddress= new EMS_MappablePagesInfo[numMappablePages];
availableFrame= new EMS_MappablePagesInfo[numMappablePages];

//
//  Get the info
//
if (ems.getAddrsMappable(pageAddress, &numMappablePages)) {
    ems_demoError("EMS_Ems::getAddrsMappable");
    }

//
//  We now allocate half of memory in order to control
//  some of the remappable pages.
//
memLeft= 327680L;
restOfMem= farmalloc(memLeft);
if (restOfMem == NULL) {
    printf("Unable to allocate conventional memory\n");
    return;
    }

//
//  Record the mappable pages which fall inside the bounds of
//  our memory block OR are part of the standard (3.0) page
//  frame area. Keep count of how many mappable pages
//  we have in total.
//
numAvailableFrames= 0;
```

```
for (i= 0; i < numMappablePages; i++) {
    if (SegToPhys(pageAddress[i].pageSegment) >= SegOffToPhys(restOfMem)
            && SegToPhys(pageAddress[i].pageSegment) + EMS_STD_PAGE_SIZE <=
                SegOffToPhys(restOfMem) + memLeft
        !! SegToPhys(pageAddress[i].pageSegment) >= SegOffToPhys(pfa[0])
            && SegToPhys(pageAddress[i].pageSegment) + EMS_STD_PAGE_SIZE <=
                SegOffToPhys(pfa[3]) + EMS_STD_PAGE_SIZE) {
        availableFrame[numAvailableFrames].physNumber=
            pageAddress[i].physNumber;
        availableFrame[numAvailableFrames].pageSegment=
            pageAddress[i].pageSegment;
        numAvailableFrames++;
        }
    }

//
//  We will be using 6 page frames. Make sure we have enough.
//
if (numAvailableFrames < 6) {
    printf("Insufficient number of available remappable pages\n");
    return;
    }

//
//  We'll be working with the first six available page frames.
//  Let's create an array which will allow us to easily
//  access them.
//
//  At the same time, set up the map list for saving the state.
//
for (i= 0; i < 6; i++) {
    frame[i]= (char *) MK_FP(availableFrame[i].pageSegment, 0);
    mapPageList[i+1]= availableFrame[i].pageSegment;
    }
mapPageList[0]= 6;

//
//  Let's put some text into the area.
//
strcpy(&frame[0][123], "CM:      In perpetrating a revolution there are two\n");
strcpy(&frame[1][456], "CM:      requirements: someone or something to revolt\n");
strcpy(&frame[2][789], "CM:      against and someone to actually show up and\n");
strcpy(&frame[3][12], "CM:      do the revolting. Dress is usually casual\n");
strcpy(&frame[4][345], "CM:\n");
strcpy(&frame[5][678], "CM:                              -- Woody Allen\n\n");

//
//  Let's the current state of these pages. Note that since
//  they (with the exception of those in the standard PFA), are
//  in the conventional memory area, they already have pages mapped
//  to them.
//
if (ems.getPMapInfoSize(6, &mapSize)) {
    ems_demoError("EMS_Ems::getPMapInfoSize");
    }

mapSave1= new char[mapSize];
mapSave2= new char[mapSize];

if (ems.savePartialMap(mapPageList, mapSave1)) {
```

```
        ems_demoError("EMS_Ems::savePartialMap");
        }

//
//   Now that we've saved the current state, let's map some
//   new pages in. We'll do it by number here.
//
for (i= 0; i < 6; i++) {
    mapByNumber[i].logicalPage= i;
    mapByNumber[i].physicalPage= availableFrame[i].physNumber;
    }

if (handle.mapPagesByNum(6, mapByNumber)) {
    ems_demoError("EMS_EmsBlk::mapPagesByNum");
    }

//
//   Now let's put some new text in:
//
strcpy(&frame[0][123],
    "EMA:    Someone did a study of the three most-often-heard phrases\n");
strcpy(&frame[1][456],
    "EMA:    in New York City. One is \"Hey taxi.\" Two is \"What train\n");
strcpy(&frame[2][789],
    "EMA:    do I take to get to Bloomingdales?\" And three is \"Don't\n");
strcpy(&frame[3][12],
    "EMA:    worry, it's only a flesh wound.\"\n");
strcpy(&frame[4][345], "EMA:\n");
strcpy(&frame[5][678], "EMA:                              -- David Letterman\n\n");

//
//   Let's save this map.
//
if (ems.savePartialMap(mapPageList, mapSave2)) {
    ems_demoError("EMS_Ems::savePartialMap");
    }

//
//   Now let's map a third set of pages, this time by segment
//
for (i= 0; i < 6; i++) {
    mapByAddress[i].logicalPage= 6 + i;
    mapByAddress[i].physicalSeg= availableFrame[i].pageSegment;
    }

if (handle.mapPagesByAddr(6, mapByAddress)) {
    ems_demoError("EMS_EmsBlk::mapPagesByAddr");
    }

//
//   Put some text in
//
strcpy(&frame[0][123],
    "EMB:    I grew up to have my father's looks, my father's\n");
strcpy(&frame[1][456],
    "EMB:    speech patterns, my father's posture, my father's\n");
strcpy(&frame[2][789],
    "EMB:    walk, my father's opinions and my mother's contempt\n");
strcpy(&frame[3][12], "EMB:    for my father.\n");
strcpy(&frame[4][345], "EMB:\n");
strcpy(&frame[5][678], "EMB:                              -- Jules Feiffer\n\n");
```

```
//
//  Now let's print out the stuff in the newest map.
//
printf("%s", &frame[0][123]);
printf("%s", &frame[1][456]);
printf("%s", &frame[2][789]);
printf("%s", &frame[3][12]);
printf("%s", &frame[4][345]);
printf("%s", &frame[5][678]);

//
//  Let's restore the second map and print the contents.
//
if (ems.restPartialMap(mapSave2)) {
    ems_demoError("EMS_Ems::restPartialMap");
    }

printf("%s", &frame[0][123]);
printf("%s", &frame[1][456]);
printf("%s", &frame[2][789]);
printf("%s", &frame[3][12]);
printf("%s", &frame[4][345]);
printf("%s", &frame[5][678]);

//
//  And finally, let's restore the original map (the conventional
//  memory pages), and print the contents.
//
if (ems.restPartialMap(mapSave1)) {
    ems_demoError("EMS_Ems::restPartialMap");
    }

printf("%s", &frame[0][123]);
printf("%s", &frame[1][456]);
printf("%s", &frame[2][789]);
printf("%s", &frame[3][12]);
printf("%s", &frame[4][345]);
printf("%s", &frame[5][678]);


//
//  Now we free that which must be freed.
//
farfree(restOfMem);
delete pageAddress;
delete availableFrame;
delete mapSave1;
delete mapSave2;

}
```

PROG4-7.CPP demonstrates the following operation:

- Moving memory between low memory and EMS

PROG4-7 shows how to use EMS_Ems.moveMemRegion() to move data between conventional memory and EMS.

Figure 4-7 presents the source code listing to PROG4-7.CPP.

4-7 The source code listing to PROG4-7.CPP

```
/////////////////////////////////////
//
// prog4-7.cpp
//
//       Demonstrates
//           - Xfer to/from EMS and Conventional memory
//
/////////////////////////////////////

extern "C" {
#include <stdio.h>
#include <stdlib.h>
#include <dos.h>
#include <string.h>
}

#include "gdefs.h"

#define Uses_EMS40
#include "ems.h"


EMS_Ems              ems;


void main()
{

    EMS_EmBlk            handle1;
    EMS_EmBlk            handle2;
    EMS_EmBlk            handle3;
    EMS_EmBlk            handle4;

    EMS_MoveMemoryInfo   movePacket;
    char                 *text;

    char                 buff[72];


    //
    //  First check for presence of EMS
    //
    if (ems.init()) {
        printf("EMS is not present\n");
        return;
        }

    //
    //  Allocate some EMS pages
    //
    if (handle1.allocEM(1)) {
        ems_demoError("EMS_EmBlk::allocEM");
        }
    if (handle2.allocEM(1)) {
        ems_demoError("EMS_EmBlk::allocEM");
        }
    if (handle3.allocEM(1)) {
        ems_demoError("EMS_EmBlk::allocEM");
        }
```

```
if (handle4.allocEM(1)) {
    ems_demoError("EMS_EmBlk::allocEM");
    }

//
//   Now let's copy some text into various places in the
//   EM blocks, and then copy it back and print it out.
//

//
//   Set \up a pointer to a string:
//
text= "     Every year when it's Chinese New Year Here in New York,\n";

//
//   Set up the move packet. Note that we round the length
//   up to an even number. The call requires an even length
//   transfer.
//
movePacket.length= strlen(text)+1;  // +1 for terminator
movePacket.srcType= EMS_MOVE_CONV;  // Conventional
movePacket.srcHandle= 0;            // indicates real memory
movePacket.srcOffset= FP_OFF(text); // actual offset
movePacket.srcPage= FP_SEG(text);   // actual segment
movePacket.destType= EMS_MOVE_EMS;  // EMS
movePacket.destHandle= handle1.num(); // 1st 1K block
movePacket.destOffset= 42;          // A random offset into block
movePacket.destPage= 0;             // page zero

//
//   Do the actual EMS call:
//
if (ems.moveMemRegion(&movePacket)) {
    ems_demoError("EMS_Ems::moveMemRegion");
    exit(1);
    }

//
//   Now put the next string into the next EM block:
//
text= "     there are fireworks going off at all hours. New York mothers\n";

movePacket.length= strlen(text)+1;  // +1 for terminator
movePacket.srcType= EMS_MOVE_CONV;  // Conventional
movePacket.srcHandle= 0;            // indicates real memory
movePacket.srcOffset= FP_OFF(text); // actual offset
movePacket.srcPage= FP_SEG(text);   // actual segment
movePacket.destType= EMS_MOVE_EMS;  // EMS
movePacket.destHandle= handle2.num(); // 1st 1K block
movePacket.destOffset= 911;         // A random offset into block
movePacket.destPage= 0;             // page zero

if (ems.moveMemRegion(&movePacket)) {
    ems_demoError("EMS_Ems::moveMemRegion");
    exit(1);
    }

//
//   And something for the the third block:
```

```
//
text= "      calm their frightened children by telling them it's just gunfire\n\n";


movePacket.length= strlen(text)+1;  // +1 for terminator
movePacket.srcType= EMS_MOVE_CONV;  // Conventional
movePacket.srcHandle= 0;            // indicates real memory
movePacket.srcOffset= FP_OFF(text); // actual offset
movePacket.srcPage= FP_SEG(text);   // actual segment
movePacket.destType= EMS_MOVE_EMS;  // EMS
movePacket.destHandle= handle3.num(); // 1st 1K block
movePacket.destOffset= 800;         // A random offset into block
movePacket.destPage= 0;             // page zero

if (ems.moveMemRegion(&movePacket)) {
    ems_demoError("EMS_Ems::moveMemRegion");
    exit(1);
    }


//
//  Now the fourth and last block:
//
text= "                            -- David Letterman\n\n";

movePacket.length= strlen(text)+1;  // +1 for terminator
movePacket.srcType= EMS_MOVE_CONV;  // Conventional
movePacket.srcHandle= 0;            // indicates real memory
movePacket.srcOffset= FP_OFF(text); // actual offset
movePacket.srcPage= FP_SEG(text);   // actual segment
movePacket.destType= EMS_MOVE_EMS;  // EMS
movePacket.destHandle= handle4.num(); // 1st 1K block
movePacket.destOffset= 212;         // A random offset into block
movePacket.destPage= 0;             // page zero

if (ems.moveMemRegion(&movePacket)) {
    ems_demoError("EMS_Ems::moveMemRegion");
    exit(1);
    }


//
//  Now we've copies four strings into EMS blocks.
//      Block 1 at offset 42,
//      Block 2 at offset 911,
//      Block 3 at offset 800,
//      Block 4 at offset 212.
//
//  Now let's retrieve them and print them out.
//
movePacket.length= 72;              // +1 for terminator
movePacket.srcType= EMS_MOVE_EMS;   // EMS
movePacket.srcHandle= handle1.num(); // First handle
movePacket.srcOffset= 42;           // A random offset into block
movePacket.srcPage= 0;              // page zero
movePacket.destType= EMS_MOVE_CONV; // Conventional memory
movePacket.destHandle= 0;           // Conventional memory
movePacket.destOffset= FP_OFF(buff);// actual offset
movePacket.destPage= FP_SEG(buff);  // actual segment

if (ems.moveMemRegion(&movePacket)) {
    ems_demoError("EMS_Ems::moveMemRegion");
```

```
    exit(1);
    }
printf("%s", buff);

//
//  Now pick up the second piece:
//
movePacket.length= 72;              // +1 for terminator
movePacket.srcType= EMS_MOVE_EMS;   // EMS
movePacket.srcHandle= handle2.num();  // First handle
movePacket.srcOffset= 911;          // A random offset into block
movePacket.srcPage= 0;              // page zero
movePacket.destType= EMS_MOVE_CONV; // Conventional memory
movePacket.destHandle= 0;           // Conventional memory
movePacket.destOffset= FP_OFF(buff);// actual offset
movePacket.destPage= FP_SEG(buff);  // actual segment

if (ems.moveMemRegion(&movePacket)) {
    ems_demoError("EMS_Ems::moveMemRegion");
    exit(1);
    }

printf("%s", buff);

//
//  Now pick up the third piece:
//
movePacket.length= 72;              // +1 for terminator
movePacket.srcType= EMS_MOVE_EMS;   // EMS
movePacket.srcHandle= handle3.num();  // Third handle
movePacket.srcOffset= 800;          // A random offset into block
movePacket.srcPage= 0;              // page zero
movePacket.destType= EMS_MOVE_CONV; // Conventional memory
movePacket.destHandle= 0;           // Conventional memory
movePacket.destOffset= FP_OFF(buff);// actual offset
movePacket.destPage= FP_SEG(buff);  // actual segment

if (ems.moveMemRegion(&movePacket)) {
    ems_demoError("EMS_Ems::moveMemRegion");
    exit(1);
    }

printf("%s", buff);

//
//  Now pick up the fourth piece:
//
movePacket.length= 72;              // +1 for terminator
movePacket.srcType= EMS_MOVE_EMS;   // EMS
movePacket.srcHandle= handle4.num();  // First handle
movePacket.srcOffset= 212;          // A random offset into block
movePacket.srcPage= 0;              // page zero
movePacket.destType= EMS_MOVE_CONV; // Conventional memory
movePacket.destHandle= 0;           // Conventional memory
movePacket.destOffset= FP_OFF(buff);// actual offset
movePacket.destPage= FP_SEG(buff);  // actual segment

if (ems.moveMemRegion(&movePacket)) {
    ems_demoError("EMS_Ems::moveMemRegion");
```

```
        exit(1);
        }

    printf("%s", buff);

}
```

Now that we have presented the source code for the EMS 4.0 demon-stration programs, it's time to present the interface functions.

C++ interface functions
Save a partial page map

Function EMS_Ems::savePartialMap() saves the state of the specified expanded page mapping registers into a designated buffer. The difference between this call and those in the 3.0 and 3.2 specifications is that here the list of physical pages for which to save mapping information must be supplied. This function calls ems_savePartialMap40(), defined in EMS4F0.ASM.

Figure 4-8 presents the source code listing to EMS4F0.ASM.

Function EMS_Ems::savePartialMap()

```
EMS_Ems   ems;
WORD      *map;
char      *buffer;

error= ems.savePartialMap(map, buffer);
```

where

map   Points to a list of segment addresses
buffer   Receives the register state information for the specified pages. The required size of this area can be determined by calling EMS_Ems::getPMapInfoSize().

4-8 The source code listing to EMS4F0.ASM

```
;******************************************************************
;***     EMS4F0.ASM                                         ***
;***                                                        ***
;***     int far ems_savePartialMap40(WORD *map,            ***
;***                              WORD *buffer);            ***
;***                                                        ***
;***     Saves the state of a subset of expanded mem page   ***
;***     mapping in buffer                                  ***
;***                                                        ***
;***     Returns 0 if no error or an error code.            ***
;***                                                        ***
;***                                                        ***
;***                                                        ***
;***     (Ems Version 4.0)                                  ***
;******************************************************************
```

4-8 Continued.

```
        .model  large,C
        include emsdefs.asm

        extrn   errno:WORD

;
;   Define entry point
;
        public  ems_savePartialMap40

        .code

ems_savePartialMap40 proc    map:Far Ptr Word, buffer:Far Ptr Word
        push    ds                           ; Save some registers
        push    si
        push    di

;
;   DS:SI needs a list of segment addresses of pages for which
;   to save the mapping state.
;
        lds     si,map

;
;   ES:DI gets the address of the buffer to save the info into
;
        les     di,buffer

        mov     ax,SavePartialMap40   ; Do the call
        int     Ems

        or      ah,ah                 ; Set flags
        jnz     error

        xor     ax,ax                 ; Return OK

        pop     di                    ; Restore regs
        pop     si
        pop     ds
        ret

error:
        pop     di                    ; Restore regs
        pop     si
        pop     ds

        mov     al,ah                 ; Transfer return code
        xor     ah,ah                 ; Zero extend
        mov     errno,ax              ; Save in errno too
        ret

ems_savePartialMap40 endp            ; End of procedure

        end                          ; End of source file
```

Restore a partial page map

The `EMS_Ems::restPartialMap()` function restores the state of the previously saved page mapping registers. This function calls `ems_restPartialMap40()`, defined in EMS4F1.ASM.

Figure 4-9 presents the source code listing to EMS4F1.ASM.

Function EMS_Ems::restPartialMap()

```
EMS_Ems    ems;
WORD       *map;
char       *buffer;

error= ems.savePartialMap(map, buffer);
...
error= ems.restPartialMap(buffer);
```

where

    `buffer`   **Holds the register state information**

4-9 The source code listing to EMS4F1.ASM

```
;****************************************************************
;***      EMS4F1.ASM                                        ***
;***                                                         ***
;***      int far ems_restPartialMap40(WORD *buffer);       ***
;***                                                         ***
;***      Restores the state of a subset of expanded mem page ***
;***      mapping from buffer                                ***
;***                                                         ***
;***      Returns 0 if no error or an error code.           ***
;***                                                         ***
;***                                                         ***
;***      (Ems Version 4.0)                                 ***
;****************************************************************

        .model  large,C

        include emsdefs.asm

        extrn   errno:WORD

;
;   Define entry point
;
        public  ems_restPartialMap40

        .code
ems_restPartialMap40 proc     buffer:Far Ptr Word
        push    ds                      ; Save registers
        push    si

        lds     si,buffer               ; DS:SI gets buffer address

        mov     ax,RestPartialMap40     ; Make EMS call
```

```
        int     Ems

        or      ah,ah                   ; Set flags
        jnz     error

        xor     ax,ax                   ; return OK

        pop     si                      ; Restore regs
        pop     ds
        ret

error:
        pop     si                      ; Restore regs
        pop     ds

        mov     al,ah                   ; AL gets error code
        xor     ah,ah                   ; Zero extend
        mov     errno,ax                ; Save in errno too

        ret

ems_restPartialMap40 endp               ; End of procedure

        end                             ; End of source file
```

Get the size of partial page map information

The EMS_Ems::getPMapInfoSize() function returns the amount of space required to save the specified number of map registers using the EMS_Ems ::savePartialMap() function. This function calls ems_getPMapInfo Size40(), defined in EMS4F2.ASM.

Figure 4-10 presents the source code listing to EMS4F2.ASM.

Function EMS_Ems::getPMapInfoSize()

```
EMS_Ems     ems;
WORD        pages;
WORD        buffSize;

error= ems.getPMapInfoSize(pages, &buffSize);
```

where

pages The number of physical pages for which state is to be saved
size   Receives the amount of space required in bytes

4-10 The source code listing to EMS4F2.ASM

```
;******************************************************************
;***     EMS4F2.ASM                                        ***
;***                                                       ***
;***     int far ems_getPMapInfoSize40(WORD pages,         ***
;***                             WORD *size);              ***
```

```
;***                                                              ***
;***       Pointer gets size of partial page map buffer in        ***
;***       bytes.                                                  ***
;***                                                              ***
;***       Returns 0 if no error or an error code.                ***
;***                                                              ***
;***                                                              ***
;***       (Ems Version 4.0)                                       ***
;*****************************************************************

          .model  large,C

          include emsdefs.asm
          extrn   errno:WORD

;
;    Define entry point
;
          public  ems_getPMapInfoSize40

          .code

ems_getPMapInfoSize40 proc pages:Word, buffSize:Far Ptr Word

          mov     bx,pages                 ; BX gets number of pages

          mov     ax,GetPMapInfoSize40     ; Make the EMS call
          int     Ems

          or      ah,ah                    ; Set flags
          jnz     error

          xor     ah,ah                    ; Zero extend size in AL
          les     bx,buffSize              ; Return it
          mov     es:[bx],ax

          xor     ax,ax                    ; Return OK
          ret

error:
          mov     al,ah                    ; AL gets error code
          xor     ah,ah                    ; Zero extend
          mov     errno,ax                 ; Save in errno too
          ret

ems_getPMapInfoSize40 endp                 ; End of procedure

          end                              ; End of source file
```

Map multiple pages by number

The EMS_EmBlk::mapPagesByNum() function maps several logical pages at one time. A mapping buffer is given which gives pairs of (logical EMS page, physical page number). This function calls ems_mapPagesByNum 40(), defined in EMS500.ASM.

Figure 4-11 presents the source code listing to EMS500.ASM.

Function EMS_EmBlk::mapPagesByNum()

```
EMS_EmBlk          block;
WORD               pages;
EMS_MapByNumber    *buffer;

error= block.mapPagesByNum(pages, buffer);
```

where

pages   The number of pages to map

buffer   Points to a table of 32-bit entries giving the logical and physical pages to be mapped (see EMS.H, FIG. 3-7 for `EMS_Map
ByNumber` structure).

4-11   The source code listing to EMS500.ASM

```
;****************************************************************
;***      EMS500.ASM                                      ***
;***                                                      ***
;***      int far ems_mapPagesByNum40(WORD handle,        ***
;***                                  WORD pages,         ***
;***                                  DWORD *buffer);     ***
;***                                                      ***
;***      Fill buffer with 32 bit entries which control pages ***
;***      to be mapped by page number                    ***
;***                                                      ***
;***      Returns 0 if no error or an error code.        ***
;***                                                      ***
;***                                                      ***
;***                                                      ***
;***      (Ems Version 4.0)                               ***
;****************************************************************

         .model  large,C

         include emsdefs.asm

         extrn   errno:WORD

;
;   Define entry point
;
         public  ems_mapPagesByNum40

         .code

ems_mapPagesByNum40 proc handle:Word, num:Word, buffer:Far Ptr Word

         push    ds                      ; Save regs
         push    si

         mov     dx,handle               ; EMS handle
         mov     cx,num                  ; Number of pages to map
         lds     si,buffer               ; Map info buffer

         mov     ax,MapPagesByNum40      ; Make the EMS call
         int     Ems
```

```
        or      ah,ah                   ; Set flags
        jnz     error

        xor     ax,ax                   ; return OK

        pop     si                      ; Restore regs
        pop     ds
        ret

error:
        pop     si                      ; Restore regs
        pop     ds

        mov     al,ah                   ; AL get error code
        xor     ah,ah                   ; Zero extend
        mov     errno,ax                ; Save in errno too

        ret

ems_mapPagesByNum40 endp                ; End of procedure

        end                             ; End of source file
```

Map multiple pages by address

The EMS_EmBlk::mapPagesByAddr() function maps several logical pages at one time. A mapping buffer is given which gives pairs of (logical EMS page, physical segment number). This function calls ems_mapPages ByAddr40(), defined in EMS501.ASM.

Figure 4-12 presents the source code listing to EMS501.ASM.

Function EMS_Ems::mapPagesByAddr()

```
EMS_EmBlk           block;
WORD                pages;
EMS_MapByAddress    *buffer;

error= block.mapPagesByAddr(pages, buffer);
```

where

pages   The number of pages to map
buffer Points to a table of 32-bit entries giving logical and phy-
        sical segment addresses (see EMS.H, FIG. 3-7 for EMS_MapByAd
        dress structure).

4-12 The source code listing to EMS501.ASM

```
;*********************************************************************
;***      EMS501.ASM                                          ***
;***                                                          ***
;***      int far ems_mapPagesByAddr40(WORD handle,           ***
;***                              WORD pages,                 ***
;***                              DWORD *buffer);             ***
```

4-12 Continued.

```
;***                                                        ***
;***    Fill buffer with 32 bit entries which control pages ***
;***    to be mapped by segment address                     ***
;***                                                        ***
;***    Returns 0 if no error or an error code.             ***
;***                                                        ***
;***                                                        ***
;***                                                        ***
;***    (Ems Version 4.0)                                   ***
;********************************************************************

        .model  large,C

        include emsdefs.asm

        extrn   errno:WORD

;
;   Define entry point
;
        public  ems_mapPagesByAddr40

        .code

ems_mapPagesByAddr40 proc handle:Word, num:Word, buffer:Far Ptr Word

        push    ds                      ; Save regs
        push    si

        mov     dx,handle               ; EMS handle
        mov     cx,num                  ; Number of pages to map
        lds     si,buffer               ; Mapping info

        mov     ax,MapPagesByAddr40     ; Make the EMS call
        int     Ems

        or      ah,ah                   ; Set flags
        jnz     error

        xor     ax,ax                   ; Return OK

        pop     si                      ; Restore regs
        pop     ds
        ret

error:
        pop     si
        pop     ds

        mov     al,ah                   ; AL get error code
        xor     ah,ah                   ; Zero extend
        mov     errno,ax                ; Save in errno too

        ret

ems_mapPagesByAddr40 endp               ; End of procedure

        end                             ; End of source file
```

Reallocate pages for handle

The function EMS_EmBlk::reallocHandPages() alters the number of pages allocated to a specified handle. This function calls ems_realloc HandlePages40(), defined in EMS51.ASM.

Figure 4-13 presents the source code listing to EMS51.ASM.

Function EMS_EmBlk::reallocHandPages()

```
EMS_EmBlk    block;
WORD         pages;

error= block.reallocHandPages(pages);
```

where

pages   Is the new handle page count

4-13 The source code listing to EMS51.ASM

```
;*****************************************************************
;***      EMS51.ASM                                      ***
;***                                                     ***
;***      int far ems_reallocHandPages40(WORD handle,    ***
;***                                WORD pages);          ***
;***                                                     ***
;***      Reallocates number of pages to EMM handle      ***
;***                                                     ***
;***      Returns 0 if no error or an error code.        ***
;***                                                     ***
;***                                                     ***
;***                                                     ***
;***      (Ems Version 4.0)                              ***
;*****************************************************************
;
        .model  large,C

        include emsdefs.asm

        extrn   errno:WORD

;
;   Define entry point
;
        public  ems_reallocHandPages40

        .code
ems_reallocHandPages40 proc handle:Word, num:Word

        mov     dx,handle               ; EMS handle
        mov     bx,num                  ; New page count

        mov     ax,ReallocHandPages40   ; Make the call
        int     Ems

        or      ah,ah                   ; Set flags
        jnz     error
```

```
        xor     ax,ax                   : Return OK
        ret

error:
        mov     al,ah                   : AL get error code
        xor     ah,ah                   : Zero extend
        mov     errno,ax                : Save in errno too
        ret

ems_reallocHandPages40 endp             : End of procedure

        end                             : End of source file
```

Get handle attribute

The function EMS_Ems::getHandleAttr() retrieves the attribute associated with a specified handle. This function calls ems_getHandleAttr 40(), defined in EMS520.ASM.

Figure 4-14 presents the source code listing to EMS520.ASM.

Function EMS_EmBlk::getHandleAttr()

```
EMS_EmBlk       block;
WORD            attribute;

error= block.getHandleAttr(&attribute);
```

where

attr 1 = nonvolatile (ems data held on warm boot)
        0 = volatile (ems data destroyed on warm boot)

4-14 The source code listing to EMS520.ASM

```
;******************************************************************
;***    EMS520.ASM                                         ***
;***                                                       ***
;***    int far ems_getHandleAttr40(WORD handle,           ***
;***                        WORD *attribute);              ***
;***                                                       ***
;***    Get volatile (0) or non-volatile (1) attribute     ***
;***    associated with the handle.                        ***
;***                                                       ***
;***    Returns 0 if no error or an error code.            ***
;***                                                       ***
;***                                                       ***
;***                                                       ***
;***    (Ems Version 4.0)                                  ***
;******************************************************************

        .model  large,C

        include emsdefs.asm

        extrn   errno:WORD
```

```
    :
    ;   Define entry point
    :

        public  ems_getHandleAttr40

        .code

ems_getHandleAttr40 proc handle:Word, attr:Far Ptr Word

        mov     dx,handle               ; DX gets EMS handle

        mov     ax,GetHandleAttr40      ; Do call
        int     Ems

        or      ah,ah                   ; Set flags
        jnz     error
        xor     ah,ah                   ; Zero extend attr to 16 bits
        les     bx,attr                 ; Return attribute
        mov     es:[bx],ax

        xor     ax,ax                   ; return OK
        ret

error:
        mov     al,ah                   ; AL get error code
        xor     ah,ah                   ; Zero extend
        mov     errno,ax                ; Save in errno too
        ret

ems_getHandleAttr40 endp                ; End of procedure

        end                             ; End of source file
```

Set handle attribute

The function EMS_EmBlk::setHandleAttr() sets the attribute associated
with a specified handle. This function calls ems_setHandleAttr40(), defined in EMS521.ASM.

Figure 4-15 presents the source code listing to EMS521.ASM.

Function EMS_EmBlk::setHandleAttr()

```
EMS_EmBlk         block;
WORD              attribute;

error= block.setHandleAttr(attribute);
```

where

```
attribute   1 = nonvolatile (ems data held on warm boot)
            0 = volatile (ems data destroyed on warm boot)
```

4-15 The source code listing to EMS521.ASM

```
;********************************************************************
;***      EMS521.ASM                                          ***
```

4-15 Continued.

```
;***                                                          ***
;***     int far ems_setHandleAttr40(WORD handle,             ***
;***                            WORD attribute);              ***
;***                                                          ***
;***     Set volatile (0) or non-volatile (1) attribute       ***
;***     associated with the handle.                          ***
;***                                                          ***
;***     Returns 0 if no error or an error code.              ***
;***                                                          ***
;***                                                          ***
;***                                                          ***
;***     (Ems Version 4.0)  ************************************
;*********************************************************************

        .model  large,C
        include emsdefs.asm

        extrn   errno:WORD

;
;   Define entry point
;
        public  ems_setHandleAttr40

        .code

ems_setHandleAttr40 proc handle:Word, attr:Word

        mov     dx,handle           ; DX gets EMS handle
        mov     bx,attr             ; BL gets attribute

        mov     ax,SetHandleAttr40  ; Make EMS call
        int     Ems

        or      ah,ah               ; Set flags
        jnz     error

        xor     ax,ax               ; Return OK
        ret

error:
        mov     al,ah               ; AL gets error code
        xor     ah,ah               ; Zero extend
        mov     errno,ax            ; Save in errno too
        ret
ems_setHandleAttr40 endp            ; End of procedure

        end                         ; End of source file
```

Get attribute capabilities

The function EMS_Ems::getAttrCapability() retrieves a flag that indicates the EMM's capability of supporting nonvolatile EMS data. This function calls ems_getAttrCapability40(), defined in EMS522.ASM.

Figure 4-16 presents the source code listing to EMS522.ASM.

Function EMS_Ems::getAttrCapability()

```
EMS_Ems   ems;
WORD      capability;

error= ems.getAttrCapability(&capability);
```

where

capability   1 = nonvolatile (ems data held on warm boot)
              0 = volatile (ems data destroyed on warm boot)

4-16 The source code listing to EMS522.ASM

```
;*****************************************************************
;***      EMS522.ASM                                       ***
;***                                                       ***
;***      int far ems_setAttrCapability40(WORD *capability);   ***
;***                                                       ***
;***      Gets EMM support status for handle volatility.   ***
;***         volatile (0) or non-volatile (1) attribute    ***
;***                                                       ***
;***      Returns 0 if no error or an error code.          ***
;***                                                       ***
;***                                                       ***
;***                                                       ***
;***      (Ems Version 4.0)                                ***
;*****************************************************************

        .model  large,C

        include emsdefs.asm

        extrn   errno:WORD

;
;   Define entry point
;
        public  ems_getAttrCapability40

        .code

ems_getAttrCapability40 proc attr:Far Ptr Word

        mov     ax,GetAttrCapability40  ; Make EMS call
        int     Ems


        or      ah,ah                   ; Set flags

        jnz     error


        xor     ah,ah                   ; Zero extend attr to 16 bits
```

```
        les     bx,attr                 ; Return it

        mov     es:[bx],ax


        xor     ax,ax                   ; Return OK

        ret

error:

        mov     al,ah                   ; AL gets error code

        xor     ah,ah                   ; Zero extend

        mov     errno,ax                ; Save in errno too

        ret



ems_getAttrCapability40 endp            ; End of procedure



        end                             ; End of source file
```

Get handle name

The `EMS_EmBlk::getHandleName()` function returns the name of a specified handle. This function calls `ems_getHandleName40()`, defined in EMS530.ASM.

Figure 4-17 presents the source code listing to EMS530.ASM.

Function EMS_EmBlk::getHandleName()

```
EMS_EmBlk   block;
char        handle_name[8];

error= block.getHandleName(handle_name);
```

where

handle_name   **An 8-byte buffer into which the name is copied**

4-17 The source code listing to EMS530.ASM

```
;****************************************************************
;***      EMS530.ASM                                        ***
;***                                                        ***
;***      int far ems_getHandleName40(WORD handle,          ***
```

```
;***                               BYTE *handle_name);        ***
;***                                                          ***
;***     Fill 8 byte handle name buffer with handle name.     ***
;***                                                          ***
;***     Returns 0 if no error or an error code.              ***
;***                                                          ***
;***                                                          ***
;***                                                          ***
;***     (Ems Version 4.0)                                    ***
;*************************************************************

        .model  large,C

        include emsdefs.asm

        extrn   errno:WORD


;
;    Define entry point
;
        public  ems_getHandleName40

        .code

ems_getHandleName40 proc handle:Word, handle_name:Far Ptr Word

        push    di                      ; Save di

        mov     dx,handle               ; DX gets EMS handle
        les     di,handle_name          ; ES:DI gets name

        mov     ax,GetHandleName40      ; Make EMS call
        int     Ems

        or      ah,ah                   ; Set flags
        jnz     error

        xor     ax,ax                   ; Return OK
        pop     di
        ret

error:
        pop     di                      ; Restore DI

        mov     al,ah                   ; AL gets error code
        xor     ah,ah                   ; Zero extend
        mov     errno,ax                ; Save in errno too
        ret
ems_getHandleName40 endp                ; End of procedure

        end                             ; End of source file
```

Set handle name

The `EMS_EmBlk::setHandleName()` function sets the name of a specified handle. This function calls `ems_setHandleName40()`, defined in EMS 531.ASM.

Figure 4-18 presents the source code listing to EMS531.ASM.

Function EMS_EmBlk::setHandleName()

```
EMS_EmBlk    block;
char         handle_name[8];

error= block.setHandleName(handle_name);
```

where

    `handle_name`   **An 8-byte buffer containing the name to be set**

4-18 The source code listing to EMS531.ASM

```
;******************************************************************
;***      EMS531.ASM                                        ***
;***                                                        ***
;***      int far ems_setHandleName40(WORD handle,          ***
;***                             BYTE *handle_name);        ***
;***                                                        ***
;***      Set handle name buffer (bytes)                    ***
;***                                                        ***
;***      Returns 0 if no error or an error code.           ***
;***                                                        ***
;***                                                        ***
;***                                                        ***
;***      (Ems Version 4.0)                                 ***
;******************************************************************
;
         .model  large,C

         include emsdefs.asm

         extrn   errno:WORD


;
;    Define entry point
;
         public  ems_setHandleName40

         .code

ems_setHandleName40 proc handle:Word, handle_name:Far Ptr Word

         push    ds                      ; Save regs
         push    si

         mov     dx,handle               ; DX gets the EMS handle
         lds     si,handle_name          ; DS:SI get handle name

         mov     ax,SetHandleName40      ; Make the EMS call
         int     Ems

         or      ah,ah                   ; Set flags
```

```
        jnz     error

        xor     ax,ax                   ; Return OK
        pop     si                      ; Restore regs
        pop     ds
        ret

error:
        pop     si                      ; Restore regs
        pop     ds
        mov     al,ah                   ; AL gets error code
        xor     ah,ah                   ; Zero extend
        mov     errno,ax                ; Save in errno too
        ret

ems_setHandleName40 endp                ; End of procedure

        end                             ; End of source file
```

Get all handle names

Function EMS_Ems::getAllHandleNames() returns a list of names for all the active handles. This function calls ems_getAllHandleNames40(), defined in EMS540.ASM.

Figure 4-19 presents the source code listing to EMS540.ASM.

Function EMS_Ems::getAllHandleNames()

```
EMS_Ems             ems;
EMS_HandleNameInfo  *info_list;
WORD                num_handles;

error= ems.getTotalHandles(&num_handles);
info_list= new EMS_HandleNameInfo[num_handles];
error= ems.getAllHandleNames(info_list);
```

where

info_list **An array of** HandleNameInfo **records (see EMS.H**, FIG. 3-7
        for EMS_HandleNameInfo **structure)**

4-19 The source code listing to EMS540.ASM

```
;***************************************************************
;***    EMS540.ASM                                          ***
;***                                                        ***
;***    int far ems_getAllHandleNames40(                    ***
;***                HandleNameInfo_type *name_list);        ***
;***                                                        ***
;***    Fill 8 byte handle names to 2550 MAX entries        ***
;***                                                        ***
;***    Returns 0 if no error or an error code.             ***
;***                                                        ***
;***                                                        ***
```

4-19 Continued.

```
;***                                                      ***
;***      (Ems Version 4.0)                               ***
;***************************************************************

        .model  large,C

        include emsdefs.asm

        extrn   errno:WORD

;
;   Define entry point
;
        public  ems_getAllHandleNames40

        extrn   errno:WORD
        .code

ems_getAllHandleNames40 proc info_list:Far Ptr Byte

        push    di                      ; Save DI

        les     di,info_list            ; ES:DI gets address of buffer

        mov     ax,GetAllHandleNames40  ; Make the EMS call
        int     Ems

        or      ah,ah                   ; Set flags
        jnz     error

        xor     ax,ax                   ; Return OK
        pop     di                      ; Restore DI
        ret

error:
        pop     di                      ; Restore DI

        mov     al,ah                   ; AL gets error code
        xor     ah,ah                   ; Zero extend
        mov     errno,ax                ; Save in errno too
        ret

ems_getAllHandleNames40 endp            ; End of procedure

        end                             ; End of source file
```

Search for handle name

Function EMS_EmBlk::searchHandleName() initializes the target EMS_Em Blk with the handle associated with the specified name. The object will not be attached to the EMS block. Thus, when the object is destroyed, the EMS block will not be released. To override this behavior, call EMS_EmBlk ::attach() after calling EMS_EmBlk::searchHandleName(). This function calls ems_searchHandleName40(), defined in EMS541.ASM.

Figure 4-20 presents the source code listing to EMS541.ASM.

Function EMS_EmBlk::searchHandleName()

```
EMS_EmBlk    block;
char         handle_name[8];

error= block.searchHandleName(handle_name);
```

where

handle_name   **Points to an 8-byte handle name**

4-20 The source code listing to EMS541.ASM

```
;****************************************************************
;***      EMS541.ASM                                       ***
;***                                                       ***
;***      int far ems_searchHandleName40(WORD *handle,     ***
;***                              BYTE *name);             ***
;***                                                       ***
;***      Returns handle number of specified handle name.  ***
;***                                                       ***
;***      Returns 0 if no error or an error code.          ***
;***                                                       ***
;***                                                       ***
;***                                                       ***
;***      (Ems Version 4.0)                                ***
;****************************************************************

        .model   large,C

        include emsdefs.asm

        extrn    errno:WORD

;
;    Define entry point
;
        public  ems_searchHandleName40

        .code

ems_searchHandleName40 proc handle:Far Ptr Word, handle_name:Far Ptr Byte

        push    ds                      ; Save regs
        push    si

        lds     si,handle_name          ; DS:SI gets handle name

        mov     ax,SearchHandleName40   ; Do EMS call
        int     Ems

        or      ah,ah                   ; Set flags
        jnz     error

        les     bx,handle               ; Return handle we found
        mov     es:[bx],dx

        xor     ax,ax                   ; Return OK
        pop     si                      ; Restore regs
        pop     ds
        ret
```

```
error:
        pop     si                      ; Restore regs
        pop     ds

        mov     al,ah                   ; AL gets error code
        xor     ah,ah                   ; Zero extend
        mov     errno,ax                ; Save in errno too
        ret

ems_searchHandleName40 endp             ; End of procedure

        end                             ; End of source file
```

Get total number of handles

Function `EMS_Ems::getTotalHandles()` returns the total number of active EMS handles. This function calls `ems_getTotalHandles40()`, defined in EMS542.ASM.

Figure 4-21 presents the source code listing to EMS542.ASM.

Function EMS_Ems::getTotalHandles()

```
EMS_Ems     ems;
WORD        handles;

error= ems.getTotalHandles();
```

where

handles   Receives total number of active EMS handles

4-21 The source code listing to EMS542.ASM

```
;*****************************************************************
;***    EMS542.ASM                                        ***
;***                                                      ***
;***    int far int far ems_getTotalHandles40(            ***
;***                            WORD *handles);           ***
;***                                                      ***
;***    Returns total number of allocated handles to      ***
;***    pointer.                                          ***
;***                                                      ***
;***    Returns 0 if no error or an error code.           ***
;***                                                      ***
;***                                                      ***
;***                                                      ***
;***    (Ems Version 4.0)                                 ***
;*****************************************************************
;
        .model  large,C

        include emsdefs.asm

        extrn   errno:WORD

;
```

```
;   Define entry point
;

        public  ems_getTotalHandles40

        .code

ems_getTotalHandles40 proc handles:Far Ptr Word

        mov     ax,GetTotalHandles40    ; Do EMS call
        int     Ems

        or      ah,ah                   ; Set flags
        jnz     error

        mov     ax,bx                   ; Number of handles
        les     bx,handles              ; Return it
        mov     es:[bx],ax

        xor     ax,ax                   ; Return OK
        ret

error:
        mov     al,ah                   ; AL gets error code
        xor     ah,ah                   ; Zero extend
        mov     errno,ax                ; Save in errno too
        ret

ems_getTotalHandles40 endp              ; End of procedure

        end                             ; End of source file
```

Map pages by number and jump

Function `EMS_EmBlk::mapPagesJumpNum()` changes the context of the EMS pages and transfers to a specified address via a JMP (jump). This function calls `ems_mapPagesJumpNum40()`, defined in EMS550.ASM.

Figure 4-22 presents the source code listing to EMS550.ASM.

Function EMS_EmBlk::mapPagesJumpNum()

```
EMS_EmBlk    block;
DWORD        *buffer;

error= block.mapPagesJumpNum(buffer);
```

where

buffer   Points to a buffer of the following form:

```
DWORD jump_target;
BYTE  num_pages_to_map;
DWORD *page_map_list;
        // pointer to logical page #,
        // physical page # pairs
```

4-22 The source code listing to EMS550.ASM

```
;******************************************************************
;***        EMS550.ASM                                     ***
;***                                                       ***
;***        int far ems_mapPagesJumpNum40(WORD handle,     ***
;***                                 WORD *buffer);        ***
;***                                                       ***
;***        Transfers control to EMS location mapped by phys.  ***
;***        page by JUMP                                   ***
;***                                                       ***
;***        Returns 0 if no error or an error code.        ***
;***                                                       ***
;***                                                       ***
;***                                                       ***
;***        (Ems Version 4.0)                              ***
;******************************************************************
;

          .model  large,C

          include emsdefs.asm
          extrn   errno:WORD

;
;    Define entry point
;
          public  ems_mapPagesJumpNum40

          .code

ems_mapPagesJumpNum40 proc handle:Word, buffer:Far Ptr DWord

          push    ds                    ; Save regs
          push    si

          mov     dx,handle             ; DX gets the EMS handle
          lds     si,buffer             ; DS:SI gets the buffer address

          mov     ax,MapPagesJumpNum40  ; Make EMS call
          int     Ems

          or      ah,ah                 ; Set flags
          jnz     error

          xor     ax,ax                 ; Return OK
          pop     si
          pop     ds
          ret

error:
          pop     si                    ; Restore regs
          pop     ds

          mov     al,ah                 ; AL gets error code
          xor     ah,ah                 ; Zero extend
          mov     errno,ax              ; Save in errno too
          ret

ems_mapPagesJumpNum40 endp              ; End of procedure

          end                           ; End of source file
```

Map pages by segment and jump

Function `EMS_EmBlk::mapPagesJumpSeg()` changes the context of the EMS pages and transfers to a specified address via a JMP (jump). This function calls `ems_mapPagesJumpSeg40()`, defined in EMS551.ASM.

Figure 4-23 presents the source code listing to EMS551.ASM.

Function EMS_Blk::mapPagesJumpSeg()

```
EMS_EmBlk    block;
DWORD        *buffer;

error= block.mapPagesJumpSeg(buffer);
```

where

buffer **Points to a buffer of the following form:**

```
DWORD jump_target;
BYTE  num_pages_to_map;
DWORD *page_map_list;
      // pointer to logical page #,
      // segment # pairs
```

4-23 The source code listing to EMS551.ASM

```
;*****************************************************************
;***     EMS551.ASM                                          ***
;***                                                         ***
;***     int far ems_mapPagesJumpSeg40(WORD handle,          ***
;***                             WORD *buffer);              ***
;***                                                         ***
;***     Transfers control to EMS location mapped by segment ***
;***     location by JUMP                                    ***
;***                                                         ***
;***     Returns 0 if no error or an error code.            ***
;***                                                         ***
;***                                                         ***
;***                                                         ***
;***     (Ems Version 4.0)                                   ***
;*****************************************************************
;
        .model  large,C

        include emsdefs.asm

        extrn   errno:WORD

;
;   Define entry point
;
        public  ems_mapPagesJumpSeg40

        .code

ems_mapPagesJumpSeg40 proc handle:Word, buffer:Far Ptr DWord

        push    ds                      ; Save regs
```

```
          push    si

          mov     dx,handle              ; DX gets the EMS handle
          lds     si,buffer              ; DS:SI gets the buffer address

          mov     ax,MapPagesJumpSeg40   ; Make the EMS call
          int     Ems

          or      ah,ah                  ; Set flags
          jnz     error

          xor     ax,ax                  ; Return OK
          pop     si                     ; Restore regs
          pop     ds
          ret

error:
          pop     si                     ; Restore regs
          pop     ds

          mov     al,ah                  ; AL gets error code
          xor     ah,ah                  ; Zero extend
          mov     errno,ax               ; Save in errno too
          ret

ems_mapPagesJumpSeg40 endp               ; End of procedure

          end                            ; End of source file
```

Map pages by number and call

Function `EMS_EmBlk::mapPagesCallNum()` changes the context of the EMS pages and transfers to a specified address via a CALL (call). This function calls `ems_mapPagesCallNum40()`, defined in EMS560.ASM.

Figure 4-24 presents the source code listing to EMS560.ASM.

Function EMS_EmBlk::mapPagesCallNum()

```
EMS_EmBlk    block;
DWORD        *buffer;

error= block.mapPagesCallNum(buffer);
```

where

buffer   Points to a buffer of the following form:
```
        DWORD call_target;
        BYTE  precall_num_pages;
DWORD   *precall_map_list;
                // pointer to logical page #,
                // physical page # pairs
        BYTE    postcall_num_pages;
        DWORD   *postcall_map_list;
```

```
                    // pointer to logical page #,
                    // physical page # pairs
```

4-24 The source code listing to EMS560.ASM

```
;*******************************************************************
;***        EMS560.ASM                                        ***
;***                                                          ***
;***        int far ems_mapPagesCallNum40(WORD handle,        ***
;***                                 WORD *buffer);           ***
;***                                                          ***
;***        Transfers control to EMS location mapped by phys. ***
;***        page by CALL                                      ***
;***                                                          ***
;***        Returns 0 if no error or an error code.           ***
;***                                                          ***
;***                                                          ***
;***                                                          ***
;***        (Ems Version 4.0)                                 ***
;*******************************************************************
        .model  large,C

        include emsdefs.asm

        extrn   errno:WORD

;
;   Define entry point
;
        public  ems_mapPagesCallNum40

        .code

ems_mapPagesCallNum40 proc handle:Word, buffer:Far Ptr DWord

        push    ds                      ; Save regs
        push    si

        mov     dx,handle               ; DX gets EMS handle
        lds     si,buffer               ; DS:SI gets buffer address

        mov     ax,MapPagesCallNum40    ; Make EMS call
        int     Ems

        or      ah,ah                   ; Set flags
        jnz     error

        xor     ax,ax                   ; Return OK
        pop     si                      ; Restore regs
        pop     ds
        ret

error:
        pop     si                      ; Restore regs
        pop     ds

        mov     al,ah                   ; AL gets error code
        xor     ah,ah                   ; Zero extend
        mov     errno,ax                ; Save in errno too
```

```
        ret

ems_mapPagesCallNum40 endp               ; End of procedure

        end                              ; End of source file
```

Map pages by segment and call

Function `EMS_Ems::mapPagesCallSeg()` changes the context of the EMS pages and transfers to a specified address via a CALL (call). This function calls `ems_mapPagesCallSeg40()`, defined in EMS561.ASM.

Figure 4-25 presents the source code listing to EMS561.ASM.

Function EMS_EmBlk::mapPagesCallSeg()

```
EMS_EmBlk    block;
DWORD        *buffer;

error= block.mapPagesCallSeg(buffer);
```

where

buffer   Points to a buffer of the following form:

```
        DWORD   call_target;
        BYTE    precall_num_pages;
        DWORD   *precall_map_list;
                // pointer to logical page #,
                // segment # pairs
        BYTE    postcall_num_pages;
        DWORD   *postcall_map_list;
                // pointer to logical page #,
                // segment # pairs
```

4-25 The source code listing to EMS561.ASM

```
;*******************************************************************
;***     EMS561.ASM                                         ***
;***                                                        ***
;***     int far ems_mapPagesCallSeg40(WORD handle,         ***
;***                                   WORD *buffer);       ***
;***                                                        ***
;***     Transfers control to EMS location mapped by segment ***
;***     location by CALL                                   ***
;***                                                        ***
;***     Returns 0 if no error or an error code.            ***
;***                                                        ***
;***                                                        ***
;***                                                        ***
;***     (Ems Version 4.0)                                  ***
;*******************************************************************
```

```
        .model  large,C

        include emsdefs.asm

        extrn   errno:WORD

;
;   Define entry point
;
        public  ems_mapPagesCallSeg40

        .code

ems_mapPagesCallSeg40 proc handle:Word, buffer:Far Ptr DWord

        push    ds                  ; Save regs
        push    si

        mov     dx,handle           ; DX gets EMS handle
        lds     si,buffer           ; DS:SI gets buffer address

        mov     ax,MapPagesCallSeg40 ; Make EMS call
        int     Ems

        or      ah,ah               ; Set flags
        jnz     error

        xor     ax,ax               ; Return OK
        pop     si                  ; Restore regs
        pop     ds
        ret

error:
        pop     si                  ; Restore regs
        pop     ds

        mov     al,ah               ; AL gets error code
        xor     ah,ah               ; Zero extend
        mov     errno,ax            ; Save in errno too
        ret

ems_mapPagesCallSeg40 endp          ; End of procedure

        end                         ; End of source file
```

Get stack space for map and call

Function EMS_Ems::getStackNeeded() retrieves the extra stack space
required by the EMS_EmBlk::mapPagesCallNum() and EMS_EmBlk::map
PagesCallSeg() functions. This function calls ems_getStackNeeded
40(), defined in EMS562.ASM.

Figure 4-26 presents the source code listing to EMS562.ASM.

Function EMS_Ems::getStackNeeded()

```
EMS_Ems    ems;
WORD       stack_space;

error= ems.getStackNeeded(&stack_space);
```

where

> stack_size **Receives the extra stack size required by the** EMS_Ems::
> mapPagesCallNum() **and** EMS_Ems::mapPagesCallSeg
> () **functions**

4-26 The source code listing to EMS562.ASM

```
;****************************************************************
;***     EMS562.ASM                                       ***
;***                                                      ***
;***     int far ems_getStackNeeded40(WORD *stack_space);  ***
;***                                                      ***
;***     Returns stack space for map page and call to      ***
;***     pointer.                                          ***
;***                                                      ***
;***     Returns 0 if no error or an error code.           ***
;***                                                      ***
;***                                                      ***
;***                                                      ***
;***     (Ems Version 4.0)                                ***
;****************************************************************

        .model  large,C

        include emsdefs.asm

        extrn   errno:WORD

;
;   Define entry point
;
        public  ems_getStackSpaceNeeded40

        .code

ems_getStackSpaceNeeded40 proc stack_space:Far Ptr Word

        mov     ax,GetStackNeeded40      ; Make EMS call
        int     Ems

        or      ah,ah                    ; Set flags
        jnz     error

        les     bx,stack_space           ; Return stack size to caller
        mov     es:[bx],dx

        xor     ax,ax                    ; Return OK
        ret

error:
```

```
        mov     al,ah               ; AL gets error code
        xor     ah,ah               ; Zero extend
        mov     errno,ax            ; Save in errno too
        ret

ems_getStackSpaceNeeded40 endp      ; End of procedure

        end                         ; End of source file
```

Move a memory region

The `EMS_Ems::moveMemRegion()` function moves a portion of expanded or conventional memory to any other location without disturbing the expanded memory page mapping context. In order to fill out the handle fields in the packet, the `EMS_EmBlk::num()` must be used to get the handle number. This function calls `ems_moveMemRegion40()`, defined in EMS 570.ASM.

Figure 4-27 presents the source code listing to EMS570.ASM.

Function EMS_Ems::moveMemRegion()

```
EMS_Ems             ems;
EMS_MoveMemoryInfo  buffer;

error= ems.moveMemRegion(buffer);
```

where

buffer   **An** `EMS_MoveMemoryInfo` **structure (see EMS.H,** FIG. **3-7 for** `EMS_MoveMemoryInfo` **structure)**

4-27 The source code listing to EMS570.ASM

```
;****************************************************************
;***                                                        ***
;***      EMS570.ASM                                        ***
;***                                                        ***
;***      int far ems_moveMemRegion40(BYTE *buffer);        ***
;***                                                        ***
;***      Moves memory region from source to destination    ***
;***      described in MoveMemoryInfo_type structure         ***
;***                                                        ***
;***      Buffer Structure                                  ***
;***      ----------------                                  ***
;***      DWORD   length;       ; memory length             ***
;***      BYTE    srce_type;    ; 0=conventional,1=expanded ***
;***      WORD    srce_handle;  ; source memory handle      ***
;***      WORD    srce_offset;  ; source memory offset      ***
;***      WORD    srce_id;      ; source seg or phys page   ***
;***      BYTE    dest_type;    ; 0=conventional,1=expanded ***
;***      WORD    dest_handle;  ; source memory handle      ***
;***      WORD    dest_offset;  ; source memory offset      ***
;***      WORD    dest_id;      ; source seg or phys page   ***
;***                                                        ***
;***      Returns 0 if no error or an error code.           ***
```

4-27 Continued.

```
;***                                                              ***
;***                                                              ***
;***                                                              ***
;***      (Ems Version 4.0)                                       ***
;****************************************************************

          .model  large,C

          include emsdefs.asm
          extrn   errno:WORD

;
;    Define entry point
;
          public  ems_moveMemRegion40

          .code

ems_moveMemRegion40 proc buffer:Far Ptr Byte

          push    ds                    ; Save regs
          push    si

          lds     si,buffer             ; DS:SI gets move buffer address

          mov     ax,MoveMemRegion40    ; Do the EMS call
          int     Ems

          or      ah,ah                 ; Set flags
          jnz     error

          xor     ax,ax                 ; Return OK
          pop     si                    ; Restore regs
          pop     ds
          ret

error:
          pop     si                    ; Restore regs
          pop     ds

          mov     al,ah                 ; AL gets error code
          xor     ah,ah                 ; Zero extend
          mov     errno,ax              ; Save in errno too
          ret

ems_moveMemRegion40 endp                ; End of procedure

          end                           ; End of source file
```

Swap memory regions

The EMS_Ems::swapMemRegion() function swaps a portion of expanded or conventional memory with any other memory without disturbing the expanded memory page mapping context. This function calls ems_swapMem Region40(), defined in ESM571.ASM.

Figure 4-28 presents the source code listing to EMS571.ASM.

Function EMS_Ems::swapMemRegion()

```
EMS_Ems              ems;
EMS_MoveMemoryInfo   buffer;

error= ems.swapMemRegion(buffer);
```

where

buffer **Points to an** EMS_MoveMemoryInfo **structure (see EMS.H,** FIG. 3-7 **for** EMS_MoveMemoryInfo **structure)**

4-28 The source code listing to EMS571.ASM

```
;******************************************************************
;***      EMS571.ASM                                       ***
;***                                                       ***
;***      int far ems_swapMemRegions40(BYTE *buffer);      ***
;***                                                       ***
;***      Swaps memory region from source to destination   ***
;***      described in MoveMemoryInfo_type structure        ***
;***                                                       ***
;***      Buffer Structure                                 ***
;***      ----------------                                 ***
;***      DWORD   length;        ; memory length           ***
;***      BYTE    srce_type;     ; 0=conventional,1=expanded ***
;***      WORD    srce_handle;   ; source memory handle      ***
;***      WORD    srce_offset;   ; source memory offset      ***
;***      WORD    srce_id;       ; source seg or phys page   ***
;***      BYTE    dest_type;     ; 0=conventional,1=expanded ***
;***      WORD    dest_handle;   ; source memory handle      ***
;***      WORD    dest_offset;   ; source memory offset      ***
;***      WORD    dest_id;       ; source seg or phys page   ***
;***                                                       ***
;***      Returns 0 if no error or an error code.          ***
;***                                                       ***
;***                                                       ***
;***                                                       ***
;***      (Ems Version 4.0)                                ***
;******************************************************************
        .model large,C

        include emsdefs.asm

        extrn  errno:WORD


;
;  Define entry point
;

        public  ems-swapMemRegions40

        .code

ems-swapMemRegions40 proc buffer: Far Ptr Byte

        push ds                     ; Save regs
        push si

        lds    si,buffer            ; DS:SI gets swap buffer address
```

```
        mov     ax,SwapMemRegions40     ; Do the EMS call
        int     Ems

        or      ah,ah                   ; Set flags
        jnz     error

        xor     ax,ax                   ; Return OK
        pop     si                      ; Restore regs
        pop     ds
        ret

error:
        pop     si                      ; Restore regs
        pop     ds

        mov     al,ah                   ; AL gets error code
        xor     ah,ah                   ; Zero extend
        mov     errno,ax                ; Save in errno too
        ret
ems_swapMemRegions40 endp               ; End of procedure

        end                             ; End of source file
```

Get addresses of mappable pages

The EMS_Ems::getAddrsMappable() function retrieves the segment base address and physical page number for each mappable page in the EMS system. This function calls ems_getAddrsMappable40(), defined in EMS580.ASM.

Figure 4-29 presents the source code listing to EMS580.ASM.

Function EMS_Ems::getAddrsMappable()

```
EMS_Ems                 ems;
EMS_MappablePagesInfo   *buffer;
WORD                    num_entries;

error= ems.getNumMappable(&num_entries);
buffer= new EMS_MappablePagesInfo[num_entries];
error= ems.getAddrsMappable(buffer, &num_entries);
```

where

buffer   An array of EMS_MappablePagesInfo records (see EMS.H, FIG. 3-7 for EMS_MappablePagesInfo structure)

num_entries   Receives the number of entries in mappable physical page array

4-29 The source code listing to EMS580.ASM

```
;*****************************************************************
;***      EMS580.ASM                                         ***
;***                                                         ***
;***      int far ems_getAddrsMappable40(                    ***
;***                  MappablePagesInfo_type *buffer,        ***
;***                  WORD *num_entries);                    ***
;***                                                         ***
;***      Returns, in the buffer specified a list of the     ***
;***      pages in memory which can be mapped. These include ***
;***      pages in the middle of the 640K area so caution    ***
;***      must be exercised in mapping them.                 ***
;***                                                         ***
;***      Returns 0 if no error or an error code.            ***
;***                                                         ***
;***      (Ems Version 4.0)                                  ***
;*****************************************************************

        .model  large,C

        include emsdefs.asm

        extrn   errno:WORD

;
;    Define entry point
;
        public  ems_getAddrsMappable40
        .code

ems_getAddrsMappable40 proc buffer:Far Ptr Byte, num_entries:Far Ptr Word

        push    di                      ; Save di

        les     di,buffer               ; Get the buffer address into ES:DI

        mov     ax,GetAddrsMappable40   ; Make the EMS call
        int     Ems

        or      ah,ah                   ; Set flags
        jnz     error

        les     bx,num_entries          ; Return number of pages
        mov     word ptr es:[bx],cx

        xor     ax,ax                   ; return OK
        pop     di                      ; restore di
        ret

error:
        pop     di                      ; restore di

        mov     al,ah                   ; AL gets error code
        xor     ah,ah                   ; Zero extend
        mov     errno,ax                ; Save in errno too
        ret

ems_getAddrsMappable40 endp             ; End of procedure

        end                             ; End of source file
```

Get number of mappable pages

The `EMS_Ems::getNumMappable()` function retrieves the number of mappable physical pages. This information may be used to calculate the size of the buffer required by the `EMS_Ems::getAddrsMappable()` function. A DWORD (4 bytes) of buffer space is required for each mappable page. This function calls `ems_getNumMappable40()`, defined in EMS581.ASM.

Figure 4-30 presents the source code listing to EMS581.ASM.

Function EMS_Ems::getNumMappable()

```
EMS_Ems    ems;
WORD       num_entries;

error= ems.getNumMappable(&num_entries);
```

where

num_entries Receives the number of mappable physical pages

4-30 The source code listing to EMS581.ASM

```
;*****************************************************************
;***      EMS581.ASM                                         ***
;***                                                         ***
;***      int far ems_getNumMappable40(DWORD *buffer);       ***
;***                                                         ***
;***      Returns total number of mappable pages to pointer. ***
;***                                                         ***
;***      Returns 0 if no error or an error code.            ***
;***                                                         ***
;***      (Ems Version 4.0)                                  ***
;*****************************************************************

        .model  large,C

        include emsdefs.asm

        extrn   errno:WORD


;
;    Define entry point
;
        public  ems_getNumMappable40

        .code

ems_getNumMappable40 proc mappable_pages:Far Ptr Word

        mov     ax,GetNumMappable40     ; Make the call
        int     Ems

        or      ah,ah                   ; Check for error
        jnz     error

        les     bx,mappable_pages       ; Return the number of...
        mov     es:[bx],cx              ; ... mappable pages
```

```
        xor     ax,ax                   ; return OK
        ret

error:
        mov     al,ah                   ; AL gets error code
        xor     ah,ah                   ; Zero extend
        mov     errno,ax                ; Save in errno too
        ret

ems_getNumMappable40    endp            ; End of procedure

        end                             ; End of source file
```

Get hardware configuration

The `EMS_Ems::getHWConfig()` function returns information about the EMM configuration. This function calls `ems_getHWConfig40()`, defined in EMS590.ASM.

Figure 4-31 presents the source code listing to EMS590.ASM.

Function EMS_Ems::getHWConfig()

```
EMS_Ems                 ems;
EMS_HardwareConfigInfo  buffer;

error= ems.getHWConfig(&buffer);
```

where

buffer **Points to** `EMS_HardwareConfigInfo` **structure (see EMS.H, FIG. 3-7 for** `EMS_HardwareConfigInfo` **structure)**

4-31 The source code listing to EMS590.ASM

```
;****************************************************************
;***    EMS590.ASM                                          ***
;***                                                        ***
;***    int far ems_getHWConfig40(                          ***
;***                    HardwareConfigInfo_type *buf);      ***
;***                                                        ***
;***    HardwareConfigInfo_type structure                  ***
;***    --------------------------------                    ***
;***    WORD    raw_p_size; ; size of raw pages in paras    ***
;***    WORD    alt_regs;   ; number of alt reg sets        ***
;***    WORD    save_area;  ; size of map sav area (bytes)  ***
;***    WORD    regs_to_dma; ; max num regs assigned to dma ***
;***    WORD    dma_type;   ; 0=alt dma regs OK,            ***
;***                        ; 1=one dma reg only            ***
;***                                                        ***
;***    Returns hardware config info to structure pointer.  ***
;***                                                        ***
;***    Returns 0 if no error or an error code.             ***
;***                                                        ***
```

4-31 Continued.

```
;***                                                      ***
;***                                                      ***
;***        (Ems Version 4.0)                             ***
;******************************************************************

            .model   large,C

            include emsdefs.asm

            extrn    errno:WORD

;
;    Define entry point
;
            public  ems_getHWConfig40

            .code

ems_getHWConfig40 proc buffer:Far Ptr Word

            push    di                    ; Save DI
            les     di,buffer             ; ES:DI gets buffer address

            mov     ax,GetHWConfig40      ; Do the EMS call
            int     Ems

            or      ah,ah                 ; Set flags
            jnz     error

            xor     ax,ax                 ; Return OK
            pop     di                    ; Restore DI
            ret

error:
            pop     di                    ; Restore DI

            mov     al,ah                 ; AL gets error code
            xor     ah,ah                 ; Zero extend
            mov     errno,ax              ; Save in errno too
            ret

ems_getHWConfig40 endp                    ; End of procedure

            end                           ; End of source file
```

Get number of raw pages

The EMS_Ems::getNumRawPages() function retrieves the number of raw pages that have been allocated and the total number of raw pages. A raw page's size may vary from the 16K page size standard. This function calls xms_getNumRawPages40, defined in EMS591.ASM.

Figure 4-32 presents the source code listing to EMS591.ASM.

Function EMS_Ems::getNumRawPages()

```
EMS_Ems   ems;
WORD      total_pages;
WORD      free_pages;

error= ems.getNumRawPages(&total_pages, &free_pages);
```

where

total_pages   **Receives the total number of raw pages**
free_pages   **Receives the number of free raw pages**

4-32   The source code listing to EMS591.ASM

```
;*****************************************************************
;***    EMS591.ASM                                           ***
;***                                                         ***
;***    int far ems_getNumRawPages40(WORD *total_pages,      ***
;***                          WORD *free_pages);             ***
;***                                                         ***
;***    Returns the total number of free raw pages and the   ***
;***    number of raw pages available.                       ***
;***                                                         ***
;***    Returns 0 if no error or an error code.              ***
;***                                                         ***
;***                                                         ***
;***    (Ems Version 4.0)                                    ***
;*****************************************************************

        .model  large,C

        include emsdefs.asm

        extrn   errno:WORD


;
;   Define entry point
;
        public  ems_getNumRawPages40

        .code
ems_getNumRawPages40 proc    total:Far Ptr Word, free:Far Ptr Word

        mov     ax,GetNumRawPages40    ;  Do the EMS call
        int     Ems

        or      ah,ah                  ; Set flags
        jnz     error

        mov     ax,bx                  ; Save free pages
        les     bx,free                ; Return it to caller
        mov     es:[bx],ax
        les     bx,total               ; Return total pages to caller
        mov     es:[bx],dx

        xor     ax,ax                  ; Return OK
        ret
```

```
error:
        mov     al,ah                     ; AL gets error code
        xor     ah,ah                     ; Zero extend
        mov     errno,ax                  ; Save in errno too
        ret
ems_getNumRawPages40 endp                 ; End of procedure

        end                               ; End of source file
```

Allocate handle and standard pages

The EMS_EmBlk::allocHandleStd() function allocates a specified number of standard (16K) pages and initializes the target EMS_EmBlk with the handle. This function calls ems_allocHandleStd40(), defined in EMS 5A0.ASM.

Figure 4-33 presents the source code listing to EMS5A0.ASM.

Function EMS_EmBlk::allocHandleStd()

```
EMS_EmBlk   block;
WORD        pages;

error= block.allocHandleStd(pages);
```

where

> pages   Holds the number of standard pages to allocate

4-33 The source code listing to EMS5A0.ASM

```
;****************************************************************
;***     EMS5A0.ASM                                         ***
;***                                                        ***
;***     int far ems_allocHandleStd40(WORD *handle,         ***
;***                             WORD pages);               ***
;***                                                        ***
;***     Allocates standards pages and returns handle to    ***
;***     pointer.                                           ***
;***                                                        ***
;***     Returns 0 if no error or an error code.            ***
;***                                                        ***
;***                                                        ***
;***                                                        ***
;***     (Ems Version 4.0)                                  ***
;****************************************************************

        .model  large,C

        include emsdefs.asm
        extrn   errno:WORD

;
;   Define entry point
;
```

```
        public  ems_allocHandleStd40

        .code

ems_allocHandleStd40 proc handle:Far Ptr Word, pages:Word

        mov     bx,pages                ; BX gets # pages to allocate

        mov     ax,AllocHandleStd40     ; Do EMS call
        int     Ems

        or      ah,ah                   ; Set flags
        jnz     error

        les     bx,handle               ; Return handle to caller
        mov     es:[bx],dx

        xor     ax,ax                   ; Return OK
        ret

error:
        mov     al,ah                   ; AL gets error code
        xor     ah,ah                   ; Zero extend
        mov     errno,ax                ; Save in errno too
        ret

ems_allocHandleStd40 endp               ; End of procedure

        end                             ; End of source file
```

Allocate handle and raw pages

The EMS_EmBlk::allocHandleRaw() function allocates a specified number of raw pages and retrieves the handles associated with those standard pages. This function calls ems_allocHandleRaw40(), defined in EMS 5A1.ASM.

Figure 4-34 presents the source code listing to EMS5A1.ASM.

Function EMS_EmBlk::allocHandleRaw()

```
EMS_EmBlk   block;
WORD        pages;

error= block.allocHandleRaw(pages);
```

where

pages   Holds the number of raw pages to allocate

4-34 The source code listing to EMS5A1.ASM

```
;****************************************************************
;***    EMS5A1.ASM                                          ***
;***                                                        ***
;***    int far ems_allocHandleRaw40(WORD *handle,          ***
```

```
;***                                 WORD pages);                    ***
;***                                                                 ***
;***     Allocates raw pages and returns handle to pointer.          ***
;***                                                                 ***
;***     Returns 0 if no error or an error code.                     ***
;***                                                                 ***
;***                                                                 ***
;***                                                                 ***
;***     (Ems Version 4.0)                                           ***
;*********************************************************************
;

         .model  large,C

         include emsdefs.asm

         extrn   errno:WORD

;
;    Define entry point
;
         public  ems_allocHandleRaw40

         .code

ems_allocHandleRaw40 proc handle:Far Ptr Word, pages:Word

         mov     bx,pages                ; BX get # pages to allocate

         mov     ax,AllocHandleRaw40     ; Do EMS call
         int     Ems

         or      ah,ah                   ; Set flags
         jnz     error

         les     bx,handle               ; Return handle to caller
         mov     es:[bx],dx

         xor     ax,ax                   ; Return OK
         ret
error:
         mov     al,ah                   ; AL gets error code
         xor     ah,ah                   ; Zero extend
         mov     errno,ax                ; Save in errno too
         ret

ems_allocHandleRaw40 endp                ; End of procedure

         end                            ; End of source file
```

Prepare EMM for warm boot

The EMS_Ems::prepEmmWarmBoot() function prepares the EMM for an impending warm boot process. This function calls ems_prepEmmWarm Boot40(), defined in EMS5C.ASM.

Figure 4-35 presents the source code listing to EMS5C.ASM.

Function EMS_Ems::prepEmmWarmBoot()

```
EMS_Ems    ems;

error= ems.prepEmmWarmBoot();
```

4-35 The source code listing to EMS5C.ASM

```
;****************************************************************
;***      EMS5C.ASM                                         ***
;***                                                        ***
;***      int far ems_PrepEmmWarmBoot40(void)               ***
;***                                                        ***
;***      Prep EMM for warm boot process                    ***
;***                                                        ***
;***      Returns 0 if no error or an error code.           ***
;***                                                        ***
;***                                                        ***
;***                                                        ***
;***      (Ems Version 4.0)                                 ***
;****************************************************************

        .model  large,C

        include emsdefs.asm

        extrn   errno:WORD

;
;    Define entry point
;
        public  ems_prepEmmWarmBoot40

        .code

ems_prepEmmWarmBoot40 proc

        mov     ax,PrepEmmWarmBoot40     ; Do the EMS call
        int     Ems

        or      ah,ah                    ; Set flags
        jnz     error

        xor     ax,ax                    ; Return OK
        ret
error:
        mov     al,ah                    ; AL gets error code
        xor     ah,ah                    ; Zero extend
        mov     errno,ax                 ; Save in errno too
        ret

ems_prepEmmWarmBoot40 endp               ; End of procedure

        end                              ; End of source file
```

EMS 4.0 operating-system-only functions

TABLE 4-1 presents a list of EMS 4.0 functions intended only for use by the operating system. These functions may be disabled at any time by the operating system. Using them in your programs is not recommended.

Table 4-1   The EMS version 4.0 OS only function list

Function	Sub.	Description
5B	00	Getting alternate map registers
5B	01	Setting alternate map registers
5B	02	Getting size of alternate map save area
5B	03	Allocating alternate map register set
5B	04	Deallocating alternate map register set
5B	05	Allocating DMA register set
5B	06	Enabling DMA on alternate map register set
5B	07	Disabling DMA on alternate map register set
5B	08	Deallocating DMA register set
5D	00	Enabling EMM operating system functions
5D	01	Disabling EMM operating system functions
5D	02	Releasing access key

Summary

Chapter 4 presented the EMS 4.0 functions that can greatly enhance your use of EMS memory in your programs. If your program is intended for commercial use, it might make sense to stick to EMS 3.0 supported functions. Although many computers do support the EMS 4.0 standard, not every computer that supports EMS conforms to the EMS 4.0 standard.

If your program is intended for an in-house application that supports the EMS 4.0 standard, then it certainly makes sense to use the functions presented in this chapter if they will make your programming task easier.

5

Extended Memory Specification (XMS) 2.0

One of the early failings for programmers attempting to use extended memory (memory addressed above 1 megabyte) was the lack of a standard. In the summer of 1988, Microsoft Corporation, Lotus Development Corporation, Intel Corporation and AST Research Inc. jointly agreed upon the XMS programming standard. This programming standard provided a series of predefined functions that permit orderly usage of extended memory.

Let's take a look at the basic vocabulary that will be used in this chapter.

Extended memory   Memory in 80286 (386, 486, etc...) computers addressed above the 1Mb boundary.

High Memory Area (HMA)   The first 64K of extended memory. HMA is unique because code can be located in it and may be executed while the computer is running in real mode. HMA really starts at address 0×FFFF:0×0010.

Upper Memory Block (UMB)   Blocks of memory available between the 640K and 1Mb addresses. The availability of UMBs depends on the hardware adapter cards installed in the computer.

Extended Memory Blocks (EMB)   Blocks of memory located above the HMA that may only be used for data storage.

A20 Line   The 21st address line of the 80x86 family of microprocessors. Enabling the A20 allows access to the HMA memory area in real mode.

Extended Memory Manager (XMM)   A DOS device driver that allows for the management of Extended Memory.

The first part of this chapter gives a brief overview of the XMS interface that we have provided.

The second part of this chapter provides a series of heavily commented demonstration programs clearly showing how to use the XMS interface. Feel free to use these demonstration programs as stepping-stones in your programs' use of extended memory.

The third part of this chapter provides the source for the XMS management functions. These functions will provide a solid foundation for your using XMS in your programs.

An overview of the XMS interface

In order to use the XMS interface effectively, the overall design of the interface must be understood.

There are four classes for XMS support: XMS_Xms, XMS_XmBlk, XMS_UmBlk, and XMS_HMA. Objects of the XMS_XmBlk class represent blocks of extended memory. The methods of this class allow allocation, deallocation, resizing, and other functions that have extended memory blocks as targets.

Objects of the XMS_UmBlk class represent blocks of upper memory. Methods of this class allow allocating and freeing upper memory blocks.

Objects of the XMS_HMA class represent the HMA. Methods of this class allow allocation of the HMA, enabling and disabling of the A20 line, and querying the A20 line status.

Finally, the XMS_Xms class contains functions not associated with any particular memory block. For example, XMS_Xms::init() is used to initialize the XMS system, and XMS_Xms::moveXM is used to move a block of data between conventional and extended memory.

Objects of the XMS_XmBlk, XMS_UmBlk, and XMS_HMA classes all represent blocks of memory. We did not use constructors to allocate the associated blocks simply because there is no simple way to return an error from a constructor. When exception handling is generally available in C++ compilers, it would be useful to rewrite these classes to use exceptions. Then errors could be returned from constructors via exceptions. The existing constructors for these classes create objects that denote no memory block. The alloc calls are used to initialize the objects to denote a memory block. Destructors are defined for these classes that release the associated memory block (if there is one). Thus, when an object passes out of scope, the associated memory block is released. In order to prevent any problems with this, we have disabled copying of these objects, either through assignment or copy-initialization. Without this, we might have a copy of an object destroyed, releasing the memory block while the original object is still accessible. Care must be taken with the XMS_HMA and XMS_UmBlk objects because the objects themselves are not absolutely necessary to access the memory they point to. If the object is destroyed, access to the previously associated memory could cause program failure or a system crash.

In order to use the XMS interface, a call must first be made to XMS_Xms::init(). This function initializes XMS, and it should be used to determine if XMS is in fact available for use by your program. If you do not initialize XMS and make a call to an XMS function, the function will return an error.

Errors are flagged by returning a non-zero error code. If a function takes an error, the error code can be determined either by saving the value returned by the function or by examining the global variable errno. Mnemonics for the error codes are defined in XMS.H. If you want to get the message associated with an error code, xms_errorText(errno) will return a string with the message.

XMS 2.0 demonstration programs

PROG5-1.CPP demonstrates the following operation:

- Initializing the XMS interface

PROG5-1 uses XMS_Xms::init() to initialize the XMS interface. It prints the address of the XMS handler before and after the initialization call. The XMS handler before the call is a handler that always returns an error. After the call, the handler is the actual XMS handler routine in the XMS driver.

Figure 5-1 presents the source code listing to PROG5-1.CPP.

5-1 The source code listing to PROG5-1.CPP

```
////////////////////////////////////////
//
// prog5-1.cpp
//
// Test to see if XMS is present
//
////////////////////////////////////////

extern "C" {
#include <stdio.h>
#include <dos.h>
}

/////////////////////////
//
// include xms memory
// management header
// files

#include "gdefs.h"
#include "xms.h"

/////////////////////////
// begin program
```

```
extern  "C" void    *xmsHandler;

void main()
{

    XMS_Xms          xms;


    //
    //  Print out the address of the XMS handler before it's
    //  initialized.
    //
    printf("Before initialization: XMS handler= %04X:%04X\n",
                FP_SEG(xmsHandler),
                FP_OFF(xmsHandler));

    //
    //  Attempt to initialize XMS. If there is an error, report it.
    //
    if(xms.init() == XMSErrOK) {
        printf("XMS is present\n");
        }
    else {
        printf("XMS is not present\n");
        }

    //
    //  Now print out the address of the XMS handler after it's been
    //  initialized.
    //
    printf("After initialization: XMS handler= %04X:%04X\n",
                FP_SEG(xmsHandler),
                FP_OFF(xmsHandler));
}
```

PROG5-2.CPP demonstrates the following operation:

- Reporting the version of the XMS driver

PROG5-2 uses XMS_Xms::getVersion() to get and print the version of XMS and XMM driver.

Figure 5-2 presents the source code listing to PROG5-2.CPP.

5-2 The source code listing to PROG5-2.CPP

```
/////////////////////////////////////
//
// prog5-2.cpp
//
// Get XMS Version Number
//
/////////////////////////////////////

extern "C" {
#include <stdio.h>
```

```c
#include <stdlib.h>
}

//////////////////////////
//
// include xms memory
// management header
// files

#include "gdefs.h"
#include "xms.h"

//////////////////////////
// begin program


void main()
{

    XMS_Xms          xms;

    extern  void   *xmsHandler;

    union   {
        struct {
            unsigned    digit4:4;
            unsigned    digit3:4;
            unsigned    digit2:4;
            unsigned    digit1:4;
            }   bcd;

        WORD    word;
        }   xmsVersion, xmmVersion;

    WORD    hmaFlag;

    //
    //  Attempt to initialize XMS. If there is an error, report it.
    //
    if(xms.init()) {
        printf("XMS is not present\n");
        return;
        }


    //
    //  Now get the version numbers:
    //
    if (xms.getVersion(&xmsVersion.word, &xmmVersion.word, &hmaFlag)) {
        xms_demoError("XMS_Xms::getVersion");
        }

    printf("XMS Version= %d%d.%d%d, XMM Version= %d%d.%d%d, HMA is %s\n",
            xmsVersion.bcd.digit1,
            xmsVersion.bcd.digit2,
            xmsVersion.bcd.digit3,
            xmsVersion.bcd.digit4,
            xmmVersion.bcd.digit1,
            xmmVersion.bcd.digit2,
            xmmVersion.bcd.digit3,
            xmmVersion.bcd.digit4,
            ((hmaFlag) ? "present" : "not present"));
}
```

PROG5-3.CPP demonstrates the following operations:

- Getting the amount of free XMS
- Allocating XMS for program use
- Freeing previously allocated XMS memory for other purposes

PROG5-3 gets two blocks of XMS using XMS_XmBlk:allocXM() and then frees them using XMS_XmBlk::freeXM(). After each operation, it uses XMS_Xms::getFreeXM() to get the amount of available XMS memory and display it.

Figure 5-3 presents the source code listing to PROG5-3.CPP.

5-3 The source code listing to PROG5-3.CPP

```
/////////////////////////////////////////
//
// prog5-3.cpp
//
// Get amount of free XMS
//
/////////////////////////////////////////

extern "C" {
#include <stdio.h>
}

////////////////////////////
//
// include xms memory
// management header
// files

#include "gdefs.h"
#include "xms.h"

////////////////////////////
// begin program


void main()
{

    WORD                totalFree;
    WORD                largestFree;


    XMS_Xms             xms;
    XMS_XmBlk           block1;
    XMS_XmBlk           block2;


    //
    //   Attempt to initialize XMS. If there is an error, report it.
    //
    if (xms.init()) {
        printf("XMS is not present\n");
        }

    //
    //   Print header:
```

```
//
printf("                                              Total      Largest
Block\n");
printf("══════════════════════════════════╤══════════╤══════════╕\n");

//
//  Report the free memory available:
//
if (xms.getFreeXM(&totalFree, &largestFree)) {
    xms_demoError("XMS_Xms::getFreeXM");
    }

printf("After initialization           |   %4d KB   |   %4d KB   |\n",
            totalFree, largestFree);
printf("──────────────────────────────────┼──────────┼──────────┤\n");

//
//  Now allocate 16KB and note the change:
//
if (block1.allocXM(16)) {
    xms_demoError("XMS_XmBlk::allocXM");
    }

if (xms.getFreeXM(&totalFree, &largestFree)) {
    xms_demoError("XMS_Xms::getFreeXM");
    }

printf("After 16 KB allocate           |   %4d KB   |   %4d KB   |\n",
            totalFree, largestFree);
printf("──────────────────────────────────┼──────────┼──────────┤\n");

//
//  Now allocate another 32KB and note the change:
//
if (block2.allocXM(32)) {
    xms_demoError("XMS_XmBlk::allocXM");
    }

if (xms.getFreeXM(&totalFree, &largestFree)) {
    xms_demoError("XMS_Xms::getFreeXM");
    }

printf("After 32 KB allocate           |   %4d KB   |   %4d KB   |\n",
            totalFree, largestFree);
printf("──────────────────────────────────┼──────────┼──────────┤\n");

//
//  Now free the FIRST block and see what happens:
//
if (block1.freeXM()) {
    xms_demoError("XMS_XmBlk::freeXM");
    }

if (xms.getFreeXM(&totalFree, &largestFree)) {
    xms_demoError("XMS_Xms::getFreeXM");
    }

printf("After free of 16 KB block      |   %4d KB   |   %4d KB   |\n",
            totalFree, largestFree);
printf("──────────────────────────────────┼──────────┼──────────┤\n");

//
//  Now free second block of 32KB
//
if (block2.freeXM()) {
    xms_demoError("XMS_XmBlk::freeXM");
    }
```

```
if (xms.getFreeXM(&totalFree, &largestFree)) {
    xms_demoError("XMS_Xms::getFreeXM");
    }
printf("After free of 32 KB block   |    %4d KB    |    %4d KB    |\n",
            totalFree, largestFree);
printf("=================================================\n");

}
```

PROG5-4.CPP demonstrates the following operation:

- Transferring data to and from XMS

PROG5-4 uses `XMS_Xms::moveXM()` to write text to various parts of XMS blocks and get the text back. This program demonstrates the basic technique of moving data between conventional and XMS memory.

Figure 5-4 presents the source code listing to PROG5-4.CPP.

5-4 The source code listing to PROG5-4.CPP

```
///////////////////////////////////////
//
// prog5-4.cpp
//
//  Demonstrates use of move to/from eXtended Memory
//
///////////////////////////////////////

/////////////////////////
// include standard
// I/O functions

extern "C" {
#include <stdio.h>
#include <stdlib.h>
#include <string.h>
}

/////////////////////////
//
// include xms memory
// management header
// files

#include "gdefs.h"
#include "xms.h"

/////////////////////////
// begin program


#define EVEN(x)     (((x)+1)&~1)
void main()
{
```

```
XMS_Xms              xms;
XMS_XmBlk            handle1;
XMS_XmBlk            handle2;
XMS_XmBlk            handle3;
XMS_XmBlk            handle4;

char    *text;

char    buff[72];


//
//  Attempt to initialize XMS. If there is an error, report it.
//
if (xms.init()) {
    printf("XMS is not present\n");
    }

//
//  Now allocate 4 1KB blocks.
//
if (handle1.allocXM(1)) {
    xms_demoError("XMS_XmBlk::allocXM");
    }
if (handle2.allocXM(1)) {
    xms_demoError("XMS_XmBlk::allocXM");
    }
if (handle3.allocXM(1)) {
    xms_demoError("XMS_XmBlk::allocXM");
    }
if (handle4.allocXM(1)) {
    xms_demoError("XMS_XmBlk::allocXM");
    }

//
//  Now let's copy some text into various places in the
//  XM blocks, and then copy it back and print it out.
//

//
//  Set up a pointer to a string:
//
text= "Fourscore and seven years ago our fathers brought forth ";

//
//  Set up the move packet. Note that we round the length
//  up to an even number. The call requires an even length
//  transfer.
//
if (xms.moveXM(handle1, 42,                  // Random offset in block
               xms_realMem, DWORD(text),     // Real memory
               EVEN(strlen(text)+1))) {      // Length (+1) for terminator
    xms_demoError("XMS_Xms::moveXM");
    exit(1);
    }

//
//  Now put the next string into the next XM block:
//
text= "on this continent a\nnew nation, ";
```

```
    if (xms.moveXM(handle2, 911,                   // Random offset in block
                   xms_realMem, DWORD(text),       // Real memory
                   EVEN(strlen(text)+1))) {        // Length (+1) for terminator
        xms_demoError("XMS_Xms::moveXM");
        exit(1);
        }

    //
    //  And something for the the third block:
    //
    text= "conceived in liberty and dedicated to the proposition ";

    if (xms.moveXM(handle3, 800,                    // Random offset in block
                   xms_realMem, DWORD(text),        // Real memory
                   EVEN(strlen(text)+1))) {         // Length (+1) for terminator
        xms_demoError("XMS_Xms::moveXM");
        exit(1);
        }

    //
    //  Now the fourth and last block:
    //
    text= "that all\nmen are created equal.\n";

    if (xms.moveXM(handle4, 212,                    // Random offset in block
                   xms_realMem, DWORD(text),        // Real memory
                   EVEN(strlen(text)+1))) {         // Length (+1) for terminator
        xms_demoError("XMS_Xms::moveXM");
        exit(1);
        }

    //
    //  Now we've copies four strings into XM blocks.
    //      Block 1 at offset 42,
    //      Block 2 at offset 911,
    //      Block 3 at offset 800,
    //      Block 4 at offset 212.
    //
    //  Now let's retrieve them and print them out.
    //
    if (xms.moveXM(xms_realMem, DWORD(buff),// Real, address of buffer
                   handle1, 42,             // Offset in block
                   72)) {                   // Max length
        xms_demoError("XMS_Xms::moveXM");
        exit(1);
        }

printf("%s", buff);

    //
    //  Now pick up the second piece:
    //
    if (xms.moveXM(xms_realMem, DWORD(buff),// Real, address of buffer
                   handle2, 911,            // Offset in block
                   72)) {                   // Max length
        xms_demoError("XMS_Xms::moveXM");
        exit(1);
        }
```

```
    printf("%s", buff);

    //
    //   Now pick up the third piece:
    //
    if (xms.moveXM(xms_realMem, DWORD(buff),// Real, address of buffer
                   handle3, 800,            // Offset in block
                   72)) {                   // Max length
        xms_demoError("XMS_Xms::moveXM");
        exit(1);
        }

    printf("%s", buff);

    //
    //   Now pick up the fourth piece:
    //
    if (xms.moveXM(xms_realMem, DWORD(buff),// Real, address of buffer
                   handle4, 212,            // Offset in block
                   72)) {                   // Max length
        xms_demoError("XMS_Xms::moveXM");
        exit(1);
        }

    printf("%s", buff);

    //
    //   Free up the blocks of memory.
    //
    if (handle1.freeXM()) {
        xms_demoError("XMS_XmBlk::freeXM");
        }
    if (handle2.freeXM()) {
        xms_demoError("XMS_XmBlk::freeXM");
        }
    if (handle3.freeXM()) {
        xms_demoError("XMS_XmBlk::freeXM");
        }
    if (handle4.freeXM()) {
        xms_demoError("XMS_XmBlk::freeXM");
        }

    }
```

PROG5-5.CPP demonstrates the following operation:

- Securing the HMA
- Getting the A20 state
- Enabling A20
- Disabling A20
- Accessing the HMA

PROG5-5 demonstrates how to use the High Memory Area. It gets the HMA using XMS_Xms::allocHMA() and then enables the A20 line using

XMS_Xms::globEnabA20(). Enabling the A20 line allows the processor to generate addresses past the 1Mb mark. By using a segment of 0×FFFF and offsets greater than 0×0010, we can access the area just past the 1Mb mark. The program generates a pointer to the beginning of the HMA and writes and reads data to it. It then disables the A20 line and attempts to access the memory. With the A20 line disabled, the addresses wrap and garbage is produced.

Figure 5-5 presents the source code listing to PROG5-5.CPP.

5-5 The source code listing to PROG5-5.CPP

```
/////////////////////////////////////
//
// prog5-5.cpp
//
//   Demonstrates use of the HMA
//
/////////////////////////////////////

//////////////////////////
// include standard
// I/O functions

extern "C" {
#include <stdio.h>
#include <stdlib.h>
#include <string.h>
#include <dos.h>
}

//////////////////////////
//
// include xms memory
// management header
// files

#include "gdefs.h"
#include "xms.h"

//////////////////////////
// begin program


void main()
{

        XMS_Xms             xms;
        XMS_Hma             hma;
        char                *text;
        char                *hmaPtr;

        WORD                a20State;

        //
        //  Attempt to initialize XMS. If there is an error, report it.
        //
        if (xms.init()) {
            printf("XMS is not present\n");
```

```
        }

    //
    //  Now try to allocate the HMA
    //
    if (hma.allocHMA(0xFFFF)) {
        xms_demoError("XMS_Hma::allocHMA");
        }

    //
    //  Now that we've got the HMA, we need to enable the A20
    //  line so that addresses won't wrap.
    //
    if (hma.globEnabA20()) {
        xms_demoError("XMS_Hma::globEnabA20");
        }

    //
    //  We've got it. Let's set up a pointer to the memory
    //  now. Note that (0xFFFF << 4) + 0x10 = 0xFFFF0 + 0x10 = 0x100000.
    //
    hmaPtr= (char *) MK_FP(0xFFFF, 0x10);

    //
    //  Now let's copy some text into various places in the
    //  HMA, and then copy it back and print it out.
    //
    text= "Oh say can you see by the dawn's early light\n";
    strcpy(&hmaPtr[0], text);
    text= "  What so proudly we hailed at the twilight's last gleaming ?\n";
    strcpy(&hmaPtr[100], text);
    text= "Whose broad stripes and bright stars ";
    strcpy(&hmaPtr[200], text);
    text= "through the perilous fight\n";
    strcpy(&hmaPtr[300], text);
    text= "  O'er the ramparts we watched were so gallantly streaming ?\n";
    strcpy(&hmaPtr[400], text);

    //
    //  Query and print out the A20 state (we know it's enabled):
    //
    if (hma.getA20State(&a20State)) {
        xms_demoError("XMS_Hma::getA20State");
        }

    printf(
"==============================A20=%s===============================\n",
            (a20State) ? "Enabled=" : "Disabled");

    //
    //  Now print the stuff right out of the HMA
    //
    printf("%s", &hmaPtr[0]);
    printf("%s", &hmaPtr[100]);
    printf("%s", &hmaPtr[200]);
    printf("%s", &hmaPtr[300]);
    printf("%s", &hmaPtr[400]);

    //
    //  Disable the A20 line.
    //
```

5-5 Continued.

```
if (hma.globDisabA20()) {
    xms_demoError("XMS_Hma::globDisabA20");
    }

//
//  Now note the garbage the same code will produce without
//  the A20 line enabled. This will be looking at addresses
//  0:0, 0:100, etc. instead of 10000:0, 10000:100, etc.
//
if (hma.getA20State(&a20State)) {
    xms_demoError("XMS_Hma::getA20State");
    }

printf(
"═══════════════════════════A20=%s═══════════════════════════\n",
        (a20State) ? "Enabled=" : "Disabled");

printf("%s", &hmaPtr[0]);
printf("%s", &hmaPtr[100]);
printf("%s", &hmaPtr[200]);
printf("%s", &hmaPtr[300]);
printf("%s", &hmaPtr[400]);

//
//  Free up the HMA
//
if (hma.freeHMA()) {
    xms_demoError("XMS_Hma::freeHMA");
    }

}
```

PROG5-6.CPP demonstrates the following operations:

- Locking and unlocking XMS blocks
- Moving data to and from XMS via the raw move

PROG5-6 demonstrates how to use `XMS_Xms::rawMove()` to move data between conventional memory and XMS memory. Raw physical moves require physical addresses. We use `XMS_XmBlk::lockXM()` to lock an XMS block's location and return its physical address. After moving data to and from the XMS blocks, we use `XMS_XmBlk::unlockXM()` to allow the XMM to reposition the blocks if it needs to. We use the macro SegOffTo-Phys to generate physical addresses from standard Segment:Offset addresses.

Figure 5-6 presents the source code listing to PROG5-6.CPP.

5-6 The source code listing to PROG5-6.CPP

```
//////////////////////////////////////
//
// prog5-6.cpp
//
//   Demonstrates use of move to/from eXtended Memory using raw move.
//
//////////////////////////////////////
/////////////////////////
// include standard
// I/O functions

extern "C" {
#include <stdio.h>
#include <stdlib.h>
#include <string.h>
#include <dos.h>
}

/////////////////////////
//
// include xms memory
// management header
// files

#include "gdefs.h"
#include "xms.h"

/////////////////////////
// begin program


#define EVEN(x)     (((x)+1)&~1)

void main()
{

    XMS_Xms         xms;

    XMS_XmBlk       handle1;
    XMS_XmBlk       handle2;
    XMS_XmBlk       handle3;
    XMS_XmBlk       handle4;

    DWORD           physAddr1;
    DWORD           physAddr2;
    DWORD           physAddr3;
    DWORD           physAddr4;

    char            *text;

    char            buff[72];


    //
    // Attempt to initialize XMS. If there is an error, report it.
```

5-6 Continued.

```
//
if (xms.init()) {
    printf("XMS is not present\n");
    }

//
//   Now allocate 4 1KB blocks.
//
if (handle1.allocXM(1)) {
    xms_demoError("XMS_XmBlk::allocXM");
    }
if (handle2.allocXM(1)) {
    xms_demoError("XMS_XmBlk::allocXM");
    }
if (handle3.allocXM(1)) {
    xms_demoError("XMS_XmBlk::allocXM");
    }
if (handle4.allocXM(1)) {
    xms_demoError("XMS_XmBlk::allocXM");
    }

//
//   Now let's lock the blocks, getting their physical addresses
//   so we can do some raw moves to and from them.
//
if (handle1.lockXM(&physAddr1)) {
    xms_demoError("XMS_XmBlk::lockXM");
    }
if (handle2.lockXM(&physAddr2)) {
    xms_demoError("XMS_XmBlk::lockXM");
    }
if (handle3.lockXM(&physAddr3)) {
    xms_demoError("XMS_XmBlk::lockXM");
    }
if (handle4.lockXM(&physAddr4)) {
    xms_demoError("XMS_XmBlk::lockXM");
    }

//
//   Now let's copy some text into various places in the
//   XM blocks, and then copy it back and print it out.
//

//
//   Set up a pointer to a string:
//
text= "Fourscore and seven years ago our fathers brought forth ";

//
//   Do the raw move. Note that the length must be an
//   even number of bytes.
//
if (xms.rawMove(physAddr1+42, SegOffToPhys(text), EVEN(strlen(text)+1))) {
    xms_demoError("XMS_Xms::rawMove");
    }

//
//   Now put the next string into the next XM block:
//
```

```
text= "on this continent a\nnew nation, ";
if (xms.rawMove(physAddr2+911, SegOffToPhys(text), EVEN(strlen(text)+1))) {
    xms_demoError("XMS_Xms::rawMove");
    }


//
//   And something for the the third block:
//
text= "conceived in liberty and dedicated to the proposition ";
if (xms.rawMove(physAddr3+800, SegOffToPhys(text), EVEN(strlen(text)+1))) {
    xms_demoError("XMS_Xms::rawMove");
    }


//
//   Now the fourth and last block:
//
text= "that all\nmen are created equal.\n";
if (xms.rawMove(physAddr4+212, SegOffToPhys(text), EVEN(strlen(text)+1))) {
    xms_demoError("XMS_Xms::rawMove");
    }


//
//   Now we've copied four strings into XM blocks.
//        Block 1 at offset 42,
//        Block 2 at offset 911,
//        Block 3 at offset 800,
//        Block 4 at offset 212.
//
//   Now let's retrieve them and print them out.
//
if (xms.rawMove(SegOffToPhys(buff), physAddr1+42, 72)) {
    xms_demoError("XMS_Xms::rawMove");
    }

printf("%s", buff);

//
//   Now pick up the second piece:
//
if (xms.rawMove(SegOffToPhys(buff), physAddr2+911, 72)) {
    xms_demoError("XMS_Xms::rawMove");
    }

printf("%s", buff);

//
//   Now pick up the third piece:
//
if (xms.rawMove(SegOffToPhys(buff), physAddr3+800, 72)) {
    xms_demoError("XMS_Xms::rawMove");
    }

printf("%s", buff);

//
//   Now pick up the fourth piece:
//
if (xms.rawMove(SegOffToPhys(buff), physAddr4+212, 72)) {
    xms_demoError("XMS_Xms::rawMove");
    }
```

```
    printf("%s", buff);

    //
    //  Now unlock the blocks.
    //
    if (handle1.unlockXM()) {
        xms_demoError("XMS_XmBlk::unlockXM");
        }
    if (handle2.unlockXM()) {
        xms_demoError("XMS_XmBlk::unlockXM");
        }
    if (handle3.unlockXM()) {
        xms_demoError("XMS_XmBlk::unlockXM");
        }
    if (handle4.unlockXM()) {
        xms_demoError("XMS_XmBlk::unlockXM");
        }


    //
    //  Free up the blocks of memory.
    //
    if (handle1.freeXM()) {
        xms_demoError("XMS_XmBlk::freeXM");
        }
    if (handle2.freeXM()) {
        xms_demoError("XMS_XmBlk::freeXM");
        }
    if (handle3.freeXM()) {
        xms_demoError("XMS_XmBlk::freeXM");
        }
    if (handle4.freeXM()) {
        xms_demoError("XMS_XmBlk::freeXM");
        }

}
```

PROG5-7.CPP demonstrates the following operations:

- Allocating and freeing upper memory
- Moving data to and from upper memory

PROG5-7 demonstrates the use of upper memory. We use XMS_Xms ::allocUM() to allocate upper memory blocks. Upper memory blocks are within the first megabytes, so no special techniques are required to read and write to them. When we are done, we can release them with XMS_ Xms::freeUM().

Figure 5-7 presents the source code listing to PROG5-7.CPP.

5-7 The source code listing to PROG5-7.CPP

```
/////////////////////////////////////
//
// prog5-7.cpp
```

```
//
//   Demonstrates use of move to/from Upper Memory
//
/////////////////////////////////////

///////////////////////
// include standard
// I/O functions

extern "C" {
#include <stdio.h>
#include <stdlib.h>
#include <string.h>
#include <dos.h>
}


///////////////////////
//
// include xms memory
// management header
// files

#include "gdefs.h"
#include "xms.h"

///////////////////////
// begin program


void main()
{

    XMS_Xms            xms;

    XMS_UmBlk          um1;
    XMS_UmBlk          um2;
    XMS_UmBlk          um3;
    XMS_UmBlk          um4;
    XMS_UmBlk          um5;

    char               *block1;
    char               *block2;
    char               *block3;
    char               *block4;
    char               *block5;

    char               *text;

    WORD               actualSize;

    //
    //   Attempt to initialize XMS. If there is an error, report it.
    //
    if (xms.init()) {
        printf("XMS is not present\n");
        }

    //
    //   Now allocate 5 128 byte blocks of Upper Memory
    //
```

```
    if (um1.allocUM(8, (void **) &block1, &actualSize)) {
        printf("    Biggest block available was %d bytes\n",
                    actualSize * 16);
        xms_demoError("XMS_UmBlk::allocUM");
        }
    if (um2.allocUM(8, (void **) &block2, &actualSize)) {
        printf("    Biggest block available was %d bytes\n",
                    actualSize * 16);
        xms_demoError("XMS_UmBlk::allocUM");
        }
    if (um3.allocUM(8, (void **) &block3, &actualSize)) {
        printf("    Biggest block available was %d bytes\n",
                    actualSize * 16);
        xms_demoError("XMS_UmBlk::allocUM");
        }
    if (um4.allocUM(8, (void **) &block4, &actualSize)) {
        printf("    Biggest block available was %d bytes\n",
                    actualSize * 16);
        xms_demoError("XMS_UmBlk::allocUM");
        }
    if (um5.allocUM(8, (void **) &block5, &actualSize)) {
        printf("    Biggest block available was %d bytes\n",
                    actualSize * 16);
        xms_demoError("XMS_UmBlk::allocUM");
        }

    //
    //   Now let's copy some text into various places in the
    //   UM blocks, and then copy it back and print it out.
    //

    //
    //   Set up a pointer to a string:
    //
    text=
"We the people of the United States, in order to form a more perfect Union,\n";

    //
    // Move it to block 1
    //
    strcpy(block1, text);

    //
    //   Now put the next string into the next UM block:
    //
    text=
"establish justice, insure domestic tranquility, provide for the common\n";
    strcpy(block2, text);

    //
    //   And something for the the third block:
    //
    text=
"defense, promote the general welfare, and secure the blessings of liberty\n";
    strcpy(block3, text);

    //
    //   Now the fourth block:
    //
```

```
    text=
"to ourselves and our posterity do ordain and establish this
Constitution\n";
    strcpy(block4, text);

    //
    //  And the fifth and final block:
    //
    text= "for the United States of America.\n";
    strcpy(block5, text);

    //
    //  Now we've copied four strings into UM blocks.
    //
    //  Let's retrieve them and print them out.
    //
    printf("%s", block1);
    printf("%s", block2);
    printf("%s", block3);
    printf("%s", block4);
    printf("%s", block5);

    //
    //  Free up the blocks of memory.
    //
    if (um1.freeUM()) {
        xms_demoError("XMS_UmBlk::freeUM");
        }
    if (um2.freeUM()) {
        xms_demoError("XMS_UmBlk::freeUM");
        }
    if (um3.freeUM()) {
        xms_demoError("XMS_UmBlk::freeUM");
        }
    if (um4.freeUM()) {
        xms_demoError("XMS_UmBlk::freeUM");
        }
    if (um5.freeUM()) {
        xms_demoError("XMS_UmBlk::freeUM");
        }

}
```

PROG5-8.CPP demonstrates the following operation:

- Resizing of XMS blocks

PROG5-8 uses `XMS_XmBlk::resizeXM()` to resize an XMS block. It displays the allocated handles, their sizes and physical addresses after each operation to investigate which blocks move when a block is resized. Note that some XMS managers do not allow block resizing. This program will report an error under these XM

Figure 5-8 presents the source code listing to PROG5-8.CPP.

5-8 The source code listing to PROG5-8.CPP

```
/////////////////////////////////////
//
// prog5-8.c
//
//  Demonstrates resizing blocks and getting block info
//
/////////////////////////////////////

////////////////////////
// include standard
// I/O functions

extern "C" {
#include <stdio.h>
#include <stdlib.h>
#include <dos.h>
}
////////////////////////
//
// include xms memory
// management header
// files

#include "gdefs.h"
#include "xms.h"

////////////////////////
// begin program


void main()
{
    XMS_Xms            xms;

    WORD               lockCount;
    WORD               numFreeHandles;
    WORD               blockSize;

    XMS_XmBlk          handle1;
    XMS_XmBlk          handle2;
    XMS_XmBlk          handle3;

    DWORD              physAddr1;
    DWORD              physAddr2;
    DWORD              physAddr3;

    //
    //  Attempt to initialize XMS. If there is an error, report it.
    //
    if (xms.init()) {
        printf("XMS is not present\n");
        }

    //
    //  Print header:
    //
    printf(
"                                Address     Size (bytes)  Locks\n");
    printf(
```

```
"━━━━━━━━━━━━━━━━━━━━━━━━━━━━━┥━━━━━━━━━━━┥━━━━━━━━━━━━━━━━\n");

//
//   Allocate three blocks:
//
if (handle1.allocXM(16)) {
    xms_demoError("XMS_XmBlk::allocXM");
    }
if (handle2.allocXM(16)) {
    xms_demoError("XMS_XmBlk::allocXM");
    }
if (handle3.allocXM(16)) {
    xms_demoError("XMS_XmBlk::allocXM");
    }


//
//   Now lock 'em and get their physical addresses.
//
if (handle1.lockXM(&physAddr1)) {
    xms_demoError("XMS_XmBlk::lockXM");
    }
if (handle2.lockXM(&physAddr2)) {
    xms_demoError("XMS_XmBlk::lockXM");
    }
if (handle3.lockXM(&physAddr3)) {
    xms_demoError("XMS_XmBlk::lockXM");
    }

//
//   Now one by one get info on them:
//
if (handle1.getHandInfo(&blockSize, &numFreeHandles, &lockCount)) {
    xms_demoError("XMS_XmBlk::getHandInfo");
    }
printf("After allocation:  block 1 |   0x%-6lX   |   0x%-6X   |  %3d |\n",
        physAddr1,
        blockSize*1024,
        lockCount);

printf(
"        ━━━━━━━━┿━━━━━━━━━━━┿━━━━━━━━━━━┥\n");

if (handle2.getHandInfo(&blockSize, &numFreeHandles, &lockCount)) {
    xms_demoError("XMS_XmBlk::getHandInfo");
    }
printf("                   block 2 |   0x%-6lX   |   0x%-6X   |  %3d |\n",
        physAddr2,
        blockSize*1024,
        lockCount);

printf(
"        ━━━━━━━━┿━━━━━━━━━━━┿━━━━━━━━━━━┥\n");

if (handle3.getHandInfo(&blockSize, &numFreeHandles, &lockCount)) {
    xms_demoError("XMS_XmBlk::getHandInfo");
    }
printf("                   block 3 |   0x%-6lX   |   0x%-6X   |  %3d |\n",
        physAddr3,
        blockSize*1024,
        lockCount);
printf(
```

```
"═══════════════════╪═══════════════╪═══════════════╡\n");


    //
    //  Now let's resize the middle block and see what happens.
    //  First, however, we want to unlock all of the blocks so
    //  that they can move as necessary.
    //
    if (handle1.unlockXM()) {
        xms_demoError("XMS_XmBlk::unlockXM");
        }
    if (handle2.unlockXM()) {
        xms_demoError("XMS_XmBlk::unlockXM");
        }
    if (handle3.unlockXM()) {
        xms_demoError("XMS_XmBlk::unlockXM");
        }
    //
    //  Do the resize:
    //
    if (handle2.resizeXM(32)) {
        xms_demoError("XMS_XmBlk::resizeXM");
        }


    //
    //  Lock them all again.
    //
    if (handle1.lockXM(&physAddr1)) {
        xms_demoError("XMS_XmBlk::lockXM");
        }
    if (handle2.lockXM(&physAddr2)) {
        xms_demoError("XMS_XmBlk::lockXM");
        }
    if (handle3.lockXM(&physAddr3)) {
        xms_demoError("XMS_XmBlk::lockXM");
        }


    //
    //  Now report on the new situation.
    //
    if (handle1.getHandInfo(&blockSize, &numFreeHandles, &lockCount)) {
        xms_demoError("XMS_XmBlk::getHandInfo");
        }
    printf("After resize:      block 1 |   0x%-6lX   |   0x%-6X   |  %3d |\n",
            physAddr1,
            blockSize*1024,
            lockCount);

    printf(
"                   ───────────────╪───────────────╪───────────────╡\n");

    if (handle2.getHandInfo(&blockSize, &numFreeHandles, &lockCount)) {
        xms_demoError("XMS_XmBlk::getHandInfo");
        }
    printf("                   block 2 |   0x%-6lX   |   0x%-6X   |  %3d |\n",
            physAddr2,
            blockSize*1024,
            lockCount);
```

```
        printf(
"——————+————————————+——————————|\n");

        if (handle3.getHandInfo(&blockSize, &numFreeHandles, &lockCount)) {
            xms_demoError("XMS_XmBlk::getHandInfo");
            }
        printf("                      block 3 |   0x%-61X   |   0x%-6X   |  %3d
|\n",
                physAddr3,
                blockSize*1024,
                lockCount);
        printf(
"══════════════════╧═══════════════╧══════════════╛\n");

        //
        //  Unlock the blocks:
        //
        if (handle1.unlockXM()) {
            xms_demoError("XMS_XmBlk::unlockXM");
            }
        if (handle2.unlockXM()) {
            xms_demoError("XMS_XmBlk::unlockXM");
            }
        if (handle3.unlockXM()) {
            xms_demoError("XMS_XmBlk::unlockXM");
            }

        //
        //  And free them
        //
        if (handle1.freeXM()) {
            xms_demoError("XMS_XmBlk::freeXM");
            }
        if (handle2.freeXM()) {
            xms_demoError("XMS_XmBlk::freeXM");
            }
        if (handle3.freeXM()) {
            xms_demoError("XMS_XmBlk::freeXM");
            }

}
```

PROG5-9.CPP demonstrates the following operation:

- Implicit freeing of extended memory blocks by the XMS_XmBlk destructor

PROG5-9 shows how XMS blocks are automatically freed by the XMS_XmBlk destructor. When the procedure destructorTest() returns, destructors are called that free the allocated XMS .

Figure 5-9 presents the source code listing to PROG5-9.CPP.

5-9 The source code listing to PROG5-9.CPP

```
/////////////////////////////////////
//
// prog5-9.cpp
//
//   Show XM destructor in action
//
/////////////////////////////////////

extern "C" {
#include <stdio.h>
}
/////////////////////////////
//
// include xms memory
// management header
// files

#include "gdefs.h"
#include "xms.h"

/////////////////////////////
// begin program

extern void destructorTest();

void main()
{

    WORD                totalFree;
    WORD                largestFree;


    XMS_Xms             xms;


    //
    //   Attempt to initialize XMS. If there is an error, report it.
    //
    if (xms.init()) {
        printf("XMS is not present\n");
        }

    //
    //   Print header:
    //
    printf("                                        Total        Largest Block\n");
    printf("========================================================\n");

    //
    //   Report the free memory available:
    //
    if (xms.getFreeXM(&totalFree, &largestFree)) {
        xms_demoError("XMS_Xms::getFreeXM");
        }

    printf("After initialization         |    %4d KB    |    %4d KB    |\n",
```

```
                        totalFree, largestFree);
        printf("─────────────────────────┼───────────────┼───────────────────┤\n");
        destructorTest();

        printf("After exiting block's scope |     %4d KB    |     %4d KB    |\n",
                        totalFree, largestFree);
        printf("═════════════════════════┼═══════════════┼═══════════════════┤\n");

}

void destructorTest()

{

    XMS_Xms                 xms;

    WORD                totalFree;
    WORD                largestFree;

    XMS_XmBlk           block1;
    XMS_XmBlk           block2;

    //
    //   Now allocate 16KB and note the change:
    //
    if (block1.allocXM(16)) {
        xms_demoError("XMS_XmBlk::allocXM");
        }

    if (xms.getFreeXM(&totalFree, &largestFree)) {
        xms_demoError("XMS_Xms::getFreeXM");
        }

    printf("After 16 KB allocate        |     %4d KB    |     %4d KB    |\n",
                totalFree, largestFree);
    printf("─────────────────────────┼───────────────┼───────────────────┤\n");

    //
    //   Now allocate another 32KB and note the change:
    //
    if (block2.allocXM(32)) {
        xms_demoError("XMS_XmBlk::allocXM");
        }

    if (xms.getFreeXM(&totalFree, &largestFree)) {
        xms_demoError("XMS_Xms::getFreeXM");
        }

    printf("After 32 KB allocate        |     %4d KB    |     %4d KB    |\n",
                totalFree, largestFree);
    printf("─────────────────────────┼───────────────┼───────────────────┤\n");

    //
    //   Note that we have not freed the XMS blocks, and they
    //   are passing out of scope when we return.
    //
}
```

The XMS interface classes

The XMS interface is built in two levels. The lowest level is a series of C callable assembly routines which call the eXtended Memory Manager. On top of these routines, we have built a class interface with four classes: XMS_Xms, XMS_XmBlk, XMS_UmBlk, and XMS_HMA.

The function prototypes, error codes, and class definitions are given in XMS.H.

Figure 5-10 presents the source code listing to XMS.H.

5-10 The source code listing to XMS.H

```
/////////////////////////////////////
//
// xms.h
//
// XMS related definitions,
// structures and function prototypes
//
/////////////////////////////////////

/***********************************************************************
***                                                                 ***
***        Constant #defines                                        ***
***                                                                 ***
***********************************************************************/

//
//   Define the XMS page size
//
#define XMS_PAGE_SIZE        1024

//
//   Define the XMS error codes.
//
#define XMSErrOK            0x00    // No Error
#define XMSErrUnimp         0x80    // Unimplemented function
#define XMSErrVDISK         0x81    // VDISK device detected
#define XMSErrA20           0x82    // A20 error
#define XMSErrNoHMA         0x90    // HMA does not exist
#define XMSErrHMAInUse      0x91    // HMA already in use
#define XMSErrHMAMin        0x92    // HMA space req. < /HMAMIN= parameter
#define XMSErrHMANotAll     0x93    // HMA not allocated
#define XMSErrA20Enab       0x94    // A20 still enabled
#define XMSErrNoXMLeft      0x0A0   // All XM allocated
#define XMSErrNoHandles     0x0A1   // All handles are allocated
#define XMSErrHandInv       0x0A2   // Invalid handle
#define XMSErrSHandInv      0x0A3   // Invalid Source Handle
#define XMSErrSOffInv       0x0A4   // Invalid Source Offset
#define XMSErrDHandInv      0x0A5   // Invalid Dest Handle
#define XMSErrDOffInv       0x0A6   // Invalid Dest Offset
#define XMSErrLenInv        0x0A7   // Invalid Length
#define XMSErrOverlap       0x0A8   // Invalid move overlap
#define XMSErrParity        0x0A9   // Parity error
#define XMSErrNoLock        0x0AA   // Handle not locked
#define XMSErrLock          0x0AB   // Handle Locked
```

```
#define XMSErrLockOvflo      0x0AC    // Lock count overflo
#define XMSErrLockFail       0x0AD    // Lock fail
#define XMSErrSmUMB          0x0B0    // Smaller UMB available
#define XMSErrNoUMB          0x0B1    // No UMB's available
#define XMSErrUMBInv         0x0B2    // Invalid UMB segment


/***********************************************************************
***                                                                 ***
***      Structure and type definitions                            ***
***                                                                 ***
***********************************************************************/

typedef struct {

    DWORD       length;         // memory length
    WORD        srcHandle;      // source handle (0 means < 1MB boundary)
    DWORD       srcOffset;      // source offset
    WORD        destHandle;     // destination handle (0 means < 1MB)
    DWORD       destOffset;     // destination offset
    }   XMS_MovePacket;

/***********************************************************************
***                                                                 ***
***      Function definitions for 'C' interface                    ***
***                                                                 ***
***********************************************************************/

extern "C" {

int     xms_init(void);
int     xms_getVersion(WORD *xmsVersion, WORD *xmmVersion, WORD *hmaFlag);
int     xms_rawMove(DWORD dest, DWORD source, WORD length);
int     xms_allocHMA(WORD hmaBytes);
int     xms_freeHMA(void);
int     xms_globEnabA20(void);
int     xms_globDisabA20(void);
int     xms_getA20State(WORD *a20State);
int     xms_getFreeXM(WORD *totalFree, WORD *largestFree);
int     xms_allocXM(WORD blockSize, WORD *handle);
int     xms_freeXM(WORD handle);
int     xms_moveXM(XMS_MovePacket *packet);
int     xms_lockXM(WORD handle, DWORD *physAddr);
int     xms_unlockXM(WORD handle);
int     xms_getHandInfo(WORD handle, WORD *blockSize,
                            WORD *handlesLeft, WORD *lockCount);
int     xms_resizeXM(WORD handle, WORD newSize);
int     xms_allocUM(WORD size, void **address, WORD *actualSize);
int     xms_freeUM(void *address);

}


/***********************************************************************
***                                                                 ***
***      Class definitions                                          ***
***                                                                 ***
***********************************************************************/

class   XMS_Xms;
class   XMS_XmBlk;
```

5-10 Continued.

```
class    XMS_UmBlk;
class    XMS_Hma;

//
//  First define the XMS_XmBlk class, which defines eXtended memory
//  blocks as objects.
//
class    XMS_XmBlk {

    WORD                handle;

    //
    //  Prevent assignment and copy-initialization:
    //
    XMS_XmBlk        &operator=(const XMS_XmBlk &);
                      XMS_XmBlk(const XMS_XmBlk &);

public:
    friend class    XMS_Xms;
        XMS_XmBlk() {
            handle= 0;
            }

      ~XMS_XmBlk() {
            if (handle) {
                xms_freeXM(handle);
                }
            }

    int allocXM(WORD blockSize);

    int freeXM();

    int lockXM(DWORD *physAddr) {
            return xms_lockXM(handle, physAddr);
            }

    int unlockXM() {
            return xms_unlockXM(handle);
            }

    int getHandInfo(WORD *blockSize, WORD *handlesLeft, WORD *lockCount) {
            return xms_getHandInfo(handle, blockSize,
                    handlesLeft, lockCount);
            }

    int resizeXM(WORD newSize) {
            return xms_resizeXM(handle, newSize);
            }
    };


//
//  Define the XMS_Xms class, which contains general XMS functions.
//
class    XMS_Xms {

    //
```

```
        //  Prevent assignment and copy-initialization:
        //
        XMS_Xms      &operator=(const XMS_Xms &);
                     XMS_Xms(const XMS_Xms &);

public:
        XMS_Xms() {};

    int init() {
            return xms_init();
            }

    int getVersion(WORD *xmsVersion, WORD *xmmVersion, WORD
*hmaFlag) {
            return xms_getVersion(xmsVersion, xmmVersion, hmaFlag);
            }

    int rawMove(DWORD dest, DWORD source, WORD length) {
            return xms_rawMove(dest, source, length);
            }

    int getFreeXM(WORD *totalFree, WORD *largestFree) {
            return xms_getFreeXM(totalFree, largestFree);
            }

    int moveXM(XMS_XmBlk &dest, DWORD destOffset,
               XMS_XmBlk &source, DWORD srcOffset,
               DWORD length) {
            XMS_MovePacket      packet;

            packet.destHandle= dest.handle;
            packet.destOffset= destOffset;
            packet.srcHandle= source.handle;
            packet.srcOffset= srcOffset;
            packet.length= length;
            return xms_moveXM(&packet);
            }
    };

//
//  Define the XMS_Hma class. This defines the High Memory Area as
//  an object.
//
class    XMS_Hma {
    int                allocated;

    //
    //  Prevent assignment and copy-initialization:
    //
    XMS_Hma      &operator=(const XMS_Hma &);
                 XMS_Hma(const XMS_Hma &);

public:
        XMS_Hma() {
            allocated= FALSE;
            }

    ~XMS_Hma() {
            if (allocated) {
```

5-10 Continued.

```
                xms_freeHMA();
                }
            allocated= FALSE;
            }

    int allocHMA(WORD hmaBytes);

    int freeHMA();
    int globEnabA20() {
            return xms_globEnabA20();
            }

    int globDisabA20(void) {
            return xms_globDisabA20();
            }

    int getA20State(WORD *a20State) {
            return xms_getA20State(a20State);
            }

    };
//
//   Define the XMS_UmBlk class. This provides an object interface
//   to blocks of upper memory.
//
class   XMS_UmBlk {

    void                *addr;

    //
    //   Prevent assignment and copy-initialization:
    //
    XMS_UmBlk   &operator=(const XMS_UmBlk &);
                XMS_UmBlk(const XMS_UmBlk &);

public:
        XMS_UmBlk() {
            addr= NULL;
            }
        ~XMS_UmBlk() {
            if (addr) {
                xms_freeUM(addr);
                }
            }

    int allocUM(WORD size, void **address, WORD *actualSize);

    int freeUM() {
            if (addr) {
                return xms_freeUM(addr);
                }
            return XMSErrOK;
            }

    };


char   *xms_errorText(WORD error);
void    xms_demoError(char *function);

extern  XMS_XmBlk   xms_realMem;
```

The class methods that are not inline are defined in XMSLIB.CPP. Figure 5-11 presents the source code listing to XMSLIB.CPP.

5-11 The source code listing to XMSLIB.CPP

```
/////////////////////////////////////
//
// xmslib.cpp
//
//      Defines non-inlined members of the XMS classes and other
//  XMS support routines.
//
/////////////////////////////////////

extern "C" {
#include "stdio.h"
#include "stdlib.h"
}

/////////////////////////
//
// include xms memory
// management header
// files

#include "gdefs.h"
#include "xms.h"


XMS_XmBlk    xms_realMem;          // An uninitialized block gives a handle
                                  // of zero which indicates real memory to
                                  // XMS_Xms::move().

/**********************************************************************
***                                                                ***
***      XMS_XmBlk::allocXM() - Allocate an eXtended Memory block   ***
***                                                                ***
**********************************************************************/

int XMS_XmBlk::allocXM(WORD blockSize)
{
    int        rval;

    //
    // If this handle already denotes a block, free that
    // block:
    //
    if (handle) {
        xms_freeXM(handle);
        }

    rval= xms_allocXM(blockSize, &handle);
    return rval;
}


/**********************************************************************
***                                                                ***
***      XMS_XmBlk::freeXM() - Frees an eXtended memory block.      ***
***                                                                ***
```

The XMS interface classes   189

5-11 Continued.

```
*********************************************************************/

int XMS_XmBlk::freeXM()
{
    int     rval;

    //
    //  If a block has been allocated, free it:
    //
    if (handle) {
        rval= xms_freeXM(handle);
        if (rval != XMSErrOK) {
            return rval;
            }
        else {
            handle= 0;
            }
        }

    return XMSErrOK;

}

/*********************************************************************
***                                                              ***
***     XMS_Hma::allocHMA() -  Allocates the High Memory Area     ***
***                                                              ***
*********************************************************************/

int XMS_Hma::allocHMA(WORD hmaBytes)
{
    int rval;

    //
    //  If we haven't already allocated the HMA, allocate it.
    //
    if (!allocated) {
        rval= xms_allocHMA(hmaBytes);
        if (rval == XMSErrOK) {
            allocated= TRUE;
            }
        else {
            return rval;
            }
        }
    return XMSErrOK;

}

/*********************************************************************
***                                                              ***
***     XMS_Hma::freeHMA() -  Release the High Memory Area        ***
***                                                              ***
*********************************************************************/

int XMS_Hma::freeHMA()
{
    int     rval;
```

```
    //
    //  If we've allocated the HMA, free it
    //
    if (allocated) {
        rval= xms_freeHMA();
        if (rval) {
            return rval;
            }
        }
    allocated= FALSE;

    return XMSErrOK;
}
/***********************************************************************
***                                                                 ***
***     XMS_UmBlk::allocUM() -  Allocate an Upper Memory block       ***
***                                                                 ***
***********************************************************************/

int XMS_UmBlk::allocUM(WORD size, void **address, WORD *actualSize)
{
    int         rval;

    if (addr) {
        xms_freeUM(addr);
        }

    rval= xms_allocUM(size, address, actualSize);
    if (rval == XMSErrOK) {
        addr= *address;
        }
    return rval;
}


/***********************************************************************
***                                                                 ***
***     xms_errorText() - Returns the text message for a given       ***
***                       XMS error.                                 ***
***                                                                 ***
***********************************************************************/

char    *xms_errorText(WORD err)

{
    static char buff[64];

    switch (err) {
    case XMSErrOK:
        return "No Error";
    case XMSErrUnimp:
        return "Unimplemented function";
    case XMSErrVDISK:
        return "VDISK device detected";
    case XMSErrA20:
        return "A20 error";
    case XMSErrNoHMA:
        return "HMA does not exist";
    case XMSErrHMAInUse:
        return "HMA already in use";
    case XMSErrHMAMin:
```

```
            return "HMA space requested < /HMAMIN= parameter";
        case XMSErrHMANotAll:
            return "HMA not allocated";
        case XMSErrA20Enab:
            return "A20 still enabled";
        case XMSErrNoXMLeft:
            return "All eXtended Memory allocated";
        case XMSErrNoHandles:
            return "All handles are allocated";
        case XMSErrHandInv:
            return "Invalid handle";
        case XMSErrSHandInv:
            return "Invalid Source Handle";
        case XMSErrSOffInv:
            return "Invalid Source Offset";
        case XMSErrDHandInv:
            return "Invalid Destination Handle";
        case XMSErrDOffInv:
            return "Invalid Destination Offset";
        case XMSErrLenInv:
            return "Invalid Length";
        case XMSErrOverlap:
            return "Invalid move overlap";
        case XMSErrParity:
            return "Parity error";
        case XMSErrNoLock:
            return "Handle not locked";
        case XMSErrLock:
            return "Handle Locked";
        case XMSErrLockOvflo:
            return "Lock count overflo";
        case XMSErrLockFail:
            return "Lock fail";
        case XMSErrSmUMB:
            return "Smaller UMB available";
        case XMSErrNoUMB:
            return "No UMB's available";
        case XMSErrUMBInv:
            return "Invalid UMB segment";
        default:
            sprintf(buff, "Unknown error 0x%X", err);
            return buff;
            }
    }


/************************************************************************
***                                                                  ***
***     xms_demoError() -  Used by demo programs to report errors    ***
***                                                                  ***
************************************************************************/

void xms_demoError(char *function)

{

    //
    //  Report the error:
    //
    printf("Error on %s(): \"%s\"\n", function, xms_errorText(errno));
```

```
    exit(0);
}
```

The XMS assembly
language definition file

Figure 5-12 presents the source code listing to XMSDEFS.ASM. This file contains definitions used by the XMS*xx*.ASM files.

5-12 The source code listing to XMSDEFS.ASMs

```
;**************************************************
;***                                            ***
;***      XmsDefs.ASM                            ***
;***                                            ***
;***      Contains definitions for XMS routines ***
;***                                            ***
;**************************************************

;
;    Define the extended function interrupt which gives us the
;    XMS handler address:
;
XFunc          equ      2fh


;
;    Define the function code for XMS, and the two sub-codes:
;
XFuncXMS            equ      43h
XFuncXMSPres        equ      0h
XFuncXMSEntry       equ      10h


;
;    Define the XMSPresent response:
;
XMSPresent          equ      80h



;
;    Now define the 2.0 XMS function codes.
;    These are 8 bit values which are loaded into
;    AH before calling the XMS handler (the address of which
;    was determined using XFuncXMSEntry int).
;
XMSGetVersion       equ      00h
XMSAllocHMA         equ      01h
XMSFreeHMA          equ      02h
XMSGlobEnabA20      equ      03h
XMSGlobDisabA20     equ      04h
XMSLocEnabA20       equ      05h
XMSLocDisabA20      equ      06h
XMSGetA20State      equ      07h
XMSGetFreeXM        equ      08h
XMSAllocXM          equ      09h
XMSFreeXM           equ      0ah
XMSMoveXM           equ      0bh
```

```
XMSLockXM        equ    0ch
XMSUnlockXM      equ    0dh
XMSGetHandInfo   equ    0eh
XMSResizeXM      equ    0fh
XMSAllocUM       equ    10h
XMSFreeUM        equ    11h
;
;    Now define the XMS error codes:
;
XMSErrOK         equ    00h    ; No error
XMSErrUnimp      equ    80h    ; Unimplemented function
XMSErrVDISK      equ    81h    ; VDISK device detected
XMSErrA20        equ    82h    ; A20 error
XMSErrNoHMA      equ    90h    ; HMA does not exist
XMSErrHMAInUse   equ    91h    ; HMA already in use
XMSErrHMAMin     equ    92h    ; HMA space req. < /HMAMIN= parameter
XMSErrHMANotAll  equ    93h    ; HMA not allocated
XMSErrA20Enab    equ    94h    ; A20 still enabled
XMSErrNoXMLeft   equ    0A0h   ; All XM allocated
XMSErrNoHandles  equ    0A1h   ; All handles are allocated
XMSErrHandInv    equ    0A2h   ; Invalid handle
XMSErrSHandInv   equ    0A3h   ; Invalid Source Handle
XMSErrSOffInv    equ    0A4h   ; Invalid Source Offset
XMSErrDHandInv   equ    0A5h   ; Invalid Dest Handle
XMSErrDOffInv    equ    0A6h   ; Invalid Dest Offset
XMSErrLenInv     equ    0A7h   ; Invalid Length
XMSErrOverlap    equ    0A8h   ; Invalid move overlap
XMSErrParity     equ    0A9h   ; Parity error
XMSErrNoLock     equ    0AAh   ; Handle not locked
XMSErrLock       equ    0ABh   ; Handle Locked
XMSErrLockOvflo  equ    0ACh   ; Lock count overflo
XMSErrLockFail   equ    0ADh   ; Lock fail
XMSErrSmUMB      equ    0B0h   ; Smaller UMB available
XMSErrNoUMB      equ    0B1h   ; No UMB's available
XMSErrUMBInv     equ    0B2h   ; Invalid UMB segment


;
;   Define the Bios interrupt and function codes
;
XMSBios          equ    15h


;
;   Define the two function codes
;
XMSBiosXMMove    equ    87h    ; Move a block of XMS
XMSBiosXMSize    equ    88h    ; Get size of extended memory


;
;   Define the access byte
;
XMSBiosAccess    equ    93h    ; The "correct" access byte
```

Initialize the XMS interface

Function XMS_Xms::init initializes XMS for use by your program. It should be called before any other XMS library functions are called. XMS_Xms::init() calls xms_init(), defined in XMSINIT.ASM.

Figure 5-13 presents the source code listing to XMSINIT.ASM.

Function XMS_Xms::init()

```
XMS_Xms    xms;

error= xms.init();
```

5-13 The source code listing to XMSINIT.ASM

```
;*****************************************************************
;***      XMSINIT.ASM                                     ***
;***                                                      ***
;***      int xms_init()                                  ***
;***                                                      ***
;***      Initializes the XMS interface. Returns a zero   ***
;***      if interface successfully initialized.          ***
;***                                                      ***
;*****************************************************************

;----------------------------------------
;
; Declare memory model and language
;

        .Model   Large,C

;----------------------------------------
;
; Include xms definition file
;

        include xmsdefs.asm

;----------------------------------------
;
; Declare error WORD as extrn to this
; module
;

        extrn    errno:WORD

;----------------------------------------
;
; Declare function as PUBLIC
```

5-13 Continued.

```
;

        public  xms_init
        public  xmsHandler

        .Data

;
;   Define the xmsHandler address which will be used
;   for calls to XMS.
;
xmsHandler      dd      xms_defaultHandler

;---------------------------------------
;
; Begin code segment
;

        .Code

xms_init    proc
        mov     ah,XFuncXMS     ; XMS functions
        mov     al,XFuncXMSPres ; Determine is XMS present
        int     XFunc           ; Call extended functions

        cmp     al,XMSPresent   ; See if it's there
        jne     noXMS           ; Nope, return an error
    ;
    ;   It's there, so let's get the handler address:
    ;
        mov     ah,XFuncXMS     ; XMS functions
        mov     al,XFuncXMSEntry; Get handler entry point
        int     XFunc           ; Call extended functions

        mov     word ptr xmsHandler,bx      ; Handler offset
        mov     word ptr xmsHandler+2,es    ; Handler segment

        mov     ax,XMSErrOK     ; no error
        ret

noXMS:
        mov     ax,XMSErrUnimp  ; No XMS (Unimplemented function)
        mov     errno,ax        ; Copy to errno
        ret

xms_init    endp                ; end of procedure


;
;   The xms_default_handler is used so that a call to
;   xmsHandler before XMS is initialized will return an
;   error. This is replaced by the actual handler when
;   xms_init is called.
;
xms_defaultHandler      proc

        xor     ax,ax           ; ax to zero means error
        mov     bl,XMSErrUnimp  ; Unimplemented function
```

```
        ret

xms_defaultHandler        endp

        End                     ; end of source file
```

Get the XMS version number

Function XMS_Xms::getVersion() returns, via WORD pointers, 16-bit BCD numbers representing the versions numbers of the XMS and the XMM, and a flag indicating the existence of the HMA. This function calls xms_getVersion(), defined in XMS00.ASM.

Figure 5-14 presents the source code listing to XMS00.ASM.

Function XMS_Xms::getVersion()

```
XMS_Xms     xms;
WORD        xmsVersion;
WORD        xmmVersion;
WORD        hmaFlag;

error= xms.getVersion(&xmsVersion, &xmmVersion, &hmaFlag);
```

where

xmsVersion   Receives the XMS version number
xmmVersion   Receives the XM Manager version number
hmaFlag   Receives a value of 1 if the HMA exists and 0 if the HMA does not
             exist

5-14 The source code listing to XMS00.ASM

```
;***************************************************************
;***     XMS00.ASM                                          ***
;***                                                        ***
;***     int xms_getVersion(WORD *xms_version,              ***
;***                        WORD *xmm_version,              ***
;***                        WORD *hma_flag);                ***
;***                                                        ***
;***     Returns the version number of the XMS, the XMM,    ***
;***     and indicates whether HMA is available.            ***
;***                                                        ***
;***************************************************************

        .model  large,C

        include xmsdefs.asm

        extrn   errno:WORD
        extrn   xmsHandler:DWord

;
;   Define entry point
```

```
;
        public   xms_getVersion

        .code

xms_getVersion  proc    xmsVer:Far Ptr Word, xmmVer: Far Ptr Word, HMAFlag:
Far Ptr Word

        mov     ah,XMSGetVersion        ; Function code
        call    xmsHandler              ; call the guy

        or      ax,ax                   ; AX=0 means error
        jz      errorReturn

;
;       Save BX, which has the XMM version.
;
        mov     cx,bx


;
;       Now return the values.
;
        les     bx,xmsVer
        mov     es:[bx],ax              ; XMS version returned
        les     bx,xmmVer
        mov     es:[bx],cx              ; XMM version returned
        les     bx,HMAFlag
        mov     es:[bx],dx              ; HMA indicator

        mov     ax,XMSErrOK             ; No error
        ret

errorReturn:
        mov     al,bl                   ; Move error code to AL
        xor     ah,ah                   ; Zero extend to 16 bits
        mov     errno,ax                ; Copy to errno
        ret

xms_getVersion  endp                    ; end of procedure

        end
```

Allocate the HMA (High Memory Area)

Function XMS_HMA::allocHMA() attempts to reserve the HMA for the calling program. The XMS_HMA object that is the target of the call will record the fact that the HMA has been allocated. When the object is destroyed, the HMA will be released. For this reason, some care must be taken in choosing where to define the XMS_HMA object. If the HMA will be temporarily used by one routine, it is appropriate to define the object locally to that routine. If the HMA will be used throughout the program, it is best to define the XMS_HMA object as a global. This function calls xms_alloc HMA(), defined in XMS01.ASM.

Figure 5-15 presents the source code listing XMS01.ASM.

Function XMS_HMA::allocHMA()

```
XMS_HMA    hma;
WORD       hmaBytes;

error= hma.allocHMA(hmaBytes);
```

where

hmaBytes Holds 0×FFFF if caller is application program, number of
bytes required if caller is TSR

5-15 The source code listing to XMS01.ASM

```
;******************************************************************
;***     XMS01.ASM                                         ***
;***                                                       ***
;***     int xms_allocHMA(WORD hmaBytes)                   ***
;***                                                       ***
;***     Allocates the High Memory Area to the program.    ***
;***     HmaBytes specifies the amount of HMA which the    ***
;***     the program intends to use. If it asks for a      ***
;***     sufficient amount, the request will be granted.   ***
;***                                                       ***
;******************************************************************
         .model  large,C

         include xmsdefs.asm

         extrn   errno:WORD
         extrn   xmsHandler:DWord

;
;   Define entry point
;
         public  xms_allocHMA

         .code

xms_allocHMA    proc    hmaBytes:Word

         mov     dx,hmaBytes      ; Amount the app expects to use
         mov     ah,XMSAllocHMA   ; Function code
         call    xmsHandler       ; call the guy

         or      ax,ax            ; AX=0 means error
         jz      errorReturn

         mov     ax,XMSErrOK      ; No error
         ret

errorReturn:
         mov     al,bl            ; Move error code to AL
         xor     ah,ah            ; Zero extend to 16 bits
         mov     errno,ax         ; Copy to errno
         ret
```

```
xms_allocHMA     endp                    ; end of procedure

        End
```

Release the HMA (High Memory Area)

Function XMS_HMA::freeHMA() allows a program to release the HMA area for use by other programs. If the target XMS_HMA object has not been the target of a previous XMS_HMA::allocHMA() call, nothing will happen. This function calls xms_freeHMA(), defined in XMS02.ASM.

Figure 5-16 presents the source code listing to XMS02.ASM.

Function XMS_HMA::freeHMA()

```
XMS_HMA     hma;

error= hma.allocHMA(0xFFFF);
...
error= hma.freeHMA();
```

5-16 The source code listing to XMS02.ASM

```
;*****************************************************************
;***      XMS02.ASM                                         ***
;***                                                        ***
;***      int xms_freeHMA()                                 ***
;***                                                        ***
;***      Frees the High Memory Area.                       ***
;***                                                        ***
;*****************************************************************

        .model  large,C

        include xmsdefs.asm

        extrn   errno:WORD
        extrn   xmsHandler:DWord

;
;   Define entry point
;
        public  xms_freeHMA

        .code

xms_freeHMA     proc

        mov     ah,XMSFreeHMA       ; Function code
        call    xmsHandler          ; call the guy

        or      ax,ax               ; AX=0 means error
```

```
        jz       errorReturn

        mov      ax,XMSErrOK         ; No error
        ret

errorReturn:
        mov      al,bl               ; Move error code to AL
        xor      ah,ah               ; Zero extend to 16 bits
        mov      errno,ax            ; Copy to errno
        ret

xms_freeHMA      endp                ; end of procedure

        End
```

Enable the global A20 line

Function XMS_HMA::globEnabA20() attempts to enable the A20 line. It should only be used by those programs that have control of the HMA. Enabling the A20 line allows overflow in address arithmetic to be used to access addresses past the 1M point. For example, with A20 enabled, the segment, offset pair 0×FFFF:0×0100 translates to physical address 0×1000F0, while with A20 disabled, it translates to physical address 0×00F0. This function calls xms_globEnabA20(), defined in XMS03.ASM.

Figure 5-17 holds the source code listing to XMS03.ASM.

Function XMS_HMA::globEnabA20()

```
XMS_HMA    hma;
error= hma.globEnabA20();
```

5-17 The source code listing to XMS03.ASM

```
;****************************************************************
;***      XMS03.ASM                                      ***
;***                                                     ***
;***      int xms_globEnabA20()                          ***
;***                                                     ***
;***      Enables the A20 address line allowing 21 bit   ***
;***      addressing and access to the HMA               ***
;***                                                     ***
;****************************************************************

        .model  large,C

        include xmsdefs.asm

        extrn   errno:WORD
        extrn   xmsHandler:DWord

;
;   Define entry point
;
```

```
        public  xms_globEnabA20

        .code

xms_globEnabA20 proc

        mov     ah,XMSGlobEnabA20    ; Function code
        call    xmsHandler           ; call the guy

        or      ax,ax                ; AX=0 means error
        jz      errorReturn

        mov     ax,XMSErrOK          ; No error
        ret

errorReturn:
        mov     al,bl                ; Move error code to AL
        xor     ah,ah                ; Zero extend to 16 bits
        mov     errno,ax             ; Copy to errno
        ret

xms_globEnabA20 endp                 ; end of procedure

        End
```

Disable the global A20 line

Function XMS_HMA::globDisabA20() attempts to disable the A20 line. It should only be used by those programs that have control of the HMA. This function calls xms_globDisabA20(), defined in XMS04.ASM.

Figure 5-18 holds the source code listing to XMS04.ASM.

Function XMS_HMA::globDisabA20()

```
XMS_HMA    hma;

error= hma.globDisabA20();
```

5-18 The source code listing to XMS04.ASM

```
;****************************************************************
;***     XMS04.ASM                                          ***
;***                                                        ***
;***     int xms_globDisabA20()                             ***
;***                                                        ***
;***     Disables the A20 address line.                     ***
;***                                                        ***
;****************************************************************

        .model  large,C

        include xmsdefs.asm

        extrn   errno:WORD
        extrn   xmsHandler:DWord
```

```
;
;   Define entry point
;
        public  xms_globDisabA20

        .code

xms_globDisabA20        proc

        mov     ah,XMSGlobDisabA20   ; Function code
        call    xmsHandler           ; call the guy

        or      ax,ax                ; AX=0 means error
        jz      errorReturn

        mov     ax,XMSErrOK          ; No error
        ret

errorReturn:
        mov     al,bl                ; Move error code to AL
        xor     ah,ah                ; Zero extend to 16 bits
        mov     errno,ax             ; Copy to errno
        ret

xms_globDisabA20        endp         ; end of procedure

        End
```

Get the current A20 line state

Function XMS_HMA::getA20State(..) checks to see if the A20 line is in fact enabled. This function calls xms_getA20State() defined in XMS 07.ASM.

Figure 5-19 presents the source code listing to XMS07.ASM.

Function XMS_HMA::getA20State()

```
XMS_HMA    hma;
WORD       a20State;

error= hma.getA20State(&a20State);
```

where

a20State   Receives 1 if A20 is enabled or 0 if A20 is disabled

5-19 The source code listing to XMS07.ASM

```
;***************************************************************
;***     XMS07.ASM                                          ***
;***                                                        ***
;***     int xms_getA20State(WORD *a20State)                ***
;***                                                        ***
;***     Returns the enable status of the A20 line.         ***
;***     A20State is TRUE (1) on return if A20 is enabled.  ***
```

5-19 Continued.

```
;***        otherwise it is FALSE (0).                          ***
;***                                                            ***
;****************************************************************

        .model  large,C

        include xmsdefs.asm

        extrn   errno:WORD
        extrn   xmsHandler:DWord

;
;   Define entry point
;
        public  xms_getA20State

        .code

xms_getA20State proc     a20State:Far Ptr Word

        mov     ah,XMSGetA20State   ; Function code
        call    xmsHandler          ; call the guy

        or      ax,ax               ; AX=0 may mean error
        jnz     goodReturn          ; AX<>0 means A20 enabled
        or      bl,bl               ; BL<>0 means error
        jnz     errorReturn

goodReturn:
        les     bx,a20State         ; Address to return result
        mov     es:[bx],ax          ; Flag gives A20 state
        mov     ax,XMSErrOK         ; No error
        ret

errorReturn:
        mov     al,bl               ; Move error code to AL
        xor     ah,ah               ; Zero extend to 16 bits
        mov     errno,ax            ; Copy to errno
        ret

xms_getA20State endp                ; end of procedure

        End
```

Get amount of free extended memory

Function XMS_HMA::getFreeXM() returns the total amount of free XMS
and the largest free XMS block in kilobytes. This function calls xms_get
FreeXM() defined in XMS08.ASM.

Figure 5-20 presents the source code listing to XMS08.ASM.

Function XMS_HMA::getFreeXM()

```
XMS_HMA    hma;
```

```
WORD        totalFree;
WORD        largestFree;

error= hma.getFreeXM(&totalFree, &largestFree);
```

where

totalFree   **Receives the total free XMS in kilobytes**
largestFree **Receives the largest free XMS block in kilobytes**

5-20 The source code listing to XMS08.ASM

```
;******************************************************************
;***    XMS08.ASM                                           ***
;***                                                        ***
;***    int xms_getFreeXM()                                 ***
;***                                                        ***
;***    Queries the amount of extended memory available.    ***
;***                                                        ***
;******************************************************************

        .model  large,C

        include xmsdefs.asm

        extrn   errno:WORD
        extrn   xmsHandler:DWord

;
;   Define entry point
;
        public  xms_getFreeXM

        .code

xms_getFreeXM   proc    total:Far Ptr Word, largest: Far Ptr Word

        mov     ah,XMSGetFreeXM     ; Function code
        call    xmsHandler          ; call the guy

        or      ax,ax               ; AX=0 means error
        jz      errorReturn

;
;   Now return the values.
;
        les     bx,total
        mov     es:[bx],dx          ; total free memory in KB
        les     bx,largest
        mov     es:[bx],ax          ; largest free block

        mov     ax,XMSErrOK         ; No error
        ret

errorReturn:
        mov     al,bl               ; Move error code to AL
        xor     ah,ah               ; Zero extend to 16 bits
        mov     errno,ax            ; Copy to errno
```

```
        ret
xms_getFreeXM    endp                    ; end of procedure

        End
```

Allocating an extended memory block

Function XMS_XmBlk.allocXM() requests a block of XMS memory in kilobytes and initializes the target XMS_XmBlk with the block's handle. If the XMS_XmBlk object is destroyed, the associated XMS block will be freed, unless it has already been freed. For this reason some care must be taken in defining the object. If it is defined locally to a function, the associated block will be released when the function is exited. In order to pass a block out of a function, the object must be allocated from the heap via the "new" operator. This function calls xms_allocXM(), defined in XMS09.ASM.

Figure 5-21 presents the source code listing to XMS09.ASM.

Xms_XmBlk::allocXM()

```
XMS_XmBlk    block;

error= block.allocXM();
```

where

    blockSize **The number of kilobytes of XMS memory to allocate**

5-21 The source code listing to XMS09.ASM

```
;*****************************************************************
;***    XMS09.ASM                                         ***
;***                                                      ***
;***    int xms_allocXM(WORD blockSize, WORD *handle)     ***
;***                                                      ***
;***    Allocates a block of extended memory blockSize KB  ***
;***    long which can be referenced via handle.          ***
;***                                                      ***
;*****************************************************************

        .model  large,C

        include xmsdefs.asm

        extrn   errno:WORD
        extrn   xmsHandler:DWord

;
;   Define entry point
;
        public  xms_allocXM

        .code
```

```
xms_allocXM      proc      blockSize:Word, handle: Far Ptr Word

        mov       dx,blockSize        ; size in KB of block
        mov       ah,XMSAllocXM       ; Function code
        call      xmsHandler          ; call the guy

        or        ax,ax               ; AX=0 means error
        jz        errorReturn

        les       bx,handle
        mov       es:[bx],dx          ; new handle

        mov       ax,XMSErrOK         ; No error
        ret

errorReturn:
        mov       al,bl               ; Move error code to AL
        xor       ah,ah               ; Zero extend to 16 bits
        mov       errno,ax            ; Copy to errno
        ret

xms_allocXM      endp                 ; end of procedure

        End
```

Free an extended memory block

Function XMS_XmBlk::freeXM() frees a previously allocated XMS memory block. If the target XMS_XmBlk object does not reference an XMS block, nothing happens. This function calls xms_freeXM(), defined in XMS0A. ASM.

Figure 5-22 presents the source code listing to XMS0A.ASM.

Function XMS_XmBlk::freeXM()
```
XMS_XmBlk    block;
error= block.allocXM(20);
...
error= block.freeXM();
```

5-22 The source code listing to XMS0A.ASM

```
;****************************************************************
;***      XMS0A.ASM                                         ***
;***                                                        ***
;***      int xms_freeXM(WORD handle)                       ***
;***                                                        ***
;***      Frees an exteded memory block referred to by      ***
;***      handle.                                           ***
;***                                                        ***
;****************************************************************

        .model    large,C

        include xmsdefs.asm

        extrn     errno:WORD
```

```
        extrn     xmsHandler:DWord

;
;   Define entry point
;
        public  xms_freeXM

        .code

xms_freeXM      proc     handle:Word

        mov     dx,handle             ; get the block's handle
        mov     ah,XMSFreeXM          ; Function code
        call    xmsHandler            ; call the guy

        or      ax,ax                 ; AX=0 means error
        jz      errorReturn

        mov     ax,XMSErrOK           ; No error
        ret

errorReturn:
        mov     al,bl                 ; Move error code to AL
        xor     ah,ah                 ; Zero extend to 16 bits
        mov     errno,ax              ; Copy to errno
        ret

xms_freeXM      endp                  ; end of procedure

        End
```

Copy an extended memory block

Function XMS_Xms::moveXM() attempts to transfer data from one location to another location. Although it is most commonly used to move memory between conventional memory and extended memory it can also be used for memory moves within conventional memory or extended memory. A special XMS_XmBlk is defined for use by this function called xms_realMem. Using this as a source (or target) indicates that the source (or target) is in real memory as opposed to extended memory. This function calls xms_moveXM(), defined in XMS0B.ASM.

Figure 5-23 presents the source code listing to XMS0B.ASM.

Function XMS_Xms.moveXM()

```
XMS_Xms      xms;
XMS_XmBlk    destBlk;
XMS_XmBlk    srcBlk;
DWORD        destOff;
DWORD        srcOff;
DWORD        length;
```

```
error= xms.moveXM(destBlk, destOff, srcBlk, srcOff, length);
```

where

destBlk   The destination XMS_XmBlk. For real memory, use xms_realMem.

destOff   The offset into the destination block. For real memory, it is the physical address (Segment*16 + Offset).

srcBlk   The source XMS_XmBlk. For real memory, use xms_realMem.

srcOff   The offset into the source block. For real memory, it is the physical address (Segment*16 + Offset).

5-23   The source code listing to XMS0B.ASM

```
;****************************************************************
;***      XMS0B.ASM                                         ***
;***                                                        ***
;***      int xms_moveXM(XMS_move_packet *packet)           ***
;***                                                        ***
;***      Frees an exteded memory block referred to by      ***
;***      handle.                                           ***
;***                                                        ***
;****************************************************************

        .model  large,C

        include xmsdefs.asm

        extrn   errno:WORD
        extrn   xmsHandler:DWord
;
;    Define entry point
;
        public  xms_moveXM

        .code

xms_moveXM      proc    packet:Far Ptr Word

    ;   We are required to pass the packet address in DS:SI.
    ;   As a result, we need to save DS. Further, we need to
    ;   copy DS to ES, so that we can find the address of the
    ;   xmsHandler when we need it.

        push    si                  ; Save SI

        push    ds                  ; Move DS to ES
        pop     es
        lds     si,packet           ; DS:SI gets packet address

        mov     ah,XMSMoveXM        ; Function code
        call    es:xmsHandler       ; call the guy

        push    es                  ; restore DS
        pop     ds

        or      ax,ax               ; AX=0 means error
        jz      errorReturn
```

5-23 Continued.

```
        mov     ax,XMSErrOK         ; No error
        pop     si                  ; Restore SI
        ret

errorReturn:
        mov     al,bl               ; Move error code to AL
        xor     ah,ah               ; Zero extend to 16 bits
        mov     errno,ax            ; Copy to errno
        pop     si                  ; Restore SI
        ret

xms_moveXM      endp                ; end of procedure

        End
```

Lock an extended memory block

Function `XMS_XmBlk::lockXM()` locks an extended memory block so it may not be moved in physical memory. The 32-bit physical address is returned. This function calls `xms_lockXM()`, defined in XMS0C.ASM.

Figure 5-24 presents the source code listing to XMS0C.ASM.

Function XMS_XmBlk::lockXM()

```
XMS_XmBlk       block;
DWORD           physAddr

error= block.lockXM(&physAddr);
```

where

physAddr   Receives the 32-bit base address of the XMS block

5-24 The source code listing to XMS0C.ASM

```
;****************************************************************
;***      XMS0C.ASM                                         ***
;***                                                        ***
;***      int xms_lockXM(WORD handle, DWORD *physAddr)      ***
;***                                                        ***
;***      Locks an extended memory block, preventing it from ***
;***      moving in physical memory, and returns its        ***
;***      physical address.                                 ***
;***                                                        ***
;****************************************************************

        .model  large,C

        include xmsdefs.asm

        extrn   errno:WORD
        extrn   xmsHandler:DWord

;
;   Define entry point
;
```

```
            public  xms_lockXM

            .code

xms_lockXM       proc      handle:Word, physAddr: Far Ptr DWord

       mov      dx,handle              ; handle of block to lock
       mov      ah,XMSLockXM           ; Function code
       call     xmsHandler             ; call the guy

       or       ax,ax                  ; AX=0 means error
       jz       errorReturn

       mov      ax,bx                  ; Save LSW ofphysical address
       les      bx,physAddr            ; Get addr of long return val
       mov      es:[bx],ax             ; LSW physical address
       mov      es:[bx+2],dx           ; MSW physical address

       mov      ax,XMSErrOK            ; No error
       ret

errorReturn:
       mov      al,bl                  ; Move error code to AL
       xor      ah,ah                  ; Zero extend to 16 bits
       mov      errno,ax               ; Copy to errno
       ret

xms_lockXM       endp                  ; end of procedure

            End
```

Unlock an extended memory block

Function XMS_Xms.unlockXM() unlocks an extended memory block so it
may be moved in physical memory. This function calls xms_unlockXM(),
defined in XMS0D.ASM.

Figure 5-25 presents the source code listing to XMS0D.ASM

Function XMS_XmBlk.unlockXM()

```
XMS_XmBlk    block;
DWORD        physAddr;

error= block.lockXM(&physAddr);
...
error= block.unlockXM();
```

5-25 The source code listing to XMS0D.ASM

```
;****************************************************************
;***     XMS0D.ASM                                          ***
;***                                                        ***
;***     int xms_unlockXM(WORD handle)                      ***
;***                                                        ***
;***     Unlocks a previously locked memory block.          ***
```

5-25 Continued.

```
;***                                                             ***
;*****************************************************************
        .model  large,C

        include xmsdefs.asm

        extrn   errno:WORD
        extrn   xmsHandler:DWord

;
;   Define entry point
;
        public  xms_unlockXM

        .code

xms_unlockXM    proc    handle:Word

        mov     dx,handle           ; handle of block to lock
        mov     ah,XMSUnlockXM      ; Function code
        call    xmsHandler          ; call the guy

        or      ax,ax               ; AX=0 means error
        jz      errorReturn

        mov     ax,XMSErrOK         ; No error
        ret

errorReturn:
        mov     al,bl               ; Move error code to AL
        xor     ah,ah               ; Zero extend to 16 bits
        mov     errno,ax            ; Copy to errno
        ret

xms_unlockXM    endp                ; end of procedure

        End
```

Get extended memory block information

Function XMS_XmBlk::getHandleInfo() returns the target block's lock count, the total number of free extended memory block handles, and the block's length in kilobytes. This function calls xms_getHandleInfo(), defined in XMS0E.ASM.

Figure 5-26 presents the source code listing to XMS0E.ASM.

Function XMS_XmBlk::getHandleInfo()

```
XMS_XmBlk    block;
WORD         blockSize;
WORD         handlesLeft;
WORD         lockCount;
```

```
        error= block.getHandInfo(&blockSize,
                            &handlesLeft, &lockCount);
```

where

blockSize   Receives the extended memory block size in kilobytes
handlesLeft Receives the number of free XMS handles
lockCount   Receives block's lock count

5-26   The source code listing to XMS0E.ASM

```
;******************************************************************
;***      XMSOE.ASM                                        ***
;***                                                       ***
;***      int    xms_getHandInfo(WORD handle,              ***
;***                        WORD *blockSize,               ***
;***                        WORD *handlesLeft,             ***
;***                        WORD *lockCount)               ***
;***                                                       ***
;***      Gets information about an allocated XM block.    ***
;***                                                       ***
;******************************************************************

        .model  large,C

        include xmsdefs.asm

        extrn   errno:WORD
        extrn   xmsHandler:DWord
;
;   Define entry point
;
        public  xms_getHandInfo

        .code

xms_getHandInfo proc     handle:Word, blSz:Far Ptr Word, nHand:Far Ptr Word, locks:Far Ptr Word

        mov     dx,handle          ; get the handle
        mov     ah,XMSGetHandInfo  ; Function code
        call    xmsHandler         ; call the guy

        or      ax,ax              ; AX=0 means error
        jz      errorReturn

    ;
    ;   Now return the values.
    ;
        mov     cx,bx              ; save BH and BL contents
        les     bx,blSz            ; Return the block size (KB)
        mov     es:[bx],dx

        les     bx,nHand           ; Return the number of free handles
        mov     al,cl              ; Zero extend to 16 bits
        xor     ah,ah
        mov     es:[bx],ax

        les     bx,locks           ; Return the number of locks on block
```

```
        mov     al,ch              ; Zero extend to 16 bits
        xor     ah,ah
        mov     es:[bx],ax

        mov     ax,XMSErrOK        ; No error
        ret

errorReturn:
        mov     al,bl              ; Move error code to AL
        xor     ah,ah              ; Zero extend to 16 bits
        mov     errno,ax           ; Copy to errno
        ret

xms_getHandInfo    endp            ; end of procedure

        End
```

Resize an extended memory block

Function XMS_XmBlk::resizeXM() alters the size of a previously allocated extended memory block. This function calls xms_resizeXM(), defined in XMS0F.ASM.

Figure 5-27 presents the source code listing to XMS0F.ASM.

Function XMS_XmBlk::resizeXM()

```
XMS_XmBlk    block;
WORD         newSize;
error= block.allocXM(1);
error= block.resizeXM(newSize);
```

where

newSize Contains the new size for the extended memory block in kilobytes

5-27 The source code listing to XMS0F.ASM

```
;****************************************************************
;***     XMS0F.ASM                                         ***
;***                                                       ***
;***     int xms_resizeXM(WORD handle, WORD newSize)       ***
;***                                                       ***
;***     Changes the size of an already allocated block.   ***
;***                                                       ***
;****************************************************************

        .model  large,C

        include xmsdefs.asm

        extrn   errno:WORD
```

```
        extrn    xmsHandler:DWord

;
;    Define entry point
;
        public   xms_resizeXM

        .code

xms_resizeXM      proc     handle:Word, newSize:Word

        mov     dx,handle            ; get handle
        mov     bx,newSize           ; new block size
        mov     ah,XMSResizeXM       ; Function code
        call    xmsHandler           ; call the guy

        or      ax,ax                ; AX=0 means error
        jz      errorReturn

        mov     ax,XMSErrOK          ; No error
        ret

errorReturn:
        mov     al,bl                ; Move error code to AL
        xor     ah,ah                ; Zero extend to 16 bits
        mov     errno,ax             ; Copy to errno
        ret

xms_resizeXM      endp               ; end of procedure

        End
```

Allocate an Upper Memory Block (UMB)

Function `XMS_UmBlk::allocUM()` requests a free upper memory block (in 16-byte paragraphs) and returns a pointer to the UMB and its actual size 16-byte paragraphs. The `XMS_UmBlk` object that is the target of this call becomes associated with the new UMB. When the object is destroyed, the UMB is released. Care must be taken not to use the address returned by this call outside the scope of the `XMS_UmBlk`. If a block is to be passed outside of a routine, the `XMS_UmBlk` should be allocated from the heap via the "new" operator. This function calls `xms_allocUM()`, defined in XMS 10.ASM.

Figure 5-28 presents the source code listing to XMS10.ASM.

Function XMS_UmBlk::allocUM()

```
XMS_UmBlk    umBlock;
WORD         size;
char         *address;
WORD         actualSize;

error= umBlock.allocUM(size, &address, &actualSize);
```

where

size   The amount of UM desired in 16-byte paragraphs
address   Receives a pointer to the allocated UMB
actualSize   Receives the actual size of the allocated UMB in 16-byte
                        paragraphs

5-28   The source code listing to XMS10.ASM

```
;*****************************************************************
;***     XMS10.ASM                                        ***
;***                                                      ***
;***     int xms_allocUM(WORD blockSize,                  ***
;***                     void **address,                  ***
;***                     WORD *actualSize)                ***
;***                                                      ***
;***     Allocates a block of upper memory blockSize      ***
;***     paragraphs long. On successful return, address has ***
;***     the address of the block. If there is not enough ***
;***     memory, actual size gives largest chunk available. ***
;***                                                      ***
;*****************************************************************

        .model  large,C

        include xmsdefs.asm

        extrn   errno:WORD
        extrn   xmsHandler:DWord

;
;   Define entry point
;
        public  xms_allocUM

        .code

xms_allocUM     proc    blockSize:Word, address:Far Ptr DWord, actual:Far Ptr Word

        mov     dx,blockSize        ; size in KB of block
        mov     ah,XMSAllocUM       ; Function code
        call    xmsHandler          ; call the guy

        or      ax,ax               ; AX=0 means error
        jz      errorReturn

        mov     ax,bx               ; Save returned segment #
        les     bx,address
        xor     cx,cx               ; Get a zero for the offset
        mov     es:[bx],cx          ; offset
        mov     es:[bx+2],ax        ; segment

        les     bx,actual           ; Return the actual size
        mov     es:[bx],dx

        mov     ax,XMSErrOK         ; No error
        ret
```

```
errorReturn:
        mov     al,bl               ; Move error code to AL
        xor     ah,ah               ; Zero extend to 16 bits
        mov     errno,ax            ; Copy to errno

        cmp     ax,XMSErrSmUMB      ; See if there's a smaller UMB
        je      errCommon           ; There is DX has it's size

        xor     dx,dx               ; Indicate size is zero

errCommon:
        les     bx,actual          ; Return the largest block size
        mov     es:[bx],dx

        ret

xms_allocUM     endp                ; end of procedure

        End
```

Release an Upper Memory Block (UMB)

Function XMS_UmBlk::freeUM() frees a previously allocated UMB. This function calls xms_freeUM(), defined in XMS11.ASM.

Figure 5-29 presents the source code listing to XMS11.ASM.

Function XMS_UmBlk::freeUM()

```
XMS_UmBlk     umBlock;

End

WORD          size;
char          *address;
WORD          actualSize;

error= umBlock.allocUM(size, &address, &actualSize);
...
error= umBlock.freeUM();
```

5-29 The source code listing to XMS11.ASM

```
****************************************************************
;***    XMS11.ASM                                           ***
;***                                                        ***
;***    int xms_freeUM(void *address)                       ***
;***                                                        ***
;***    Frees a previously allocated Upper Memory Block     ***
;***                                                        ***
;****************************************************************
```

5-29 Continued.

```
        .model  large,C

        include xmsdefs.asm

        extrn   errno:WORD
        extrn   xmsHandler:DWord

;
;   Define entry point
;
        public  xms_freeUM

        .code
xms_freeUM      proc    addressLo:Word, addressHi:Word

        mov     ax,addressLo        ; Get offset
        or      ax,ax               ; See if it's zero (better be)
        jnz     offsetError         ; It's no good

        mov     dx,addressHi        ; Block segment address
        mov     ah,XMSFreeUM        ; Function code
        call    xmsHandler          ; call the guy

        or      ax,ax               ; AX=0 means error
        jz      errorReturn

        mov     ax,XMSErrOK         ; No error
        ret

offsetError:
        mov     bl,XMSErrUMBInv     ; bogus UMB

errorReturn:
        mov     al,bl               ; Move error code to AL
        xor     ah,ah               ; Zero extend to 16 bits
        mov     errno,ax            ; Copy to errno

        ret

xms_freeUM      endp                ; end of procedure
```

Move raw XMS memory

Function `XMS_Xms::rawMove()` moves memory by use of physical addresses. Note that the memory blocks must be locked. The physical addresses are found by using the `XMS_XmBlk::lockXM()` function. This function calls `xms_rawMove()`, defined in XMSRAW.ASM.

Figure 5-30 presents the source code listing to XMSRAW.ASM.

Function XMS_Xms::rawMove()

```
DWORD   dest;
DWORD   source;
DWORD   length;
error= xms.rawMove(dest, source, length);
```

where

    dest   Gives the physical address of destination buffer

source   **Gives the physical address of source buffer**
length   **Gives the number of bytes to be moved**

5-30 The source code listing to XMSRAW.ASM

```
;****************************************************************
;***      XMSRAW.ASM                                      ***
;***                                                      ***
;***      int xms_rawMove(dest, source, length)           ***
;***                                                      ***
;***      Move a block of XM from source to dest. This call ***
;***      uses physical addresses, and so the blocks must  ***
;***      be locked.                                       ***
;***                                                      ***
;****************************************************************

        .model  large,C

        include xmsdefs.asm

        extrn   errno:WORD
        extrn   xmsHandler:DWord

;
;   Define entry point
;
        public  xms_rawMove

        .data

;
;   Define the raw move packet:
;
movePacket  dd  0,0,0,0
segLength1  dw  ?
sourceAddr  db  ?,?,?
            db  XMSBiosAccess
            dw  0
segLength2  dw  ?
destAddr    db  ?,?,?
            db  XMSBiosAccess
            dw  0,0,0,0,0,0,0,0,0

        .code
xms_rawMove     proc    destLo:Word, destHi:Word, sourceLo:Word, sourceHi:WORD, xferLen:Word

        push    si                  ; Save SI

        mov     cx,xferLen          ; length in bytes of xfer
        mov     segLength1,cx
        mov     segLength2,cx

    ;
    ;   The bios call takes a number of words to move, so
    ;   we need to convert the byte count into a word count.
    ;   we give an error if the byte count was odd. We don't
    ;   want to round up, because this may be destructive.
    ;
        clc
        rcr     cx,1                ; shift right into carry
        jc      oddLength           ; special error case

    ;
    ;   Transfer the three byte (24 bit) physical addresses:
    ;
        mov     ax,destLo           ; LSB 2 bytes of dest
        mov     Word Ptr destAddr,ax
```

The XMS assembly language definition file   **219**

```
            mov     ax,destHi           ; MSB byte of dest
            mov     destAddr+2,al

            mov     ax,sourceLo         ; LSB 2 bytes of source
            mov     Word Ptr sourceAddr,ax
            mov     ax,sourceHi         ; MSB byte of source
            mov     sourceAddr+2,al

    :
    :       We're ready to do the call:
    :
            push    ds                  ; get ES:SI = packet
            pop     es
            lea     si,movePacket

            mov     ah,XMSBiosXMMove    ; Function code
            int     XMSBios

            jc      errorReturn         ; Carry means error occurred

            mov     ax,XMSErrOK         ; No error
            pop     si                  ; restore SI
            ret

oddLength:
            mov     ah,XMSErrLenInv     ; Invalid length

errorReturn:
            mov     al,ah               ; Move error to AL
            xor     ah,ah               ; Zero extend error
            mov     errno,ax            ; Save in errno
            pop     si                  ; Restore SI
            ret

xms_rawMove     endp                    ; end of procedure

        end
```

XMS function error reporting

The function xms_errorText() allows the programmer to get the text
message associated with an error code.

Function XMS_Xms.errorText()

WORDerror;

cout << "XMS Error: " << xms_errorText(error);

where

error   Holds the error code

Summary

Chapter 5 presented the XMS 2.0 interface that facilitates the use of extended memory in your DOS real mode programs. Use the heavily documented XMS demonstration programs (FIGS. 5-1 through 5-9) as guides for understanding how the XMS related functions are used.

The XMS functions presented in this chapter are used as building blocks for the Virtual Memory Manager used in Chapter 6.

6

The Virtual
Memory Manager

This chapter begins with an overview of the Virtual Memory Manager. Once the Virtual Memory Manager has been described, the six simple-to-use VMM function prototypes for the applications programmer are presented. The VMM demonstration programs follow, and the chapter ends with the full source code for the VMM's internal operations.

The VMM presented in this last chapter is quite sophisticated in its operation. If you don't quite catch all the VMM concepts in the first reading, be patient. You'll catch on to what's happening in the VMM in time.

An overview of the
Virtual Memory Manager

A Virtual Memory Manager (VMM) facilitates a program's use of all the available memory in its host computer system. For purposes of this chapter, "all the memory" means all the unallocated conventional memory, EMS, XMS and hard disk space. This unallocated space will be referred to as the "memory pool."

The memory pool

Conventional memory
Unallocated EMS
Unallocated XMS
Unallocated hard disk

Let's say you need to work with 5Mb of data. It's pretty obvious that conventional memory will not fill the bill. Suppose your computer's memory pool is over 5Mb. Managing the way your 5Mb of data is dispersed in the memory pool can become quite nightmarish. What data is held in conventional memory? What data is held in EMS? What data is held in XMS? What data is held on disk?

The VMM isolates you from these hairy memory pool management requirements. It allows you to work with large amounts of data by using a few simple functions. Pretty nifty, indeed.

Overview of the VMM's architecture

The purpose of this overview is to give you a feel for the basic design principles of the VMM. This discussion is designed to help you visualize how the VMM system operates. The demonstration programs will show the simple VMM interface in use, and the heavily documented VMM source code will explain the nitty gritty of VMM system.

One of the first decisions that had to be made centered on the size of the memory pages we were going to use in the VMM. The page is the basic unit of virtual memory. Although we considered using pages as small as 2K, ultimately we decided that 16K was best as it greatly simplified the building of the VMM. The 16K unit proves to be the least common multiple of EMS, XMS, and disk page sizes.

VMM page size

16K page size

Once you have initialized the VMM, the next task is to allocate blocks of virtual memory (via a VMM function) where data can be stored. The VMM lets you wire virtual memory into conventional memory. Wiring an area of virtual memory means that you are bringing it into conventional memory where the data in the page is available to be read or written.

Unwiring a page makes it unavailable for reading or writing data and makes buffer space available for wiring other pages. If you want to write data to or read data from the unwired page, you must wire it again. An area of virtual memory may be wired and unwired an unlimited number of times.

When you request wiring an area, the pages covered by that area must be wired. Note that if even one byte of the area resides in a given page, that page must be wired.

Wiring a page

Imports a 16K page to memory where data may be read or written.

Unwiring a page

Making a page unavailable for reading or writing data.

If you attempt to wire a new area from your VMM allocated memory block and there is no room, one of the VMM unwired pages will be kicked out of the buffer. If there isn't enough buffer space to wire the area, you will receive an error.

For purposes of this chapter, conventional memory is called *fast memory*. EMS and XMS are called *slow memory*. Disk memory is called *slowest memory*.

Memory access speed

Fast   ->   Conventional
Slow   ->   EMS, XMS
Slowest ->   Disk

The rule of thumb for 16K page location management is called the Least Recently Used (LRU) rule. When the VMM needs to throw an unwired page out of memory, it chooses the least recently used. The theory is that the less recently a page was used, the less likely it is to be used in the near future. If EMS and XMS are filled, then the LRU page in slow memory goes to disk and is replaced by the VMM allocated fast-memory block kicked-out page. Phew . . .

Least Recently Used (LRU) principle

The less recently a 16K page was used, the higher the probability it will wind up in slowest memory. The most recently a 16K page was used, the higher the probability it will remain in fast memory.

The VMM keeps track of page status through an intricately crafted series of structures and linked lists. Fortunately for you, the entire page management scheme proves invisible to the programmer using the VMM. To use the VMM, you only need to use a few simple functions.

First, the prototypes for the VMM interface functions are presented, and then the demonstration programs follow. The demonstration programs will help you see the VMM in action. After the demonstration programs are presented, the complete and heavily documented source code to the VMM is presented. No secrets!

One final note: the VMM uses an error reporting system in the same fashion as the EMS and XMS functions. An error is flagged by returning True from a function. When an error has occurred, the error code can be found in the global variable `errno`.

Here is the VMM error code list.

VMM error code list

Name	Code	Meaning
VMErrOK	0	There is no error
VMErrEMS	1	There is an EMS-related error
VMErrXMS	2	There is an XMS-related error
VMErrDisk	3	There is a disk-related error
VMErrNoConv	4	No conventional memory is available
VMErrBadWire	5	There is a problem wiring a VMM area
VMErrNotWired	6	Attempted to unwire a page not wired
VMErrBounds	7	Tried to wire or unwire a page not in block

Initialize the VMM

Function `VM_Vm::init()` initializes the VMM. Looking at the function prototypes will help to facilitate its use in your programs. For detailed help, see the heavily documented demonstration program source code. If the `VM_Vm` object has been initialized and it is destroyed, the VMM system is shut down.

Function VM_Vm::init()

```
VM_Vm     vm;
DWORD     maxSpace;

error= vm.init(maxSpace);
```

where

>   `maxSpace`   The amount of conventional memory that the VMM is permitted to use for buffer space

Shut down the VMM

Function `VM_Vm::shutdown` shuts down all VMM operations and frees up the memory (both conventional, EMS, XMS, and disk) that had been allocated by the VMM. This function is also called when the `VM_Vm` object is destroyed.

Function VM_Vm::shutdown()

```
VM_Vm     vm;

error= vm.shutdown();
```

Allocate a VMM block

Function `VM_VmBlk::alloc()` allocates a block of virtual memory. Physical memory doesn't get allocated until you wire an area. The target `VM_Vm Blk` is initialized to represent the new block.

By default, the object is attached to the VM block. Thus, if the object is destroyed, the VM block is released. To override this behavior, the `VM_Vm Blk::detach()` function must be used to detach the object from the VM block.

Function VM_VmBlk.alloc()

```
VM_VmBlk   block;
DWORD      size;

error= block.alloc(size);
```

where

>   `size`   Gives the amount of virtual memory desired in bytes

Free a previously allocated VMM block

Function `VM_VmBlk::free` frees up a previously allocated block.

Function VM_VmBlk::free

```
VM_VmBlk    block;
DWORD       size;

error= block.alloc(size);
...
error= block.free();
```

Wire a VMM area for reading and writing

Function `VM_VmBlk::wire()` allows you to make a specified amount of memory from a VMM block available for reading and writing.

Function VM_VmBlk::wire()

```
VM_VmBlk    block;
DWORD       areaOffset;
DWORD       areaSize;
void        *areaAddress;

error= block.wire(areaOffset, areaSize, &areaAddress);
```

where

`areaOffset`	Gives, in bytes, the offset into the VMM block of the area that you want to access
`areaSize`	Gives, in bytes, the size of the VMM area you want to access
`areaAddress`	Receives a pointer to the conventional memory containing the wired area

Unwire a VMM page

Function `VM_VmBlk::unwire()` signals to the VMM that the specified area might be kicked out to slower memory if a new VMM area is to be wired and insufficient space is available. The buffer address returned by wiring the area becomes invalid after the area is unwired.

Function VM_VmBlk::unwire()

```
VM_VmBlk    block;
DWORD       areaOffset;
DWORD       areaSize;
int         dirty;

error= block.unwire(areaOffset, areaSize, dirty);
```

where

areaOffset   Gives, in bytes, the offset into the VMM block of the area that you want released from conventional memory

areaSize   Gives, in bytes, the size of the VMM area you want released from conventional memory

dirty   Is a flag that tells the VMM system if the area has been modified since it was wired

VMM demonstration programs

This chapter presents two demonstration programs. Great care has been taken to document the VMM functions. By examining the source code, you'll be able to easily discern how the VMM functions are used.

PROG6-1.CPP demonstrates the following operations:

- Initializing the VMM
- Allocating a block of memory via a VMM function
- Wiring a VMM page

PROG6-1 initializes the VMM with VM_Vm::init(). It then allocates some memory using VM_VmBlk::alloc(). It wires virtual memory into conventional memory using VM_VmBlk::wire() and then writes to the memory. Finally, it wires and reads what it wrote.

Figure 6-1 presents the source code listing to PROG6-1.CPP.

6-1 The source code listing to PROG6-1.CPP

```
//////////////////////////////////////
//
// prog6-1.cpp --     VM demo
//
//      This test program demonstrates
//          - vm intialization
//          - allocation
//          - wiring
//
//////////////////////////////////////

//
// include standard I/O functions
//
extern "C" {
#include <stdio.h>
#include <stdlib.h>
#include <string.h>
#include <dos.h>
}

//
//  Convenient "call" macro keeps track of error codes.
//
#define call(cond)  if ((error= (cond)) != 0)

//
```

```
// include memory management header files
//
#include "gdefs.h"
#include "vm.h"

void main()

{

    VM_Vm       vm;
    VM_VmBlk    handle;
    char        *addr;

    int         error;


    addr= NULL;
    call (vm.init(245760L)) {
        goto err;
        }

    call (handle.alloc(100000L)) {
        goto err;
        }

    //
    //  Write some text to various places in the VM block
    //
    call (handle.wire(54320L, 80L, &addr)) {
        goto err;
        }
    strcpy(addr, "     Americans are broad minded people. They'll\n");
    call (handle.unwire(54320L, 80L, TRUE)) {
        goto err;
        }

    call (handle.wire(660L, 80L, &addr)) {
        goto err;
        }
    strcpy(addr, "     accept the fact that a person can be an alcoholic,\n");
    call (handle.unwire(660L, 80L, TRUE)) {
        goto err;
        }

    call (handle.wire(9878L, 80L, &addr)) {
        goto err;
        }
    strcpy(addr, "     a dope fiend, a wife beater, and even a newspaperman,\n");
    call (handle.unwire(9878L, 80L, TRUE)) {
        goto err;
        }

    call (handle.wire(76654L, 80L, &addr)) {
        goto err;
        }
    strcpy(addr, "     but if a man doesn't drive, there's something wrong\n");
    call (handle.unwire(76654L, 80L, TRUE)) {
        goto err;
        }
    call (handle.wire(10L, 80L, &addr)) {
        goto err;
        }
```

```
strcpy(addr, "        with him.\n\n");
call (handle.unwire(10L, 80L, TRUE)) {
    goto err;
    }


call (handle.wire(24000L, 80L, &addr)) {
    goto err;
    }
strcpy(addr, "                        -- Art Buchwald\n");
call (handle.unwire(24000L, 80L, TRUE)) {
    goto err;
    }



//
//  Now let's recall the blocks.
//
call (handle.wire(54320L, 80L, &addr)) {
    goto err;
    }
printf("%s", addr);
call (handle.unwire(54320L, 80L, TRUE)) {
    goto err;
    }

call (handle.wire(660L, 80L, &addr)) {
    goto err;
    }
printf("%s", addr);
call (handle.unwire(660L, 80L, TRUE)) {
    goto err;
    }

call (handle.wire(9878L, 80L, &addr)) {
    goto err;
    }
printf("%s", addr);
call (handle.unwire(9878L, 80L, TRUE)) {
    goto err;
    }

call (handle.wire(76654L, 80L, &addr)) {
    goto err;
    }
printf("%s", addr);
call (handle.unwire(76654L, 80L, TRUE)) {
    goto err;
    }

call (handle.wire(10L, 80L, &addr)) {
    goto err;
    }
printf("%s", addr);
call (handle.unwire(10L, 80L, TRUE)) {
    goto err;
    }
call (handle.wire(24000L, 80L, &addr)) {
    goto err;
    }
```

```
    printf("%s", addr);
    call (handle.unwire(24000L, 80L, TRUE)) {
        goto err;
        }

    handle.free();

    vm.shutdown();

    return;
err:
    printf("Died: Error #%d\n", error);
}
```

PROG6-2.PAS demonstrates the following operations:

- Allocating two very large blocks of virtual memory
- Running through them twice—first initializing them, then reading them (making sure they were correctly initialized)

PROG6-2 uses the same calls as PROG6-1. However, it allocates a much larger area of virtual memory and exercises the memory manager more strenuously. It is instructive to run this program with one or both of EMS and XMS disabled to note the performance differences.

Figure 6-2 presents the source code listing to PROG6-2.CPP.

6-2 The source code listing to PROG6-2.CPP

```
//////////////////////////////////////
//
// prog6-2.c --      VM exerciser
//
//      This test program allocates two big blocks of virtual memory
//      and runs through them twice, first initializing them and then
//      reading them to make sure they were correctly initialized.
//
//////////////////////////////////////

//
// include standard I/O functions
//
#include <stdio.h>
#include <stdlib.h>
#include <string.h>
#include <dos.h>

//
// include memory management header files
//
#include "gdefs.h"
#include "vm.h"

//
```

6-2 Continued.

```
//  A handy macro for calling functions:
//
#define call(cond)  if ((error= (cond)) != 0)


VM_Vm        vm;


int     main()

{

    VM_VmBlk      handle1;
    VM_VmBlk      handle2;
    char          *addr;

    long          i;
    long          j;

    int           error;


    addr= NULL;
    call (vm.init(245760L)) {
        goto err;
        }

    call (handle1.alloc(2113536L)) {
        goto err;
        }
    call (handle2.alloc(2113536L)) {
        goto err;
        }

    for (i= 0; i < 32; i++) {
        //
        //  Wire a chunk of the first block and initialize it.
        //
        call (handle1.wire(i*65536L, 65536L, &addr)) {
            goto err;
            }
        printf("--> %2ld: wire #1, %04X:%04X\n", i,
                    FP_SEG(addr), FP_OFF(addr));

        for (j= 0; j < 65534L; j+= 8192) {
            addr[(WORD) 1L]= 0;
            addr[(WORD) 16385L]= 1;
            addr[(WORD) 32769L]= 2;
            addr[(WORD) 49153L]= 3;
            if (addr[(WORD) j]) {
                printf("Error: handle1, i= %ld, addr[j]= %d, j= %ld\n",
                    i, addr[(WORD) j], j);
                }
            addr[(WORD) j]= (char) i;
            }
        call (handle1.unwire(i*65536L, 65536L, TRUE)) {
            goto err;
            }
        printf("--> %2ld: unwire #1\n", i);
```

```
//
//   Wire a chunk of the second block and initialize it.
//
call (handle2.wire(i*65536L, 65536L, &addr)) {
    goto err;
    }
printf("--> %2ld: wire #2, %04X:%04X\n", i,
            FP_SEG(addr), FP_OFF(addr));
for (j= 0; j < 65534L; j+= 8192) {
    addr[(WORD) 1L]= 0;
    addr[(WORD) 16385L]= 1;
    addr[(WORD) 32769L]= 2;
    addr[(WORD) 49153L]= 3;
    if (addr[(WORD) j]) {
        printf("Error: handle1, i= %ld, addr[j]= %d, j= %ld\n",
            i, addr[(WORD) j], j );
        }
    addr[(WORD) j]= (char) (i + 10L);
    }
call (handle2.unwire(i*65536L, 65536L, TRUE)) {
    goto err;
    }
printf("--> %2ld: unwire #2\n", i);
    }

for (i= 0; i < 32; i++) {
//
//   Wire a chunk of the first block and make sure we get
//   the values we expect.
//
call (handle1.wire(i*65536L, 65536L, &addr)) {
    goto err;
    }
printf("<-- %2ld: wire #1, %04X:%04X\n", i,
            FP_SEG(addr), FP_OFF(addr));
printf("    %d, %d, %d, %d\n",
    addr[(WORD) 1L],
    addr[(WORD) 16385L],
    addr[(WORD) 32769L],
    addr[(WORD) 49153L]);
for (j= 0; j < 65534L; j+= 8192) {
    if (addr[(WORD) j] != (char) i) {
        printf("Error: handle1, i= %ld, addr[j]= %d, j= %ld\n",
            i, addr[(WORD) j], j );
        }
    }
call (handle1.unwire(i*65536L, 65536L, TRUE)) {
    goto err;
    }
printf("<-- %2ld: unwire #1\n", i);

//
//   Now validate a chunk of the second block.
//
call (handle2.wire(i*65536L, 65536L, &addr)) {
    goto err;
    }
printf("<-- %2ld: wire #2, %04X:%04X\n", i, FP_SEG(addr), FP_OFF(addr));
printf("    %d, %d, %d, %d\n",
    addr[(WORD) 1L],
    addr[(WORD) 16385L],
```

```
            addr[(WORD) 32769L],
            addr[(WORD) 49153L]);
    for (j= 0; j < 65534L; j+= 8192) {
        if (addr[(WORD) j] != (char) (10L + i)) {
            printf("Error: handle2, i= %ld, addr[j]= %d, j= %ld\n",
                    i, addr[(WORD) j], j);
            }
        }
    call (handle2.unwire(i*65536L, 65536L, TRUE)) {
        goto err;
        }
    printf("<-- %2ld: unwire #2\n", i);
    }


handle1.free();
handle2.free();



vm.shutdown();

return 0;
err:
    printf("Died: Error #%d\n", error);
    return 0;
}
```

The complete VMM source code listings

The VMM source code listing is broken up into five files. These files are
heavily documented and might appear complex to those uninitiated in virtual memory management techniques. Take your time when exploring the
source code. The real meat of the book falls in the source presented in this
section of the book.

Figure 6-3 presents the VM.H header file listing for the VMM. This file
defines all of the types, objects, and function prototypes externally visible
from the VMM system.

6-3 The source code listing to VM.H

```
///////////////////////////////////////
//
// vm.h
//
//  External definitions for the virtual memory module
//
///////////////////////////////////////

//
//  Define some error codes
//
```

```
#define     VMErrOK        0
#define     VMErrEMS       1
#define     VMErrXMS       2
#define     VMErrDisk      3
#define     VMErrNoConv    4
#define     VMErrBadWire   5
#define     VMErrNotWired  6
#define     VMErrBounds    7


//
//  Define the class
//
class VM_Vm {
    int     initialized;

public:
            VM_Vm() {
                initialized= FALSE;
                }

            ~VM_Vm() {
                if (initialized) {
                    this->shutdown();
                    }
                }

    int     init(DWORD maxMemory);

    int     shutdown();
    };

class VM_VmBlk {
    DWORD   handle;
    int     attached;

public:
        VM_VmBlk() {
            handle= 0;
            attached= FALSE;
            }

        VM_VmBlk(const VM_VmBlk &old) {
            handle= old.handle;
            attached= FALSE;
            }

        ~VM_VmBlk() {
            if (attached) {
                this->free();
                }
            }

    VM_VmBlk &operator=(const VM_VmBlk &rhs) {
            if (attached) {
                this->free();
                }
            handle= rhs.handle;
            attached= FALSE;
            return *this;
            }
```

```
int     alloc(DWORD size);

int     free();

int     wire(DWORD start, DWORD size, char **addr);

int     unwire(DWORD start, DWORD size, int dirty);

void    attach() {
            attached= TRUE;
            }

void    detach() {
            attached= FALSE;
            }

};
```

Figure 6-4 presents the source code listing to VMINTERN.H. This header file gives the internal types, objects, and functions for the VMM. This header file is for use only by the VMM, not users of the VMM.

6-4 The source code listing to VMINTERN.H

```
/////////////////////////////////////
//
// vmintern.h
//
//   Internal definitions for the virtual memory module
//
/////////////////////////////////////

//
//   Include the external definitions
//
#include    "vm.h"

//
//   Do a little compiler dependent stuff
//
#if     defined(MSC)

#define farmalloc(n)    halloc(n, 1)
#define farfree(p)      hfree(p)

#endif

#undef max
#undef min
#define max(a,b)        (((a) >= (b)) ? (a) : (b))
#define min(a,b)        (((a) < (b)) ? (a) : (b))

//
//   First let's define some important constants:
//
```

```
#define     VM_PAGE_SIZE          16384
#define     VM_PAGE_SHIFT         14
#define     VM_PAGE_OFFSET_MASK (VM_PAGE_SIZE-1)
#define     VM_PAGE_NUM_MASK      (~VM_PAGE_OFFSET_MASK)

#define     VM_MAX_BUFF_SPACE    131072L

//
//  Define our ENQUE macro
//
#define ENQUE_H(type, item, head, tail) \

            vm_enque  ((char *) (item), \

                      (char **) &(head),\

                      (char **) &(tail),\

                      (int) &((type *) 0)->next,\

                      (int) &((type *) 0)->prev)

#define ENQUE_T(type, item, head, tail) \

            vm_enque( (char *) (item), \

                      (char **) &(tail),\

                      (char **) &(head), \

                      (int) &((type *) 0)->prev, \

                      (int) &((type *) 0)->next)

#define DEQUE(type, item, head, tail) \

            vm_deque( (char *) (item), \

                      (char **) &(head), \

                      (char **) &(tail),  \

                      (int) &((type *) 0)->next,  cx\

                      (int) &((type *) 0)->prev)

//
//  Define the types of secondary memory
//
typedef enum {
    VM_SEC_UNALLOCATED= 0,
    VM_SEC_DISK= 1,
    VM_SEC_XMS= 2,
    VM_SEC_EMS= 3
    }   SecondaryKind;

//
//  Define the queues on which we may find a physical page.
//
typedef enum {
    VM_Q_FREE=  0,
```

```
    VM_Q_LRU=   1,
    VM_Q_WIRED= 2
    }   SecondaryQueue;

//
//  Define a free area descriptor
//
typedef struct  freeArea {

    struct freeArea    *next;         // Next free area
    struct freeArea    *prev;         // Prev free area

    DWORD              handle;        // EMS/XMS Buff addr (if appropriate)
    DWORD              start;         // Start address
    DWORD              size;          // Size of area

    }   FreeArea;


//
//  Define a conventional memory buffer descriptor.
//
typedef struct  convBuff {

    struct convBuff    *next;         // Next buffer (mru first)
    struct convBuff    *prev;         // Prev buffer

    WORD               buffSize;      // Size in pages
    char huge          *address;      // Address of buffer

    struct vmBlock     *vmBlock;      // Where the pages are from
    WORD               startPage;     // First page in buffer

    WORD               wiredPages;    // Number of wired pages

    }   ConvBuff;

//
//  A -1 convBuff means page is in PFA
//
#define PFABUFF          ((ConvBuff *) -1)

//
//  Define an EMS buffer descriptor.
//
typedef struct  emsBuff {

    struct emsBuff     *next;         // Next buffer
    struct emsBuff     *prev;

    WORD               buffSize;      // Size in pages
    EMS_EmBlk          handle;        // EMS handle

    WORD               useCount;      // Number of pages in use

    }   EmsBuff;


//
//  Define an XMS buffer descriptor.
```

```
//
typedef struct  xmsBuff {

    struct xmsBuff       *next;          // Next buffer
    struct xmsBuff       *prev;

    WORD                 buffSize;       // Size in pages
    XMS_XmBlk            handle;         // XMS handle

    WORD                 useCount;       // Number of pages in use

    }   XmsBuff;

//
//  Define the EMS page descriptor.
//
typedef struct  emsPage {

    struct emsPage       *next;          // Next EMS page (mru order)
    struct emsPage       *prev;          // Prev EMS page

    struct vmPage        *vmPage;        // Corresponding VM page

    EmsBuff              *emsBuff;       // EMS buffer descriptor
    WORD                 pageNum;        // Page in buffer

    SecondaryQueue       secondaryQueue; // Queue page is on

    }   EmsPage;

typedef struct  xmsPage {

    struct xmsPage       *next;          // Next XMS page (mru order)
    struct xmsPage       *prev;          // Prev EMS page

    struct vmPage        *vmPage;        // Corresponding VM page

    XmsBuff              *xmsBuff;       // XMS buffer descriptor
    WORD                 pageNum;        // Offset into buffer

    SecondaryQueue       secondaryQueue; // Queue page is on

    }   XmsPage;

typedef struct  diskPage {

    struct diskPage      *next;          // Next disk page
    struct diskPage      *prev;          // Prev disk page

    struct vmPage        *vmPage;        // Corresponding VM page

    WORD                 pageNum;        // Offset into file (in pages)

    }   DiskPage;

//
//  Define a vitual memory page
//
typedef struct  vmPage {

    WORD                 pageNum;        // Number of page in VM block
    SecondaryKind        secondaryKind;  // Type of secondary
```

6-4 Continued.

```
union {
    DiskPage          *disk;          // Disk secondary page
    XmsPage           *xms;           // XMS secondary page
    EmsPage           *ems;           // EMS secondary page
    }                 sec;

    ConvBuff          *convBuff;      // Conventional memory buffer
    DWORD             offset;         // Offset in buffer

    WORD              wired;          // Wire count

    unsigned          dirty:1;        // Page modified

    }   VmPage;


//
//  Define a virtual memory block.
//
typedef struct  vmBlock {

    struct vmBlock    *next;          // Next VM block
    struct vmBlock    *prev;          // Prev VM block

    WORD              size;           // Size in pages
    VmPage            *pages;         // Virtual pages

    }   VmBlock;


//
//  Define the EMS Descriptor
//
typedef struct  emsDesc {

    EMS_PageFrame     pageFrame;      // Address of Page Frame

    EmsPage           *contents[EMS_PAGE_FRAME_SIZE];
                                      // Pages in Page frame

    EmsPage           *mruPage;       // Page LRU queue
    EmsPage           *lruPage;

    EmsPage           *firstWired;    // Wired page list
    EmsPage           *lastWired;

    FreeArea          *firstFree;     // Free page chain
    FreeArea          *lastFree;

    EmsBuff           *firstBuff;     // Buffer queue
    EmsBuff           *lastBuff;

    EMS_EmBlk         pageBuffHandle; // One page handle for buffering

    WORD              emsBlockSize;   // Preferred block size

    }   EmsDesc;
//
//  Define the XMS descriptor.
```

```
//
typedef struct  xmsDesc {

    XmsPage             *mruPage;       // Page LRU queue
    XmsPage             *lruPage;

    XmsPage             *firstWired;    // Wired page list
    XmsPage             *lastWired;

    FreeArea            *firstFree;     // Free page chain
    FreeArea            *lastFree;

    XmsBuff             *firstBuff;     // Buffer queue
    XmsBuff             *lastBuff;

    WORD                xmsBlockSize;   // Preferred block size

    }  XmsDesc;

//
//  Define the Disk descriptor.
//
typedef struct  diskDesc {

    DiskPage            *firstPage;     // Page queue
    DiskPage            *lastPage;

    FreeArea            *firstFree;     // Free page chain
    FreeArea            *lastFree;

    FILE                *channel;       // File channel

    DWORD               fileSize;       // Current size of file

    }  DiskDesc;

//
//  Define the conventional memory descriptor.
//
typedef struct  convDesc {

    ConvBuff            *mruBuff;       // Buffer LRU chain
    ConvBuff            *lruBuff;

    ConvBuff            *firstWired;
    ConvBuff            *lastWired;

    DWORD               spaceAvail;     // maxSpace - Memory allocated for buffers

    }  ConvDesc;

//
//  Declare some extern functions
//
extern void     vm_enque(char *item, char **head, char **tail,
                         int next_offset, int prev_offset);
extern void     vm_deque(char *item, char **head, char **tail,
                         int next_offset, int prev_offset);

extern void     vm_addFree(DWORD handle, DWORD offset, DWORD size,
                           FreeArea **firstFree, FreeArea **lastFree);
```

6-4 Continued.

```
extern void      vm_freeVmPage(VmPage *page);
extern void      vm_freeEmsPage(EmsPage *page);
extern void      vm_freeXmsPage(XmsPage *page);
extern void      vm_freeDiskPage(DiskPage *page);
extern void      vm_freeConvBuff(ConvBuff *buff);
extern void      vm_freeEmsBuff(EmsBuff *buff);
extern void      vm_freeXmsBuff(XmsBuff *buff);

extern int       vm_faultInPages(VmBlock *, WORD, WORD);
extern int       vm_faultToEMS(VmBlock *, WORD, WORD);
extern int       vm_faultToXMS(VmBlock *, WORD, WORD);
extern int       vm_faultToDisk(VmBlock *, WORD, WORD);
extern int       vm_tryMapPFA(VmBlock *, WORD, WORD);
extern int       vm_tryMapConv(VmBlock *, WORD, WORD);
extern void      vm_getEMSPages(int, EmsPage **);
extern void      vm_getXMSPages(int, XmsPage **);
extern void      vm_getDiskPages(int, DiskPage **);
extern void      vm_promoteToEMS(VmPage *, EmsPage *);
extern void      vm_promoteToXMS(VmPage *, XmsPage *);
extern void      vm_promoteToDisk(VmPage *, DiskPage *);
extern void      vm_demoteFromEMS(EmsPage *);
extern void      vm_demoteFromXMS(XmsPage *);
extern void      vm_flushVmPage(VmPage *);
extern void      vm_loadVmPage(VmPage *, ConvBuff *);
extern int       vm_freeLRUConvBuff(void);
extern void      vm_moveSecPageToWired(VmPage *);
extern void      vm_dequeSecPage(VmPage *);
extern void      vm_fatal(char *);

//
//   Now declare global data
//
extern EmsDesc         emsInf;
extern XmsDesc         xmsInf;
extern DiskDesc        diskInf;
extern ConvDesc        convInf;

extern VmBlock         *firstVmBlock;
extern VmBlock         *lastVmBlock;

extern int             emsPresent;
extern int             xmsPresent;

extern EMS_Ems         ems;
extern XMS_Xms         xms;
```

Figure 6-5 presents the source code listing to VMINIT.CPP. This source file contains the code to functions that initialize the VMM's data structures.

6-5 The source code listing to VMINIT.CPP

```
/////////////////////////////////////
//
```

```
//  vminit.cpp --     VM initialization
//
//      Initialization and termination of VM module
//
//////////////////////////////////////////

//
// include standard I/O functions
//
extern "C" {
#include <stdio.h>
#include <stdlib.h>
#include <dos.h>
}


//
// include memory management header files
//
#include "gdefs.h"
#include "xms.h"

#define Uses_EMS40
#include "ems.h"
#include "vmintern.h"


//
//   Define all of the global stuff
//
EmsDesc         emsInf;
XmsDesc         xmsInf;
DiskDesc        diskInf;
ConvDesc        convInf;

VmBlock         *firstVmBlock;
VmBlock         *lastVmBlock;

int             emsPresent;
int             xmsPresent;

XMS_Xms         xms;
EMS_Ems         ems;

VM_Vm::init(DWORD maxSpace)
{

    int             i;
    WORD            numHandles;
    WORD            totalPages;
    WORD            freePages;
    WORD            activeHandles;
    WORD            freeKXM;
    WORD            contiguousKXM;
    XMS_XmBlk       xmsHandle;
    WORD            blockSize;
    WORD            lockCount;

    //
    //   First look into initializing EMS
    //
```

```
emsInf.mruPage= NULL;
emsInf.lruPage= NULL;
emsInf.firstWired= NULL;
emsInf.lastWired= NULL;
emsInf.firstFree= NULL;
emsInf.lastFree= NULL;
emsInf.firstBuff= NULL;
emsInf.lastBuff= NULL;

emsPresent= FALSE;
if (ems.init() == EMSErrOK && ems.getStatus() == EMSErrOK) {
    emsPresent= TRUE;


    //
    //  Get the page frame address
    //
    if (ems.getPFA(&emsInf.pageFrame)) {
        return VMErrEMS;
        }

    //
    //  Indicate that the page frame area is empty
    //
    for (i= 0; i < EMS_PAGE_FRAME_SIZE; i++) {
        emsInf.contents[i]= NULL;
        }

    //
    //  Allocate a one page buffer which we will use for
    //  reading and writing pages between XMS and DISK.
    //
    //  This is to avoid spending valuable conventional memory on
    //  the buffer.
    if (emsInf.pageBuffHandle.allocEM(1)) {
        emsInf.pageBuffHandle= 0;
        }

    //
    //  Let's figure out how big blocks we should allocate.
    //  We do this by dividing the total available pages by the
    //  total available handles.
    //
    if (ems.getTotalHandles(&numHandles)) {
        //
        //  Probably not 4.0 EMS. Just assume 64 handles.
        //
        numHandles= 64;
        }
    if (ems.getNumActiveHandles(&activeHandles)) {
        vm_fatal("EMS_Ems::getNumActiveHandles");
        }
    if (ems.getFreeEM(&totalPages, &freePages)) {
        vm_fatal("EMS_Ems::getFreeEM");
        }

    emsInf.emsBlockSize= (freePages + numHandles - 1) /
                         (numHandles - activeHandles);
```

```
        emsInf.emsBlockSize= max(emsInf.emsBlockSize, 8);
        }

//
//  Now let's look at XMS.
//
xmsInf.mruPage= NULL;
xmsInf.lruPage= NULL;
xmsInf.firstWired= NULL;
xmsInf.lastWired= NULL;
xmsInf.firstFree= NULL;
xmsInf.lastFree= NULL;

xmsPresent= FALSE;
if (xms.init() == XMSErrOK) {
    xmsPresent= TRUE;

    //
    //  Let's figure out how big blocks we should allocate.
    //  We do this by dividing the total available pages by the
    //  total available handles.
    //
    //  Start by just getting a handle.
    //
    if (xms.getFreeXM(&freeKXM, &contiguousKXM)) {
        if (errno == XMSErrNoXMLeft) {
            freeKXM= 0;
            }
        else {
            vm_fatal("XMS_Xms::getFreeXM");
            }
        }

    if (freeKXM) {
        if (xmsHandle.allocXM(1)) {
            vm_fatal("XMS_XmBlk::allocXM");
            }
        if (xmsHandle.getHandInfo(&blockSize, &numHandles, &lockCount)) {
            vm_fatal("XMS_XmBlk::getHandleInfo");
            }

        freePages= freeKXM / (VM_PAGE_SIZE / XMS_PAGE_SIZE);
        xmsInf.xmsBlockSize= (freePages + numHandles - 1) / numHandles;

        xmsInf.xmsBlockSize= max(xmsInf.xmsBlockSize, 8);

        if (xmsHandle.freeXM()) {
            vm_fatal("XMS_XmBlk::freeXM");
            }
        }
    else {
        xmsInf.xmsBlockSize= 8;
        }
    }
//
//  Now initialize the disk
//
diskInf.firstPage= NULL;
diskInf.lastPage= NULL;
```

```
    diskInf.firstFree= NULL;
    diskInf.lastFree= NULL;
    diskInf.fileSize= 0;

    diskInf.channel= fopen("TMPFILE", "w+b");
    if (diskInf.channel == NULL) {
        return VMErrDisk;
        }

    //
    //   Initialize conventional memory descriptor:
    //
    convInf.mruBuff= NULL;
    convInf.lruBuff= NULL;
    convInf.firstWired= NULL;
    convInf.lastWired= NULL;
    convInf.spaceAvail= maxSpace;

    //
    //   Now initialize the VM block queue
    //
    firstVmBlock= NULL;
    lastVmBlock= NULL;

    initialized= TRUE;

    return VMErrOK;
}

int     VM_Vm::shutdown()

{

    WORD                    i;

    FreeArea            *currFreeArea;
    FreeArea            *nextFreeArea;

    ConvBuff            *currConvBuff;
    ConvBuff            *nextConvBuff;

    EmsBuff             *currEmsBuff;
    EmsBuff             *nextEmsBuff;

    XmsBuff             *currXmsBuff;
    XmsBuff             *nextXmsBuff;

    VmPage              *currVmPage;

    VmBlock             *currVmBlock;
    VmBlock             *nextVmBlock;

    //
    //   Start by going through the VM blocks.
    //
    for (currVmBlock= firstVmBlock; currVmBlock; currVmBlock= nextVmBlock)
{

        nextVmBlock= currVmBlock->next;

        //
```

```
    //  Now go through the pages for the block
    //
    for (i= 0; i < currVmBlock->size; i++) {
        currVmPage= &currVmBlock->pages[i];

        if (currVmPage->secondaryKind != VM_SEC_UNALLOCATED) {
            delete currVmPage->sec.disk;
            }
        }
    delete currVmBlock->pages;
    delete currVmBlock;
    }


//
//  Now free up the various buffers and buffer descriptors
//
for (currConvBuff= convInf.mruBuff; currConvBuff; currConvBuff= nextConvBuff) {
    nextConvBuff= currConvBuff->next;

    //
    //  Free the actual buffer
    //
    farfree((char *) currConvBuff->address);

    //
    //  Free the buffer descriptor
    //
    delete currConvBuff;
    }

for (currEmsBuff= emsInf.firstBuff; currEmsBuff; currEmsBuff= nextEmsBuff) {
    nextEmsBuff= currEmsBuff->next;

    //
    //  Free the buffer descriptor, the destructor will do the freeing
    //  of the EMS block.
    //
    delete currEmsBuff;
    }

for (currXmsBuff= xmsInf.firstBuff; currXmsBuff; currXmsBuff= nextXmsBuff) {
    nextXmsBuff= currXmsBuff->next;

    //
    //  Free the buffer descriptor, the destructor will do the freeing
    //  of the XMS block.
    //
    delete currXmsBuff;
    }

//
//  Now free various free chains.
//
for (currFreeArea= emsInf.firstFree; currFreeArea; currFreeArea= nextFreeArea) {
    nextFreeArea= currFreeArea->next;
    delete currFreeArea;
    }

for (currFreeArea= xmsInf.firstFree; currFreeArea; currFreeArea= nextFreeArea) {
    nextFreeArea= currFreeArea->next;
    delete currFreeArea;
```

The complete VMM source code listings   245

```
        }

    for (currFreeArea= diskInf.firstFree; currFreeArea; currFreeArea= nextFreeArea) {
        nextFreeArea= currFreeArea->next;
        delete currFreeArea;
        }

    //
    //  Free up the one page EMS buffer
    //
    if (emsPresent) {
        if (emsInf.pageBuffHandle.freeEM()) {
            vm_fatal("EMS_EmBlk::freeEM");
            }
        }

    //
    //  Now close the temp file and delete it.
    //
    fclose(diskInf.channel);
    unlink("TMPFILE");

    initialized= FALSE;

    //
    //  All done.
    //
    return VMErrOK;
}
```

Figure 6-6 presents the source code listing to VMUTIL.CPP. This source file contains the code to functions that maintain the linked lists that keep track of where pages are located.

6-6 The source code listing to VMUTIL.CPP

```
////////////////////////////////////////
//
// vmutil.cpp --          Utility functions for VM
//
//      vm_enque()      -- Enque to a doubly linked list
//      vm_deque()      -- Deque from a double linked list
//      vm_addFree()    -- Add to a free chain
//      vm_fatal()      -- Handles a fatal VM error
//
////////////////////////////////////////

//
//  Include basic headers
//
extern "C" {
#include <stdio.h>
#include <stdlib.h>
}

//
```

```c
//   Include memory management header files
//
#include "gdefs.h"
#include "xms.h"
#include "ems.h"
#include "vmintern.h"

//
//   Define the tres ugly OFFSET macro which takes a char * and an int
//   and gives the char * starting at int bytes from the start of
//   the structure.
//
#define OFFSET(structure, offset)   (*((char **) &(structure)[offset]))


void    vm_enque(
    char        *item,
    char        **head,
    char        **tail,
    int         next,
    int         prev)
{

    OFFSET(item, prev)= NULL;
    OFFSET(item, next)= *head;
    if (*head) {
        OFFSET(*head, prev)= item;
        }
    else {
        *tail= item;
        }
    *head= item;
}


void    vm_deque(
    char        *item,
    char        **head,
    char        **tail,
    int         next,
    int         prev)
{

    //
    //   DEQUEing an element from a list which isn't on the list
    //   can cause all kinds of problems. Let's do a sanity check.
    //
    if (OFFSET(item,prev) == NULL) {
        if (*head != item) {
            vm_fatal("deque error");
            }
        }
    else {
        if (OFFSET(OFFSET(item,prev), next) != item) {
            vm_fatal("deque error");
            }
        }

    if (OFFSET(item,next) == NULL) {
        if (*tail != item) {
            vm_fatal("deque error");
```

6-6 Continued.

```
                }
            }
        else {
            if (OFFSET(OFFSET(item,next), prev) != item) {
                vm_fatal("deque error");
                }
            }


        if (OFFSET(item, prev) == NULL) {
            *head= OFFSET(item, next);
            }
        else {
            OFFSET(OFFSET(item, prev), next)= OFFSET(item, next);
            }
        if (OFFSET(item, next) == NULL) {
            *tail= OFFSET(item, prev);
            }
        else {
            OFFSET(OFFSET(item, next), prev)= OFFSET(item, prev);
            }
}

void    vm_addFree(
    DWORD               handle,
    DWORD               start,
    DWORD               size,
    FreeArea            **head,
    FreeArea            **tail)
{

    FreeArea            *nextArea;
    FreeArea            *prevArea;
    FreeArea            *newArea;


    //
    //  Find the right place to insert it.
    //
    prevArea= NULL;
    for (nextArea= *head; nextArea; nextArea= nextArea->next) {
        if (nextArea->handle > handle ||
                nextArea->handle == handle &&
                    nextArea->start >= start + size) {
            break;
            }
        prevArea= nextArea;
        }

    //
    //  See if we merge with previous area
    //
    if (prevArea &&
            prevArea->handle == handle &&
            prevArea->start + prevArea->size == start) {
        //
        //  See if we merge with next area
        //
```

```
        if (nextArea &&
                nextArea->handle == handle &&
                start + size == nextArea->start) {
            //
            //  New area is sandwiched between prev and next.
            //  Merge them all into prev.
            //
            prevArea->size= prevArea->size + size + nextArea->size;
            DEQUE(FreeArea, nextArea, *head, *tail);
            delete nextArea;
            }
        else {
            //
            //  Merge with previous area
            //
            prevArea->size= prevArea->size + size;
            }
        }
    else {
        //
        //  See if we merge with next area
        //
        if (nextArea &&
                nextArea->handle == handle &&
                start + size == nextArea->start) {
            //
            //  We merge with next area.
            //
            nextArea->start= start;
            nextArea->size= size + nextArea->size;
            }
        else {
            //
            //  No merging. We need to insert a new element.
            //
            newArea= new FreeArea;
            newArea->handle= handle;
            newArea->start= start;
            newArea->size= size;
            newArea->next= nextArea;
            newArea->prev= prevArea;
            if (prevArea) {
                prevArea->next= newArea;
                }
            else {
                *head= newArea;
                }
            if (nextArea) {
                nextArea->prev= newArea;
                }
            else {
                *tail= newArea;
                }
            }
        }
}


void    vm_fatal(char *string)
{
```

```
    fprintf(stderr, "Fatal error: %s, %d\n", string, errno);
    exit(1);
}
```

Figure 6-7 presents the source code listing to VMALLOC.CPP. This source file contains the code to functions that allocate and free VM blocks.

6-7 The source code listing to VMALLOC.CPP

```
/////////////////////////////////////////
//
// vmalloc.cpp --    Allocate and Free VM blocks
//
//      Defines routines for allocating and freeing VM blocks
//
/////////////////////////////////////////

//
// include standard I/O functions
//
extern "C" {
#include <stdio.h>
#include <stdlib.h>
#include <dos.h>
}

//
// include memory management header files
//
#include "gdefs.h"
#include "xms.h"
#include "ems.h"
#include "vmintern.h"

int VM_VmBlk::alloc(DWORD size)
{

    VmBlock             *newVmBlock;
    VmPage              *page;
    WORD                i;

    WORD                numPages;
    //
    // Before allocating a new block, release the old one, if
    // appropriate.
    //
    if (attached) {
        this->free();
        }

    //
    // Start by changing size to number of pages
    //
    numPages= (WORD) ((size + VM_PAGE_OFFSET_MASK) >> VM_PAGE_SHIFT);
```

```
    //
    //   Allocate the vm block and pages
    //
    newVmBlock= new VmBlock;
    if (newVmBlock == NULL) {
        goto noMem1;
        }

    newVmBlock->size= numPages;
    newVmBlock->pages= new VmPage[numPages];
    if (newVmBlock->pages == NULL) {
        goto noMem2;
        }

    for (i= 0; i < numPages; i++) {
        page= &newVmBlock->pages[i];

        page->pageNum= i;
        page->secondaryKind= VM_SEC_UNALLOCATED;
        page->sec.disk= NULL;
        page->convBuff= NULL;
        page->offset= 0;
        page->wired= 0;
        page->dirty= FALSE;
        }

    //
    //   Link it into the list of blocks
    //
    ENQUE_H(VmBlock, newVmBlock, firstVmBlock, lastVmBlock);

    //
    //   Finally return the handle
    //
    handle= (DWORD) newVmBlock;
    attached= TRUE;

    return VMErrOK;

    //
    //   Error handling
    //
noMem2:
    delete newVmBlock;

noMem1:
    return VMErrNoConv;
}
int VM_VmBlk::free()
{

    WORD                i;

    VmBlock             *vmBlock;

    if (handle == 0) {
        return VMErrOK;
        }

    vmBlock= (VmBlock *) handle;
```

```
    //
    //  One by one, free up the pages.
    //
    for (i= 0; i < vmBlock->size; i++) {
        vm_freeVmPage(&vmBlock->pages[i]);
        }

    //
    //  Free the page array
    //
    delete vmBlock->pages;

    //
    //  Unlink the block
    //
    DEQUE(VmBlock, vmBlock, firstVmBlock, lastVmBlock);

    //
    //  Finally, free it up
    //
    delete vmBlock;

    //
    //  Make sure it doesn't get freed again.
    //
    attached= FALSE;
    handle= 0;

    return VMErrOK;
}


void vm_freeVmPage(VmPage *vmPage)
{

    //
    //  First free the secondary memory page
    //
    switch (vmPage->secondaryKind) {
    case VM_SEC_UNALLOCATED:
        break;

    case VM_SEC_DISK:
        vm_freeDiskPage(vmPage->sec.disk);
        break;
    case VM_SEC_EMS:
        vm_freeEmsPage(vmPage->sec.ems);
        break;

    case VM_SEC_XMS:
        vm_freeXmsPage(vmPage->sec.xms);
        break;
        }

    //
    //  Now free the primary memory page (if it's in memory)
    //
    if (vmPage->convBuff && vmPage->convBuff != PFABUFF) {
        vm_freeConvBuff(vmPage->convBuff);
```

```
        }

    }


void vm_freeDiskPage(DiskPage *diskPage)
{

    //
    //  First remove it from the list of disk pages.
    //
    DEQUE(DiskPage, diskPage, diskInf.firstPage, diskInf.lastPage);

    //
    //  Now add the space to the free list
    //
    vm_addFree(0, diskPage->pageNum, 1,
                    &diskInf.firstFree, &diskInf.lastFree);

    //
    //  Finally free the actual memory.
    //
    delete diskPage;

}

void vm_freeEmsPage(EmsPage *emsPage)
{

    //
    //  First remove it from the list of disk pages.
    //
    if (emsPage->vmPage->wired) {
        DEQUE(EmsPage, emsPage, emsInf.firstWired, emsInf.lastWired);
        }
    else {
        DEQUE(EmsPage, emsPage, emsInf.mruPage, emsInf.lruPage);
        }

    //
    //  Now add the space to the free list
    //
    vm_addFree((DWORD) emsPage->emsBuff,
                emsPage->pageNum,
                1,
              &emsInf.firstFree,
              &emsInf.lastFree);
    emsPage->emsBuff->useCount--;

    //
    //  This may have emptied the buffer. If so, free the buffer.
    //
    if (emsPage->emsBuff->useCount == 0) {
        vm_freeEmsBuff(emsPage->emsBuff);
        }

    //
    //  Finally free the actual memory.
    //
    delete emsPage;
```

```
}

void vm_freeXmsPage(XmsPage *xmsPage)
{

    //
    //  First remove it from the list of disk pages.
    //
    if (xmsPage->vmPage->wired) {
        DEQUE(XmsPage, xmsPage, xmsInf.firstWired, xmsInf.lastWired);
        }
    else {
        DEQUE(XmsPage, xmsPage, xmsInf.mruPage, xmsInf.lruPage);
        }

    //
    //  Now add the space to the free list
    //
    vm_addFree((DWORD) xmsPage->xmsBuff,
                xmsPage->pageNum,
                1,
              &xmsInf.firstFree,
              &xmsInf.lastFree);
    xmsPage->xmsBuff->useCount--;


    //
    //  This may have emptied the buffer. If so, free the buffer.
    //
    if (xmsPage->xmsBuff->useCount == 0) {
        vm_freeXmsBuff(xmsPage->xmsBuff);
        }

    //
    //  Finally free the actual memory.
    //
    delete xmsPage;

}

void vm_freeConvBuff(ConvBuff *convBuff)
{

    DWORD               i;
    WORD                pageNum;
    //
    //  First go through all of the pages in the buffer
    //  removing references to this buffer.
    //
    for (i= 0, pageNum= convBuff->startPage;
                i < convBuff->buffSize;
                    i++, pageNum++) {
        convBuff->vmBlock->pages[pageNum].convBuff= NULL;
        convBuff->vmBlock->pages[pageNum].offset= 0;
        }

    //
    //  Remove the buffer from the buffer list
    //
```

```
        if (convBuff->wiredPages) {
            DEQUE(ConvBuff, convBuff, convInf.firstWired, convInf.lastWired);
            }
        else {
            DEQUE(ConvBuff, convBuff, convInf.mruBuff, convInf.lruBuff);
            }

        //
        //   Free the buffer memory
        //
        farfree((char *) convBuff->address);

        //
        //   Finally, free the descriptor itself
        //
        delete convBuff;

}

void vm_freeEmsBuff(EmsBuff *emsBuff)
{

    FreeArea            *currFreeArea;
    FreeArea            *nextFreeArea;


    //
    //   First remove it from the ems buffer list
    //
    DEQUE(EmsBuff, emsBuff, emsInf.firstBuff, emsInf.lastBuff);

    //
    //   Now go through the free memory chain removing any references
    //   to this buffer
    //
    for (currFreeArea= emsInf.firstFree; currFreeArea; currFreeArea= nextFreeArea)
    {

        nextFreeArea= currFreeArea->next;

        if (currFreeArea->handle == (DWORD) emsBuff) {
            DEQUE(FreeArea, currFreeArea, emsInf.firstFree, emsInf.lastFree);
            delete currFreeArea;
            }
        }

    //
    //   Now release the buffer descriptor. The destructor will release
    //   the EMS memory.
    //
    delete emsBuff;

}

void vm_freeXmsBuff(XmsBuff *xmsBuff)
{

    FreeArea            *currFreeArea;
    FreeArea            *nextFreeArea;

    //
    //   First remove it from the xms buffer list
```

```
    //
    DEQUE(XmsBuff, xmsBuff, xmsInf.firstBuff, xmsInf.lastBuff);

    //
    //  Now go through the free memory chain removing any references
    //  to this buffer
    //
    for (currFreeArea= xmsInf.firstFree; currFreeArea; currFreeArea= nextFreeArea) {
        nextFreeArea= currFreeArea->next;

        if (currFreeArea->handle == (DWORD) xmsBuff) {
            DEQUE(FreeArea, currFreeArea, xmsInf.firstFree, xmsInf.lastFree);
            delete currFreeArea;
            }
        }

    //
    //  Now release the buffer descriptor. The destructor will release
    //  the XMS memory.
    //
    delete xmsBuff;

}
```

Figure 6-8 presents the source code listing to VMWIRE.CPP. This source file contains the code to functions that permit the wiring and un-wiring of VMM pages.

6-8 The source code listing to VMWIRE.CPP

```
//////////////////////////////////////
//
// vmwire.cpp --      Wire and unwire VM pages
//
//      Defines routines for wiring and unwiring VM pages.
// wiring a page makes it accessable to a program. Unwiring
// indicates that the page is will not be needed until it is
// wired again.
//
//////////////////////////////////////

//
// include standard I/O functions
//
extern "C" {
#include <stdio.h>
#include <stdlib.h>
#include <string.h>
#include <dos.h>
}

//
// include memory management header files
//
#include "gdefs.h"
#include "xms.h"
```

```
#include "ems.h"
#include "vmintern.h"


int VM_VmBlk::wire(
    DWORD               areaOffset,
    DWORD               areaSize,
    char                **areaAddress)
{

    WORD                startPage;
    WORD                endPage;
    WORD                pageNum;
    WORD                offset;

    ConvBuff            *blockBuffer;

    VmBlock             *vmBlock;
    VmPage              *vmPage;

    int                 error;
    int                 contiguous;
    int                 pageWired;
    int                 resident;


    //
    //  Start by casting the handle into an appropriate pointer.
    //
    vmBlock= (VmBlock *) handle;

    //
    //  Let's translate the offset and size into page
    //  values.
    //  The offset is truncated to a page number, and the
    //  size is rounded up to a page number.
    //
    startPage= (WORD) (areaOffset >> VM_PAGE_SHIFT);
    endPage= (WORD) ((areaOffset + areaSize - 1) >> VM_PAGE_SHIFT);
    offset= (WORD) (areaOffset & VM_PAGE_OFFSET_MASK);

    //
    //  Make sure the pages are within the bounds of the block:
    //
    if (endPage >= vmBlock->size) {
        return (errno= VMErrBounds);
        }

    //
    //  We need to see whether the pages are wired or resident already.
    //  If there is an already wired page in the set, it cannot be moved.
    //  Otherwise, we would invalidate the address returned to the caller
    //  who wired it. Since it cannot be moved, we must have room in its
    //  buffer for all of the other pages that we are loading. If there
    //  is room in the buffer, then the other pages we are mapping will
    //  be there, since we do not replace individual pages in a buffer.
    //  This, though, does not hold true for the PFA, so we make an
    //  exception.
    //

    //
    //  blockBuffer will hold the convBuff address for the resident
```

```
//   pages. contiguous will flag whether all of the resident pages
//   are in the same buffer. If there is a wired page, they must
//   be.
//
contiguous= TRUE;
resident= TRUE;
pageWired= FALSE;
blockBuffer= vmBlock->pages[startPage].convBuff;
for (pageNum= startPage; pageNum <= endPage; pageNum++) {
    vmPage= &vmBlock->pages[pageNum];

    if (!vmPage->convBuff) {
        resident= FALSE;
        }

    if (vmPage->wired) {
        if (!contiguous) {
            goto badWireError;
            }
        pageWired= TRUE;
        }

    if (vmPage->convBuff != blockBuffer) {
        if (pageWired) {
            goto badWireError;
            }
        contiguous= FALSE;
        }
    }


//
//   OK, we're good. Either we already have the pages in a
//   contiguous block, or none of them are wired.
//   blockBuffer tells us which is the case.
//
if (!resident || !contiguous) {
    //
    //   Oh well, we have to do some work. I hate it when that happens.
    //
    //   Where to begin, where to begin ?  I know, let's call another
    //   routine to do the mapping. This will give the appearance of
    //   progress.
    //
    error= vm_faultInPages(vmBlock, startPage, endPage);
    if (error) {
        return (error);
        }
    }
else {
    //
    //   We need to move stuff from the LRU queues to
    //   the wired queues.
    //
    if (!vmBlock->pages[startPage].convBuff->wiredPages) {
        DEQUE(ConvBuff, vmBlock->pages[startPage].convBuff,
                        convInf.mruBuff, convInf.lruBuff);
        ENQUE_T(ConvBuff, vmBlock->pages[startPage].convBuff,
                        convInf.firstWired, convInf.lastWired);
        }
```

```
            }

    //
    //  Everythings resident. Let's go through, upping the
    //  wire counts, and then return the address of the first page
    //
    for (pageNum= startPage; pageNum <= endPage; pageNum++) {
        if (!vmBlock->pages[pageNum].wired &&
                vmBlock->pages[pageNum].convBuff != PFABUFF) {
            vmBlock->pages[pageNum].convBuff->wiredPages++;
            }

        vmBlock->pages[pageNum].wired++;

        vm_moveSecPageToWired(&vmBlock->pages[pageNum]);
        }

    //
    //  We're set, let's return the address.
    //
    vmPage= &vmBlock->pages[startPage];
    if (vmPage->convBuff == PFABUFF) {
        *areaAddress= emsInf.pageFrame[0] + (WORD) vmPage->offset + offset;
        }
    else {
        *areaAddress= (char *) (vmPage->convBuff->address +
                                    vmPage->offset + offset);
        }

    return (errno= VMErrOK);

badWireError:
    return (errno= VMErrBadWire);
}

int     vm_faultInPages(
    VmBlock             *vmBlock,
    WORD                startPage,
    WORD                endPage)
{

    //
    //  Let's promote these pages to EMS or XMS (if possible and
    //  necessary).
    //  This achieves two purposes. First, we get the pages into
    //  EMS if possible so that we can map them into the PFA, which
    //  is our fastest mapping method. Second, if the pages are on
    //  disk, they are promoted to EMS or XMS so that we maintain
    //  the most recently used pages in EMS or XMS as opposed to disk.
    //
    //  We'll try EMS, if that fails, for example, because the system
    //  has no EMS, we'll try XMS. If that fails, then OK, we'll get
    //  the pages from disk. The only real reason for vm_faultToDisk
    //  is to handle the possibility that the pages are unallocated.
    //
    if (vm_faultToEMS(vmBlock, startPage, endPage)) {
        if (vm_faultToXMS(vmBlock, startPage, endPage)) {
            vm_faultToDisk(vmBlock, startPage, endPage);
            }
        }
    //
```

```
        //   OK, the pages are in the best secondary memory we have.
        //   Let's see if we can map them into the EMS PFA
        //
        if (vm_tryMapPFA(vmBlock, startPage, endPage) == VMErrOK) {
            return (errno= VMErrOK);
            }


        //
        //   That didn't work. Let's put it into a normal buffer
        //
        if (vm_tryMapConv(vmBlock, startPage, endPage) == VMErrOK) {
            return (errno= VMErrOK);
            }


        //
        //   That didn't work either. We're out of luck.
        //
        return (errno);
}


int      vm_faultToEMS(
    VmBlock               *vmBlock,
    WORD                   startPage,
    WORD                   endPage)
{

    EmsPage               *emsPage;
    EmsPage               *nextEmsPage;
    EmsPage               *emsPageChain;

    VmPage                *vmPage;

    WORD                   pageNum;
    int                    nonEMSPages;

    if (!emsPresent) {
        //
        //   We don't even have EMS. Let's give an error
        //
        return TRUE;
        }


    //
    //   First go through and see how many pages are not in EMS
    //
    nonEMSPages= 0;
    for (pageNum= startPage; pageNum <= endPage; pageNum++) {
        if (vmBlock->pages[pageNum].secondaryKind < VM_SEC_EMS) {
            nonEMSPages++;
            }
        else {
            vm_moveSecPageToWired(&vmBlock->pages[pageNum]);
            }
        }


    //
    //   Now let's get as many pages as we can. This will include
```

```
        //   swapping older pages from EMS to disk.
        //
        vm_getEMSPages(nonEMSPages,  ageChain);

        //
        //   Let's promote as many pages as possible.
        //
        pageNum= startPage;
        emsPage= emsPageChain;
        for (pageNum= startPage; pageNum <= endPage; pageNum++) {

            vmPage= &vmBlock->pages[pageNum];

            //
            //   If this is one of the nonEMS pages, we need to take
            //   an emsPage and promote it.
            //
            if (vmPage->secondaryKind < VM_SEC_EMS) {
                //
                //   Before anything else, let's see if there's a
                //   page left.
                //
                if (emsPage == NULL) {
                    break;
                    }

                //
                //   Promotion will enque the page, so we need to get
                //   its "next" pointer now.
                //
                nextEmsPage= emsPage->next;

                vm_promoteToEMS(vmPage, emsPage);

                emsPage= nextEmsPage;
                }
            }

        if (pageNum <= endPage) {
            //
            //   We weren't able to promote all of the pages. Return
            //   a flag to that effect.
            //
            return TRUE;
            }

        return FALSE;
    }


int     vm_faultToXMS(
    VmBlock             *vmBlock,
    WORD                 startPage,
    WORD                 endPage)
{

    XmsPage             *xmsPage;
    XmsPage             *nextXmsPage;
    XmsPage             *xmsPageChain;

    VmPage              *vmPage;
```

```
WORD                    pageNum;
int                     nonXMSPages;

if (!xmsPresent) {
    //
    //  We don't even have XMS. Let's give an error
    //
    return TRUE;
    }


//
//  First go through and see how many pages are not in XMS
//
nonXMSPages= 0;
for (pageNum= startPage; pageNum <= endPage; pageNum++) {
    if (vmBlock->pages[pageNum].secondaryKind < VM_SEC_XMS) {
        nonXMSPages++;
        }
    }

//
//  Now let's get as many pages as we can. This will include
//  swapping older pages from XMS to disk.
//
vm_getXMSPages(nonXMSPages, &xmsPageChain);

//
//  Let's promote as many pages as possible.
//
pageNum= startPage;
xmsPage= xmsPageChain;
for (pageNum= startPage; pageNum <= endPage; pageNum++) {

    vmPage= &vmBlock->pages[pageNum];

    //
    //  If this is one of the nonXMS pages, we need to take
    //  a emsPage and promote it.
    //
    if (vmPage->secondaryKind < VM_SEC_XMS) {
        //
        //  Before anything else, let's see if there's a
        //  page left.
        //
        if (xmsPage == NULL) {
            break;
            }

        //
        //  Promotion will enque the page, so we need to get
        //  its "next" pointer now.
        //
        nextXmsPage= xmsPage->next;

        vm_promoteToXMS(vmPage, xmsPage);

        xmsPage= nextXmsPage;
        }
```

```
            }

      if (pageNum <= endPage) {
          //
          //  We weren't able to promote all of the pages. Return
          //  a flag to that effect.
          //
          return TRUE;
          }

      return FALSE;
}

int     vm_faultToDisk(
    VmBlock             *vmBlock,
    WORD                 startPage,
    WORD                 endPage)
{

    DiskPage            *diskPage;
    DiskPage            *nextDiskPage;
    DiskPage            *diskPageChain;

    WORD                 pageNum;
    int                  nonDiskPages;

    //
    //  First go through and see how many pages are not allocated
    //
    nonDiskPages= 0;
    for (pageNum= startPage; pageNum <= endPage; pageNum++) {
        if (vmBlock->pages[pageNum].secondaryKind < VM_SEC_DISK) {
            nonDiskPages++;
            }
        }

    //
    //  Now let's get as many pages as we can. This will include
    //  swapping older pages from Disk to disk.
    //
    vm_getDiskPages(nonDiskPages, &diskPageChain);
    //
    //  Let's promote as many pages as possible.
    //
    pageNum= startPage;
    diskPage= diskPageChain;
    while (diskPage) {
        //
        //  If this is one of the non Disk pages, we need to take
        //  an diskPage and promote it.
        //
        if (vmBlock->pages[pageNum].secondaryKind < VM_SEC_DISK) {
            //
            //  Promotion will enque the Disk page, so we need to
            //  get the "next" pointer now.
            //
            nextDiskPage= diskPage->next;

            vm_promoteToDisk(&vmBlock->pages[pageNum], diskPage);

            diskPage= nextDiskPage;
```

```
            }

        pageNum++;
        }

    if (pageNum <= endPage) {
        //
        //  We weren't able to promote all of the pages. Return
        //  a flag to that effect.
        //
        return TRUE;
        }

    return FALSE;
}

void    vm_getEMSPages(
    int                 number,
    EmsPage             **chain)
{

    EmsPage             *newEmsPage;
    EmsPage             *tmpEmsPage;
    EmsBuff             *newEmsBuff;

    WORD                freePages;
    WORD                totalPages;
    WORD                requestNum;

    //
    //  Start by making the return chain empty.
    //
    *chain= NULL;

    //
    //  Now try to get as many pages as we can up to the number requested.
    //
    while (number) {
        if (emsInf.firstFree) {
            //
            //  We've got some free pages.
            //  Create an EmsPage and fill it in.
            //
            newEmsPage= new EmsPage;
            newEmsPage->emsBuff= (EmsBuff *) emsInf.firstFree->handle;
            newEmsPage->pageNum= (WORD) emsInf.firstFree->start;
            newEmsPage->secondaryQueue= VM_Q_FREE;

            //
            //  Bump the buffer's use count.
            //
            newEmsPage->emsBuff->useCount++;

            //
            //  Remove the page from the free chain.
            //
            emsInf.firstFree->size--;
            emsInf.firstFree->start++;
```

```
        if (emsInf.firstFree->size == 0) {
            DEQUE(FreeArea, emsInf.firstFree, emsInf.firstFree, emsInf.lastFree);
            }

        //
        //   Add our new page to the return list.
        //
        newEmsPage->next= *chain;
        *chain= newEmsPage;

        //
        //   We've added a page. Decrement "number";
        //
        number--;
        }
    else {
        //
        //   Nothing on the free chain. Look into EMS from the
        //   EMS manager.
        //
        if (ems.getFreeEM(&totalPages, &freePages)) {
            ems_demoError("EMS_Ems::getNumPages");
            }

        if (freePages) {
            //
            //   We've got some EMS left.
            //   Allocate a block of EMS. We've computed this size
            //   so that we can use all of EMS with the available
            //   handles.
            //
            requestNum= min(emsInf.emsBlockSize, freePages);
            newEmsBuff= new EmsBuff;
            if (newEmsBuff->handle.allocEM(requestNum)) {
                ems_demoError("EMS_EmBlk::allocEM");
                }
            newEmsBuff->buffSize= requestNum;
            newEmsBuff->useCount= 0;
            ENQUE_H(EmsBuff, newEmsBuff, emsInf.firstBuff, emsInf.lastBuff);
            //
            //   Put the pages on the free chain.
            //
            vm_addFree((DWORD) newEmsBuff, 0,
                        requestNum, &emsInf.firstFree, &emsInf.lastFree);

            //
            //   We haven't actually returned a page, so
            //   we don't decrement "number"
            //
            }
        else {
            //
            //   We've got no EMS. Let's start throwing stuff out.
            //
            if (emsInf.lruPage) {
                //
                //   Pull the least recently used page.
                //
                tmpEmsPage= emsInf.lruPage;
                DEQUE(EmsPage, tmpEmsPage, emsInf.mruPage, emsInf.lruPage);
```

```
                    tmpEmsPage->secondaryQueue= VM_Q_FREE;

                    //
                    //  Demote it to Disk or disk.
                    //
                    vm_demoteFromEMS(tmpEmsPage);

                    //
                    //  Enque the newly available page to the return chain.
                    //
                    tmpEmsPage->next= *chain;
                    *chain= tmpEmsPage;

                    number--;
                    }
                else {
                    //
                    //  We're totally out of EMS. Let's just return.
                    //  We've done the best we could.
                    //
                    return;
                    }
                }
            }
        }
}

void    vm_getXMSPages(
    int                 number,
    XmsPage            **chain)
{

    XmsPage            *newXmsPage;
    XmsPage            *tmpXmsPage;
    XmsBuff            *newXmsBuff;
    WORD                freePages;
    WORD                contiguousPages;
    WORD                requestNum;

    //
    //  Start by making the return chain empty.
    //
    *chain= NULL;

    //
    //  Now try to get pages as we can up to the number requested.
    //
    while (number) {
        if (xmsInf.firstFree) {
            //
            //  We've got some free pages.
            //  Create an XmsPage and fill it in.
            //
            newXmsPage= new XmsPage;
            newXmsPage->xmsBuff= (XmsBuff *) xmsInf.firstFree->handle;
            newXmsPage->pageNum= (WORD) xmsInf.firstFree->start;
            newXmsPage->secondaryQueue= VM_Q_FREE;
            //
            //  Bump the buffer's use count.
```

```
        //
        newXmsPage->xmsBuff->useCount++;

        //
        //   Remove the page from the free chain.
        //
        xmsInf.firstFree->size--;
        xmsInf.firstFree->start++;
        if (xmsInf.firstFree->size == 0) {
            DEQUE(FreeArea, xmsInf.firstFree, xmsInf.firstFree, xmsInf.lastFree);
            }

        //
        //   Add our new page to the return list.
        //
        newXmsPage->next= *chain;
        *chain= newXmsPage;

        //
        //   We've added a page. Decrement "number";
        //
        number--;
        }
    else {
        //
        //   Nothing on the free chain. Look into XMS from the
        //   XMS manager.
        //
        if (xms.getFreeXM(&freePages, &contiguousPages)) {
            if (errno == XMSErrNoXMLeft) {
                contiguousPages= 0;
                }
            else {
                xms_demoError("XMS_Xms::getFreeXM");
                }
            }
        contiguousPages/= VM_PAGE_SIZE/XMS_PAGE_SIZE;

        if (contiguousPages) {
            //
            //   We've got some XMS left.
            //   Try to allocate as much as we can to satisfy
            //   our needs.
            //
            requestNum= min(xmsInf.xmsBlockSize, contiguousPages);
            newXmsBuff= new XmsBuff;
            if (newXmsBuff->handle.allocXM(
                        requestNum*(VM_PAGE_SIZE/XMS_PAGE_SIZE))) {
                xms_demoError("XMS_XmBlk::allocXM");
                }
            newXmsBuff->>buffSize= requestNum;
            newXmsBuff->useCount= 0;
            ENQUE_H(XmsBuff, newXmsBuff, xmsInf.firstBuff, xmsInf.lastBuff);

            //
            //   Put the pages on the free chain.
            //
            vm_addFree((DWORD) newXmsBuff, 0,
                        requestNum, &xmsInf.firstFree, &xmsInf.lastFree);

            //
```

```
                        //   We haven't actually returned a page, so
                        //   we don't decrement "number"
                        //
                        }
                else {
                        //
                        //   We've got no XMS. Let's start throwing stuff out.
                        //
                        if (xmsInf.lruPage) {
                            //
                            //   Pull the least recently used page.
                            //
                            tmpXmsPage= xmsInf.lruPage;
                            DEQUE(XmsPage, tmpXmsPage, xmsInf.mruPage,
xmsInf.lruPage);

                            tmpXmsPage->secondaryQueue= VM_Q_FREE;


                            //
                            //   Demote it to disk.
                            //
                            vm_demoteFromXMS(tmpXmsPage);

                            //
                            //   Enque the newly available page to the return chain.
                            //
                            tmpXmsPage->next= *chain;
                            *chain= tmpXmsPage;

                            number--;
                            }
                    else {
                            //
                            //   We're totally out of XMS. Let's just return.
                            //   We've done the best we could.
                            //
                            return;
                            }
                        }
                    }
                }
}

void    vm_getDiskPages(
    int                 number,
    DiskPage            **chain)
{

    DiskPage            *newDiskPage;
    DiskPage            *lastDiskPage;

    //
    //   Start by making the return chain empty.
    //
    *chain= NULL;
    lastDiskPage= NULL;

    //
    //   Now try to get as many pages as we can up to the number requested.
    //   We enque pages in order rather than in reverse order as in
```

```
//   the getXMS and getEMS functions because we want to write
//   pages in order to minimize disk access if we're extending EOF.
//
while (number) {
    if (diskInf.firstFree) {
        //
        //   We've got some free pages.
        //   Create an DiskPage and fill it in.
        //
        newDiskPage= new DiskPage;
        newDiskPage->pageNum= (WORD) diskInf.firstFree->start;

        //
        //   Remove the page from the free chain.
        //
        diskInf.firstFree->size--;
        diskInf.firstFree->start++;
        if (diskInf.firstFree->size == 0) {
            DEQUE(FreeArea, diskInf.firstFree,
                        diskInf.firstFree, diskInf.lastFree);
            }

        //
        //   Add our new page to the return list.
        //
        newDiskPage->next= NULL;
        if (lastDiskPage) {
            lastDiskPage->next= newDiskPage;
            }
        else {
            *chain= newDiskPage;
            }
        lastDiskPage= newDiskPage;

        //
        //   We've added a page. Decrement "number";
        //
        number--;
        }
    else {
        //
        //   Put an appropriate number of pages on the free chain
        //   starting at the current end of file.
        //
        vm_addFree(0, diskInf.fileSize,
                        number, &diskInf.firstFree,
                        &diskInf.lastFree);

        //
        //   Advance the EOF marker.
        //
        diskInf.fileSize+= number;

        //
        //   We haven't actually returned a page, so
        //   we don't decrement "number"
        //
        }
    }
}
```

```
void     vm_promoteToEMS(
    VmPage              *vmPage,
    EmsPage             *emsPage)
{


    //
    //  First off, let's see if the page is already in EMS. If so
    //  we're done.
    //
    if (vmPage->secondaryKind == VM_SEC_EMS) {
        return;
        }


    //
    //  We need to save the page map (pages in PFA), map the page, and then
    //  xfer the data to the mapped page, then restore the page map.
    //


    //
    //  Save the current state of the PFA
    //
    if (emsPage->emsBuff->handle.savePageMap()) {
        ems_demoError("EMS_EmBlk::savePageMap");
        }


    //
    //  Map the EMS page into the first page of the PFA
    //
    if (emsPage->emsBuff->handle.mapPage(0, emsPage->pageNum)) {
        ems_demoError("EMS_EmBlk::mapPage");
        }


    //
    //  Let's do the xfer:
    //
    switch (vmPage->secondaryKind) {
    case VM_SEC_UNALLOCATED:
        //
        //  The page is as yet unallocated. Zero it out.
        //
        memset(emsInf.pageFrame[0], 0, VM_PAGE_SIZE);
        break;

    case VM_SEC_DISK:
        //
        //  The page is on disk. Read it in.
        //
        if (fseek(diskInf.channel, (DWORD) vmPage->sec.disk->pageNum * VM_PAGE_SIZE, SEEK_SET))
            vm_fatal("fseek");
            }
        if (!fread(emsInf.pageFrame[0], VM_PAGE_SIZE, 1, diskInf.channel)) {
            vm_fatal("fread");
            }

        //
        //  Free the disk page.
        //
        vm_addFree(0, vmPage->sec.disk->pageNum, 1,
```

```
                    &diskInf.firstFree, &diskInf.lastFree);

        //
        //   Release the disk page descriptor.
        //
        vm_dequeSecPage(vmPage);
        delete vmPage->sec.disk;

        break;

    case VM_SEC_XMS:
        //
        //   The page is in XMS. Let's xfer it in.
        //
        if (xms.moveXM(xms_realMem, (DWORD) emsInf.pageFrame[0],
                        vmPage->sec.xms->xmsBuff->handle,
                        (DWORD) vmPage->sec.xms->pageNum * VM_PAGE_SIZE,
                        VM_PAGE_SIZE)) {
            xms_demoError("XMS_Xms::moveXM");
            }

        //
        //   Free the xms page.
        //
        vm_addFree((DWORD) vmPage->sec.xms->xmsBuff,
                        vmPage->sec.xms->pageNum, 1,
                        &xmsInf.firstFree, &xmsInf.lastFree);

        //
        //   Release the xms page descriptor.
        //
        vm_dequeSecPage(vmPage);
        delete vmPage->sec.xms;

        break;

    default:
        vm_fatal("Bogus vmPage->secondaryKind");
        }

    //
    //   Set up the EMS page descriptor.
    //
    emsPage->vmPage= vmPage;
    vmPage->secondaryKind= VM_SEC_EMS;
    vmPage->sec.ems= emsPage;

    //
    //   Let's just restore the PFA map.
    //
    if (emsPage->emsBuff->handle.restorePageMap()) {
        ems_demoError("EMS_EmBlk::restorePageMap");
        }

}

void    vm_promoteToXMS(
    VmPage              *vmPage,
    XmsPage             *xmsPage)
{
```

```
char                 *pageBuff;

//
//  If EMS is initialized, we have a page of EMS to use as
//  a buffer. Otherwise we need to use conventional memory.
//
if (emsPresent && emsInf.pageBuffHandle.num()) {
    //
    //  Save the current page frame map.
    //
    if (emsInf.pageBuffHandle.savePageMap()) {
        ems_demoError("EMS_EmBlk::savePageMap");
        }

    //
    //  Map the EMS page into the first page of the PFA
    //
    if (emsInf.pageBuffHandle.mapPage(0, 0)) {
        ems_demoError("EMS_EmBlk::mapPage");
        }

    pageBuff= emsInf.pageFrame[0];
    }
else {
    //
    //  No EMS, we need to use conventional memory.
    //
    pageBuff= new char[VM_PAGE_SIZE];
    }

//
//  Let's do the xfer:
//
switch (vmPage->secondaryKind) {
case VM_SEC_UNALLOCATED:
    //
    //  The page is as yet unallocated. Zero it out.
    //
    memset(pageBuff, 0, VM_PAGE_SIZE);
    break;

case VM_SEC_DISK:
    //
    //  The page is on disk. Read it in.
    //
    if (fseek(diskInf.channel, (DWORD) vmPage->sec.disk->pageNum *
VM_PAGE_SIZE, SEEK_SET)) {
        vm_fatal("fseek");
        }
    if (!fread(pageBuff, VM_PAGE_SIZE, 1, diskInf.channel)) {
        vm_fatal("fread");
        }

    //
    //  Free the disk page.
    //
    vm_addFree(0, vmPage->sec.disk->pageNum, 1,
                &diskInf.firstFree, &diskInf.lastFree);

    //
```

```
                // Release the disk page descriptor.
                //
                vm_dequeSecPage(vmPage);
                delete vmPage->sec.disk;

                break;

        default:
            vm_fatal("Bogus vmPage->secondaryKind");
            }

    //
    // We have the page in memory. Let's transfer it to
    // XMS now.
    //
    if (xms.moveXM(xmsPage->xmsBuff->handle,
                   (DWORD) xmsPage->pageNum * VM_PAGE_SIZE,
                   xms_realMem,
                   (DWORD) pageBuff,
                   VM_PAGE_SIZE)) {
        xms_demoError("XMS_Xms::moveXM");
        }

    //
    // Set up the XMS page descriptor.
    //
    xmsPage->vmPage= vmPage;
    vmPage->secondaryKind= VM_SEC_XMS;
    vmPage->sec.xms= xmsPage;
    //
    // Now release the buffer
    //
    if (emsPresent && emsInf.pageBuffHandle.num()) {
        //
        // Let's just restore the PFA map.
        //
        if (emsInf.pageBuffHandle.restorePageMap()) {
            ems_demoError("EMS_EmBlk::restorePageMap");
            }
        }
    else {
        //
        // Free the conventional memory buffer
        //
        delete pageBuff;
        }

}

void    vm_promoteToDisk(
    VmPage              *vmPage,
    DiskPage           *diskPage)
{

    char               *pageBuff;

    //
    // If EMS is initialized, we have a page of EMS to use as
    // a buffer. Otherwise we need to use conventional memory.
    //
    if (emsPresent && emsInf.pageBuffHandle.num()) {
        //
```

```
        //   Save the current page frame map.
        //
        if (emsInf.pageBuffHandle.savePageMap()) {
            ems_demoError("EMS_EmBlk::savePageMap");
            }


        //
        //   Map the EMS page into the first page of the PFA
        //
        if (emsInf.pageBuffHandle.mapPage(0, 0)) {
            ems_demoError("EMS_EmBlk::mapPage");
            }

        pageBuff= emsInf.pageFrame[0];
        }
    else {
        //
        //   No EMS, we need to use conventional memory.
        //
        pageBuff= new char[VM_PAGE_SIZE];
        }

//
//   Let's do the xfer:
//
switch (vmPage->secondaryKind) {
case VM_SEC_UNALLOCATED:
    //
    //   The page is as yet unallocated. Zero it out.
    //
    memset(pageBuff, 0, VM_PAGE_SIZE);
    break;

default:
    vm_fatal("Bogus vmPage->secondaryKind");
    }

//
//   Let's write the thing to disk now.
//
if (fseek(diskInf.channel, (DWORD) diskPage->pageNum * VM_PAGE_SIZE, SEEK_SET)) {
    vm_fatal("fseek");
    }
if (!fwrite(pageBuff, VM_PAGE_SIZE, 1, diskInf.channel)) {
    vm_fatal("write");
    }

//
//   Set up the Disk page descriptor.
//
diskPage-.>vmPage= vmPage;
vmPage->secondaryKind= VM_SEC_DISK;
vmPage->sec.disk= diskPage;

//
//   Enque to the list of pages
//
ENQUE_T(DiskPage, diskPage, diskInf.firstPage, diskInf.lastPage);
```

```
        //
        //   Now release the buffer
        //
        if (emsPresent && emsInf.pageBuffHandle.num()) {
            //
            //   Let's just restore the PFA map.
            //
            if (emsInf.pageBuffHandle.restorePageMap()) {
                ems_demoError("EMS_EmBlk::restorePageMap");
                }
            }
        else {
            //
            //   Free the conventional memory buffer
            //
            delete pageBuff;
            }

    }

void    vm_demoteFromEMS(EmsPage *emsPage)
{

    VmPage              *vmPage;
    XmsPage             *xmsPage;
    DiskPage            *diskPage;
    SecondaryKind        pageType;


    //
    //   Just get a handy pointer to the VM page
    //
    vmPage= emsPage->vmPage;

    //
    //   This page could possibly be in the PFA. If so we need to
    //   remove it.
    //
    if (vmPage->convBuff == PFABUFF) {
        //
        //   OK. It's in the PFA. It's OK to leave the EMS page there,
        //   because we're going to need it anyway. However, we want
        //   to indicate that the virtual page is no longer there, since
        //   it is being disconnected from the EMS page.
        //
        vmPage->convBuff= NULL;
        vmPage->offset= 0;
        }


    //
    //   The first thing we need to do is to try to find a
    //   page to go to. We first try XMS, if that fails, we
    //   go to Disk.
    //
    vm_getXMSPages(1, &xmsPage);
    pageType= VM_SEC_XMS;
    if (xmsPage == NULL) {
        vm_getDiskPages(1, &diskPage);
```

```
        pageType= VM_SEC_DISK;
        }


//
//   We need to map the page. We'll save the current page map
//   so we can restore it later.
//

//
//   Save the current page frame map.
//
if (emsPage->emsBuff->handle.savePageMap()) {
    ems_demoError("EMS_EmBlk::savePageMap");
    }


//
//   Map the EMS page into the first page of the PFA
//
if (emsPage->emsBuff->handle.mapPage(0, emsPage->pageNum)) {
    ems_demoError("EMS_EmBlk::mapPage");
    }


//
//   Let's do the xfer:
//
switch (pageType) {
case VM_SEC_DISK:
    //
    //   We're demoting to disk. Write the page out.
    //
    if (fseek(diskInf.channel, (DWORD) diskPage->pageNum * VM_PAGE_SIZE, SEEK_SET)) {
        vm_fatal("fseek");
        }
    if (!fwrite(emsInf.pageFrame[0], VM_PAGE_SIZE, 1, diskInf.channel)) {
        vm_fatal("write");
        }


    //
    //   Update the VM page, etc.
    //
    diskPage->vmPage= vmPage;
    vmPage->secondaryKind= VM_SEC_DISK;
    vmPage->sec.disk= diskPage;


    //
    //   Enque the disk page. Note that is will be the most
    //   recently used on disk.
    //
    ENQUE_H(DiskPage, diskPage, diskInf.firstPage, diskInf.lastPage);

    break;

case VM_SEC_XMS:
    //
    //   We're demoting to XMS, let's move it on out.
    //
    if (xms.moveXM(xmsPage->xmsBuff->handle,
                    (DWORD) xmsPage->pageNum * VM_PAGE_SIZE,
```

```
                                xms_realMem,
                                (DWORD) emsInf.pageFrame[0],
                                VM_PAGE_SIZE)) {
                    xms_demoError("XMS_Xms::moveXM");
                    }

            //
            //   Update the VM page, etc.
            //
            xmsPage->vmPage= vmPage;
            vmPage->secondaryKind= VM_SEC_XMS;
            vmPage->sec.xms= xmsPage;

            //
            //   Enque the XMS page. Note that is will be the most
            //   recently used on XMS.
            //
            ENQUE_H(XmsPage, xmsPage, xmsInf.mruPage, xmsInf.lruPage);
            xmsPage->secondaryQueue= VM_Q_LRU;

            break;

        default:
            vm_fatal("Bogus vmPage->secondaryKind");
            }
        //
        //   Let's just restore the PFA map.
        //
        if (emsPage->emsBuff->handle.restorePageMap()) {
            ems_demoError("EMS_EmBlk::restorePageMap");
            }

}


void     vm_demoteFromXMS(XmsPage *xmsPage)

{

    VmPage              *vmPage;
    DiskPage            *diskPage;

    char                *pageBuff;


    //
    //   Just get a handy pointer to the VM page
    //
    vmPage= xmsPage->vmPage;

    //
    //   The first thing we need to do is to try to find a
    //   page to go to.
    //
    vm_getDiskPages(1, &diskPage);


    //
    //   If EMS is initialized, we have a page of EMS to use as
    //   a buffer. Otherwise we need to use conventional memory.
```

```
//
if (emsPresent && emsInf.pageBuffHandle.num()) {
    //
    //   Save the current page frame map.
    //
    if (emsInf.pageBuffHandle.savePageMap()) {
        ems_demoError("EMS_EmBlk::savePageMap");
        }

    //
    //   Map the EMS page into the first page of the PFA
    //
    if (emsInf.pageBuffHandle.mapPage(0, 0)) {
        ems_demoError("EMS_EmBlk::mapPage");
        }

    pageBuff= emsInf.pageFrame[0];
    }
else {
    //
    //   No EMS, we need to use conventional memory.
    //
    pageBuff= new char[VM_PAGE_SIZE];
    }

//
//   First let's transfer from the XMS page to the
//   buffer.
//
if (xms.moveXM(xms_realMem, (DWORD) pageBuff,
               xmsPage->xmsBuff->handle,
               (DWORD) xmsPage->pageNum * VM_PAGE_SIZE,
               VM_PAGE_SIZE)) {
    xms_demoError("XMS_Xms::moveXM");
    }

//
//   Now transfer the page to disk
//
if (fseek(diskInf.channel, (DWORD) diskPage->pageNum * VM_PAGE_SIZE, SEEK_SET)) {
    vm_fatal("fseek");
    }
if (!fwrite(pageBuff, VM_PAGE_SIZE, 1, diskInf.channel)) {
    vm_fatal("write");
    }

//
//   Update the VM page, etc.
//
diskPage->vmPage= vmPage;
vmPage->secondaryKind= VM_SEC_DISK;
vmPage->sec.disk= diskPage;

//
//   Enque the disk page. Note that is will be the most
//   recently used on disk.
//
ENQUE_H(DiskPage, diskPage, diskInf.firstPage, diskInf.lastPage);

//
```

```
        //   Now release the buffer
        //
        if (emsPresent && emsInf.pageBuffHandle.num()) {
            //
            //   Let's just restore the PFA map.
            //
            if (emsInf.pageBuffHandle.restorePageMap()) {
                ems_demoError("EMS_EmBlk::restorePageMap()");
                }
            }
        else {
            //
            //   Free the conventional memory buffer
            //
            delete pageBuff;
            }

    }

int      vm_tryMapPFA(
    VmBlock             *vmBlock,
    WORD                 startPage,
    WORD                 endPage)
{

    EmsPage             *emsPage;

    WORD                 pageCount;
    WORD                 pageNum;

    WORD                 freeString;
    WORD                 offset;
    WORD                 i;

    //
    //   First, let's make a couple of quick checks:
    //      Can the pages fit in the PFA ?
    //      Are the page all in EMS ?
    //
    pageCount= endPage - startPage + 1;
    if (pageCount > EMS_PAGE_FRAME_SIZE) {
        return (errno= VMErrNoConv);
        }

    for (pageNum= startPage; pageNum <= endPage; pageNum++) {
        if (vmBlock->pages[pageNum].secondaryKind != VM_SEC_EMS) {
            return (errno= VMErrNoConv);
            }
        }

    //
    //   OK, the initial checks have passed. Let's see whether we
    //   actually have a block of pages in the PFA which we can use.
    //
    //   Note that we do not concern ourselves with lru-ness. Mapping
    //   pages is too fast to worry about it, since there is no
    //   data movement.
    //
    freeString= 0;
    for (offset= 0; offset < EMS_PAGE_FRAME_SIZE; offset++) {
        if (emsInf.contents[offset] == 0 ||
                !emsInf.contents[offset]->vmPage->wired) {
```

```
                freeString++;
                }
        else {
            freeString= 0;
            }

        if (freeString >= pageCount) {
            offset= offset - freeString + 1;
            break;
            }
        }

    //
    //  If offset isn't in the PFA, we can't do anything.
    //
    if (offset >= EMS_PAGE_FRAME_SIZE) {
        return (errno= VMErrNoConv);
        }

    //
    //  Now we need to take any pages out of conventional memory
    //  buffers and flush them back to EMS.
    //
    for (pageNum= startPage; pageNum <= endPage; pageNum++) {
        vm_flushVmPage(&vmBlock->pages[pageNum]);
        }

    //
    //  Now let's mark the pages we're replacing as history.
    //
    for (pageNum= offset, i= 0; i < pageCount; i++, pageNum++) {
        if (emsInf.contents[pageNum]) {
            emsInf.contents[pageNum]->vmPage->convBuff= NULL;
            emsInf.contents[pageNum]->vmPage->offset= 0;
            }
        }

    //
    //  We're finally ready to map the pages.
    //
    for (pageNum= startPage; pageNum <= endPage; pageNum++) {
        emsPage= vmBlock->pages[pageNum].sec.ems;
        if (emsPage->emsBuff->handle.
                mapPage(offset+(pageNum-startPage),
                        emsPage->pageNum)) {
            ems_demoError("EMS_EmBlk::mapPage");
            }

        //
        //  Note where we've mapped them.
        //
        emsInf.contents[offset+(pageNum-startPage)]= emsPage;
        emsPage->vmPage->convBuff= PFABUFF;
        emsPage->vmPage->offset= (offset+(pageNum-startPage)) * VM_PAGE_SIZE;
        }

    return (errno= VMErrOK);

}
```

```
int      vm_tryMapConv(
    VmBlock              *vmBlock,
    WORD                  startPage,
    WORD                  endPage)
{

    ConvBuff             *newConvBuff;

    WORD                  pageNum;
    WORD                  pageCount;
    DWORD                 memNeeded;

    char                 *newBuffSpace;


    //
    //  Get the number of pages.
    //
    pageCount= endPage - startPage + 1;

    //
    //  Free up buffers till we can get the buffer space.
    //
    memNeeded= (DWORD) pageCount * VM_PAGE_SIZE;
    while (memNeeded > convInf.spaceAvail
            ¦¦ (newBuffSpace= (char *) farmalloc(memNeeded)) == NULL) {
        if (vm_freeLRUConvBuff()) {
            return (errno= VMErrNoConv);
            }
        }
    convInf.spaceAvail-= memNeeded;

    //
    //  We've got memory for the buffer. Let's create a buffer header.
    //
    newConvBuff= new ConvBuff;
    newConvBuff->buffSize= pageCount;
    newConvBuff->address= newBuffSpace;
    newConvBuff->vmBlock= vmBlock;
    newConvBuff->startPage= startPage;
    newConvBuff->wiredPages= 0;
    ENQUE_T(ConvBuff, newConvBuff, convInf.firstWired, convInf.lastWired);

    //
    //  OK, we've got a buffer. Let's bring in the pages.
    //
    for (pageNum= startPage; pageNum <= endPage; pageNum++) {
        vm_loadVmPage(&vmBlock->pages[pageNum], newConvBuff);
        }

    return (errno= VMErrOK);
}

void     vm_flushVmPage(VmPage *vmPage)

{

    EmsPage              *emsPage;

    char                 *pageAddr;
```

```
//
//  If the page is dirty, and resident, write it to secondary
//
if (vmPage->dirty && vmPage->convBuff &&
            vmPage->convBuff != PFABUFF) {

    pageAddr= (char *) (vmPage->convBuff->address + vmPage->offset);

    switch(vmPage->secondaryKind) {
    case VM_SEC_UNALLOCATED:
        //
        //  The page is as yet unallocated. This is a NOP
        //
        break;

    case VM_SEC_DISK:
        //
        //  The page is on disk. Write it out
        //
        if (fseek(diskInf.channel, (DWORD) vmPage->sec.disk->pageNum * VM_PAGE_SIZE,
                    SEEK_SET)) {
            vm_fatal("fseek");
            }
        if (!fwrite(pageAddr, VM_PAGE_SIZE, 1, diskInf.channel)) {
            vm_fatal("fwrite");
            }

        break;

    case VM_SEC_XMS:
        //
        //  The page is in XMS. Let's xfer it out.
        //
        if (xms.moveXM(vmPage->sec.xms->xmsBuff->handle,
                    (DWORD) vmPage->sec.xms->pageNum * VM_PAGE_SIZE,
                    xms_realMem, (DWORD) pageAddr,
                    VM_PAGE_SIZE)) {
            xms_demoError("XMS_Xms::moveXM");
            }

        break;

    case VM_SEC_EMS:
        //
        //  Get convenient handle on the emsPage.
        //
        emsPage= vmPage->sec.ems;

        //
        //  We need to save the PFA for a bit.
        //
        if (emsPage->emsBuff->handle.savePageMap()) {
            ems_demoError("EMS_EmBlk::savePageMap");
            }

        //
        //  Map the EMS page in.
        //
        if (emsPage->emsBuff->handle.mapPage(0, emsPage->pageNum)) {
```

```
                    ems_demoError("EMS_EmBlk::mapPage");
                        }

            //
            //  Copy the memory.
            //
            memcpy(emsInf.pageFrame[0], pageAddr, VM_PAGE_SIZE);

            //
            //  Restore the page map.
            //
            if (emsPage->emsBuff->handle.restorePageMap()) {
                ems_demoError("EMS_EmBlk::restorePageMap()");
                    }

            break;

        default:
            vm_fatal("Bogus vmPage->secondaryKind");
                }
            }

    }

void    vm_loadVmPage(
    VmPage              *vmPage,
    ConvBuff            *convBuff)
{

    EmsPage              *emsPage;

    char                 *pageAddr;

    //
    //  First figure out the address of the buffer.
    //
    vmPage->convBuff= convBuff;
    vmPage->offset= (DWORD) (vmPage->pageNum - convBuff->startPage) * VM_PAGE_SIZE;
    pageAddr= (char *) (vmPage->convBuff->address + vmPage->offset);

    switch(vmPage->secondaryKind) {
    case VM_SEC_DISK:
        //
        //  The page is on disk. Read it in.
        //
        if (fseek(diskInf.channel, (DWORD) vmPage->sec.disk->pageNum * VM_PAGE_SIZE,
                    SEEK_SET)) {
            vm_fatal("fseek");
            }
        if (!fread(pageAddr, VM_PAGE_SIZE, 1, diskInf.channel)) {
            vm_fatal("fread");
            }

        break;

    case VM_SEC_XMS:
        //
        //  The page is in XMS. Let's xfer it in.
        //
        if (xms.moveXM(xms_realMem, (DWORD) pageAddr,
                        vmPage->sec.xms->xmsBuff->handle,
```

```
                        (DWORD) vmPage->sec.xms->pageNum * VM_PAGE_SIZE,
                        VM_PAGE_SIZE)) {
            xms_demoError("XMS_Xms::moveXM");
            }

        break;

    case VM_SEC_EMS:
        //
        //   Get convenient handle on the emsPage.
        //
        emsPage= vmPage->sec.ems;

        //
        //   We need to save the PFA for a bit.
        //
        if (emsPage->emsBuff->handle.savePageMap()) {
            ems_demoError("EMS_EmBlk::savePageMap");
            }

        //
        //   Map the EMS page in.
        //
        if (emsPage->emsBuff->handle.mapPage(0, emsPage->pageNum)) {
            ems_demoError("EMS_EmBlk::mapPage");
            }

        //
        //   Copy the memory.
        //
        memcpy(pageAddr, emsInf.pageFrame[0], VM_PAGE_SIZE);

        //
        //   Restore the page map.
        //
        if (emsPage->emsBuff->handle.restorePageMap()) {
            ems_demoError("EMS_EmBlk::restorePageMap()");
            }

        break;

    default:
        vm_fatal("Bogus vmPage->secondaryKind");
        }

}


int     vm_freeLRUConvBuff()

{

    ConvBuff            *convBuff;
    VmBlock             *vmBlock;

    WORD                pageNum;
    WORD                i;


    //
```

```
    //  First, see if there is an unwired buffer, otherwise we're
    //  out of luck.
    //
    if (convInf.lruBuff == NULL) {
        return (errno= VMErrNoConv);
        }

    //
    //  O.K, let's get rid of the LRU buffer.
    //
    convBuff= convInf.lruBuff;
    DEQUE(ConvBuff, convBuff, convInf.mruBuff, convInf.lruBuff);

    //
    //  Flush, and mark the virtual pages as gone.
    //
    vmBlock= convBuff->vmBlock;
    for (pageNum= convBuff->startPage, i= 0; i < convBuff->buffSize; pageNum++, i++) {
        vm_flushVmPage(&vmBlock->pages[pageNum]);
        vmBlock->pages[pageNum].convBuff= NULL;
        vmBlock->pages[pageNum].offset= 0;
        }

    //
    //  Free up the memory.
    //
    farfree((char *) convBuff->address);
    convInf.spaceAvail+= (DWORD) convBuff->buffSize * VM_PAGE_SIZE;
    delete convBuff;

    return (errno= VMErrOK);
}

int     VM_VmBlk::unwire(
    DWORD               areaOffset,
    DWORD               areaSize,
    int                 dirty)
{

    WORD                startPage;
    WORD                endPage;
    WORD                pageNum;

    VmBlock             *vmBlock;
    VmPage              *vmPage;

    //
    //  Start by casting the handle into an appropriate pointer.
    //
    vmBlock= (VmBlock *) handle;

    //
    //  Let's translate the offset and size into page
    //  values.
    //  The offset is truncated to a page number, and the
    //  size is rounded up to a page number.
    //
    startPage= (WORD) (areaOffset >> VM_PAGE_SHIFT);
    endPage= (WORD) ((areaOffset + areaSize - 1) >> VM_PAGE_SHIFT);

    //
    //  Make sure the pages are within the bounds of the block:
```

```
    //
    if (endPage >= vmBlock->size) {
        return (errno= VMErrBounds);
        }


    //
    //  Now let's go through and make sure they're wired.
    //
    for (pageNum= startPage; pageNum <= endPage; pageNum++) {
        if (!vmBlock->pages[pageNum].wired) {
            return (errno= VMErrNotWired);
            }
        }


    //
    //  OK, all of the pages are wired. Let's unwire the pages and
    //  mark them dirty as necessary.
    //  If a buffer becomes totally unwired, we move it to the LRU
    //  queue.
    //
    for (pageNum= startPage; pageNum <= endPage; pageNum++) {
        vmPage= &vmBlock->pages[pageNum];

        vmPage->dirty= vmPage->dirty || dirty;

        vmPage->wired--;
        if (!vmPage->wired && vmPage->convBuff != PFABUFF) {
            vmPage->convBuff->wiredPages--;
            if (vmPage->convBuff->wiredPages == 0) {
                //
                //  Move the buffer to the LRU.
                //
                DEQUE(ConvBuff, vmPage->convBuff, convInf.firstWired, convInf.lastWired);
                ENQUE_H(ConvBuff, vmPage->convBuff, convInf.mruBuff, convInf.lruBuff);
                }
            }

        //
        //  If the page is in EMS or XMS, move it from the wired
        //  queue to the LRU chain.
        //
        switch (vmPage->secondaryKind) {
        case VM_SEC_EMS:
            DEQUE(EmsPage, vmPage->sec.ems, emsInf.firstWired, emsInf.lastWired);
            ENQUE_H(EmsPage, vmPage->sec.ems, emsInf.mruPage, emsInf.lruPage);
            vmPage->sec.ems->secondaryQueue= VM_Q_LRU;
            break;
        case VM_SEC_XMS:
            DEQUE(XmsPage, vmPage->sec.xms, xmsInf.firstWired, xmsInf.lastWired);
            ENQUE_H(XmsPage, vmPage->sec.xms, xmsInf.mruPage, xmsInf.lruPage);
            vmPage->sec.xms->secondaryQueue= VM_Q_LRU;
            break;
        default:
            break;
            }
        }
```

```
        return (errno= VMErrOK);
}
void vm_moveSecPageToWired(VmPage *vmPage)
{

    switch (vmPage->secondaryKind) {
    case VM_SEC_EMS:
        if (vmPage->sec.ems->secondaryQueue == VM_Q_LRU) {
            DEQUE(EmsPage, vmPage->sec.ems, emsInf.mruPage, emsInf.lruPage);
            }
        if (vmPage->sec.ems->secondaryQueue != VM_Q_WIRED) {
            ENQUE_T(EmsPage, vmPage->sec.ems, emsInf.firstWired, emsInf.lastWired);
            }
        vmPage->sec.ems->secondaryQueue= VM_Q_WIRED;
        break;
    case VM_SEC_XMS:
        if (vmPage->sec.xms->secondaryQueue == VM_Q_LRU) {
            DEQUE(XmsPage, vmPage->sec.xms, xmsInf.mruPage, xmsInf.lruPage);
            }
        if (vmPage->sec.xms->secondaryQueue != VM_Q_WIRED) {
            ENQUE_T(XmsPage, vmPage->sec.xms, xmsInf.firstWired, xmsInf.lastWired);
            }
        vmPage->sec.xms->secondaryQueue= VM_Q_WIRED;
        break;
    default:
        break;
        }
}

void vm_dequeSecPage(VmPage *vmPage)

{

    switch (vmPage->secondaryKind) {
    case VM_SEC_EMS:
        if (vmPage->sec.ems->secondaryQueue == VM_Q_LRU) {
            DEQUE(EmsPage, vmPage-..sec.ems, emsInf.mruPage, emsInf.lruPage);
            }
        else if (vmPage->sec.ems->secondaryQueue == VM_Q_WIRED) {
            DEQUE(EmsPage, vmPage->sec.ems, emsInf.firstWired, emsInf.lastWired);
            }
        vmPage->sec.ems->secondaryQueue= VM_Q_FREE;
        break;
    case VM_SEC_XMS:
        if (vmPage->sec.xms->secondaryQueue == VM_Q_LRU) {
            DEQUE(XmsPage, vmPage->sec.xms, xmsInf.mruPage, xmsInf.lruPage);
            }
        else if (vmPage->sec.xms->secondaryQueue == VM_Q_WIRED) {
            DEQUE(XmsPage, vmPage->sec.xms, xmsInf.firstWired, xmsInf.lastWired);
            }
        vmPage->sec.xms->secondaryQueue= VM_Q_FREE;
        break;
    case VM_SEC_DISK:
        DEQUE(DiskPage, vmPage->sec.disk, diskInf.firstPage, diskInf.lastPage);
        break;
    default:
        break;
        }
}
```

Summary

In a very real sense, the VMM is the crown jewel of this book because its foundation lies in the EMS and XMS functions presented earlier. Standard library I/O disk functions were used as a last resort when there wasn't enough EMS and XMS memory available to meet the needs of the program's VMM requests.

The virtual memory manager (VMM) allows you to allocate and use blocks of memory far beyond the normal size associated with standard DOS-based memory allocation functions. The VMM pools EMS, XMS, and disk memory to meet the needs of the VMM block size request. The beauty of the VMM lies in the fact that it makes the complex task of tracking which data is held in EMS, XMS, and on disk invisible to the applications programmer.

Epilogue

Please feel free to use the memory management functions presented in the book in your personal and commercial code. We hope that you had as much enjoyment from reading this book as we had in writing it.

We're always interested in how readers might use or react to the code presented in our books. Feel free to write us via TAB Books if you have any comments or code you'd like to share with us. We'll try our best to write back as time permits.

Namaste',

Len and Marc

Index